MASSACRE IN NORWAY

MASSACRE IN NORWAY

THE 2011 TERROR ATTACKS ON
OSLO & THE UTØYA YOUTH CAMP

Stian Bromark | *Translated by Hon Khiam Leong*

Potomac Books | *An imprint of the University of Nebraska Press*

Contents

I've Had the Time of My Life

Imagine your most cherished memories from childhood. You may remember a particular summer camp on an island. Staying up all night, the swear words you uttered for the first time, and the water acrobatics with which you impressed your fellow campers. Or the memories may be from another camp and another place, with your older sister and parents. The frivolous laughter throughout the evening when the adults didn't care whether you were in your sleeping bag or not; the girls your sister got to know and with whom you fell head over heels in love one by one; the chewy, sour candy from the store, the kind that you couldn't get back home. Minigolf, dancing on the lawn, boat trips on the Oslo fjord. The memories may be from the cabin by the sea. The first time you went there in spring, the expectations in the Volvo, the stuffy but promising scent you recognize when you opened the front door. Will he be there this year? Will she? Small changes in the landscape, big changes in the siblings in the neighboring cabin, changes in yourself that you didn't notice before meeting the others and seeing where their eyes came to rest. Not to mention Line, whom you could really talk to late into the night, even though you were a boy and she was a girl. There were no hormones in the way. Just pure friendship. Titillating, everlasting, and sun-warmed summer friendship.

Imagine that it were possible to prolong such experiences, take them with you into the convoluted teenage years to a safe place where, for one brief week each July, you met kids of the same age who thought like you, dreamed your dreams, laughed at the same embarrassing jokes, dove into the sea when you did, dressed as half-trendy as you, and sang "My Rainbow Race" when you strummed the chords on the guitar. Without irony. That is what the summer camp at Utøya is like—one big, warm cliché. The stuff that summer memories are made of. Right up there with the chugging boat in the sunset over the islands on the fjord. Carefree children on the pier with mussels on the line. The very refreshing morning swim before breakfast. It's the prosaic moments to which we return because they are safe, predictable, and pleasant. And because the sun always shines. "When it's summer, our dreams come true," sing the members of the AUF (Arbeidernes Ungdomsfylking, the Workers' Youth League—the youth wing of the Labor Party) on Utøya.

On Friday, July 22, 2011, the cloud cover over the island is so low that it almost touches the heads sticking out of the tents. The rain is pouring down in buckets. The campground has turned into a mud bath. The encouraging news is that the mosquitoes are not as persistent as they were the night before. The bad news is that the frogs sound like the coming of the seventh plague. The small brown creatures can be found creeping all over the tents, the forest, and Lovers' Lane. The lilies of the valley hang limply with their leaves down to the forest floor, next to the moss, cranberry, rose hip bushes, and pine cones under an insufferably energetic and loud woodpecker. As "The Utøya Song" says, "When summer is here, the lily of the valley comes into bloom and welcomes you as a friend."

Hundreds of youths crawl out of the tents to a techno version of the Gummy Bears theme song over the PA system. Some did not sleep well because of the rain or because they'd slept on earth, roots, and pebbles. Others talked politics and love most of the night. It wasn't possible to break up the camaraderie around the barbecue pit, where one fine song led to another: Nordahl Grieg's "To Youth" and "Victor Jara," which is Lillebjørn Nilsen's tribute to the eponymous Chilean folksinger. The campfire is significant in Utøya mythology, albeit not as significant as in the old days because of "unsexy inventions" such as fire regulations and pink, laminated A4 sheets saying "All open fires are forbidden on Utøya." The tents have become more spacious with the rise in prosperity over time, but the size of the campsite has remained constant. Brown, green, and blue tents are pitched too close to conform to regulations, with white tent ropes tangled together. The campers playfully step through the ropes and pretend they are laser beams. The barbecue pits, with benches around them, can create the illusion of a campfire, especially when there's a hookah in the middle that glows faintly at the top and spreads the scent of apples, lemons, and cinnamon. One of the camp participants from Hedmark County has decorated his tent with a hookah, Persian carpets, and fake flowers. Karaoke in the main hall has become a somewhat tacky substitute for campfire camaraderie, and there you can also enjoy hamburgers, fries, and vegetarian spring rolls. Everything can be washed down with politically incorrect sweeteners such as Sunett and a bottle of Coke.

Towels, bikinis, and swimming trunks that were hung up to dry on the clotheslines on Thursday have not dried yet. On Lovers' Lane, there's some evidence of the evening's many promising expeditions. Two by two, hand in hand, they appear out of the "love fog" of frogs that crunch underfoot. A smaller group remembers how inspiring it was to sit around the hookah and learn the Arabic vocabulary while karaoke enthusiasts filled the air on the island with pop oldies. Others remember how Oslo boy Tore Sinding Bekkedal impressed everyone with the phrase "Hawwāmtī mumtil'ah bi'anqalaysūn," which means "My hovercraft is full of eels." Some wake up in the wrong tent without having to clear up any misunderstandings, while others check whether daddy's half worn out military brown two-man tent from the '70s has held up over the night. Have I been soaked right through in the sleeping bag? Is my mobile phone dry? Camera!

Johanne Butenschøn Lindheim is, surprisingly, awake in her turquoise three-man tent. Last night she got into her sleeping bag sensibly early, right after the Datarock concert. Johanne set the alarm clock to ring at a quarter to seven to be first in line for the shower. For a while after getting into her sleeping bag, she lay and listened to the buzz of camp life, with varied karaoke singing in the background, before she inserted the iPhone's earphones and fell asleep to the voice of Melissa Horn. In the middle of the night, she woke up feeling bruised. Johanne always freezes at night on Utøya, but that night was especially bad. The tent, the sleeping mat, and the sleeping bag were all wet. There wasn't much she could do to alleviate the harshness of the environment, so she remained prone and endured the cold until the alarm clock rang. And then she needed a hot shower.

Johanne felt a little old on Utøya. That's why she didn't come on Tuesday like many others but on Thursday morning. Wearing a crisp pink dress and white shoes, the nineteen-year-old had been picked up outside the family villa at Blindern by a film director and a cameraman at half past eight. The film crew was supposed to follow her to Utøya in connection with a documentary about student election debates. As they stood on the mainland waiting for the old military landing craft MS *Thorbjørn*, to take her and the film crew over to Utøya, she felt a tingling in her stomach. Johanne wondered whether she'd see many familiar faces or whether she'd feel lonely. She was both proud and embarrassed to have a cameraman in tow. Johanne was mostly feeling embarrassed when the director asked the camp administrator to wait before casting off so she could be filmed at the right angle while she got on board with a fully loaded bag over her shoulder onto the rough iron deck that had once been green. Johanne strongly resented the fact that others had to wait for her, and she didn't like that Utøya's camp administrator (whom she was already afraid of because she could be strict) had openly demonstrated her impatience. As the boat backed out into Lake Tyri, she glanced over at a boy wearing saggy pants and a cap. He bragged that he had slept in a parked car by the registration booth on the mainland because he and his buddy had missed the last boat over the previous evening. Not everyone goes to summer camp because of an interest in politics.

Johanne takes out shampoo, soap, and a towel from her red bag. She fishes out the new pink dress from the right side of the tent. Her jacket is in a bag outside, and it is certainly soaked through. She walks out of the tent toward the lavatory block. There she not only has hot water, which is a luxury in Utøya, but she can also be by herself for some minutes, which is just as scarce a commodity. In the dining hall, she eats salami on crisp bread for the first time in her life. It tastes surprisingly good together with cold milk. If she has mobile phone reception, she thinks, she can update her status on Facebook: "Am enjoying myself on Utøya."

Jorid Nordmelan rises at dawn from the top bunk in the schoolhouse's only bedroom. The twenty-year-old from Namsos is allergic to cigarette smoke, and that fact qualifies her to sleep indoors as there are always some people who pretend they haven't been informed that the island has designated smoking zones. Moreover, she has earned it. Currently Jorid works in Oslo as the campaign secretary for the Labor Party, deployed to the youth organization. She didn't really have time to come to Utøya, and she felt that she was done with summer camp. In the context of AUF, twenty can feel old. However, it was decided that she should go as it was considered a part of her job. When the AUF members become more familiar with the campaign secretary, it'll be easier to ask them to put in an extra effort during the election campaign. It should be mentioned that Jorid slept outside last year, in a borrowed tent where the owner had forgotten to put in any flooring. That same year someone thought it would be great fun to collect as many frogs as possible and throw them into targeted tents. It's not that Jorid has anything against frogs per se, but she left the camp in summer 2010 with one resolution: "No more sleeping in tents on Utøya."

Jorid belongs to the Registration and Parking work crew. The name has been shortened to Mainland since the seven or eight in the group are the only party members who stay on the mainland. Their tasks are to register participants and guests, park cars, and check baggage. Jorid climbs down the steps of her bunk at around seven and fishes out her clothes from the bag on the chair. All members of the crew must have the same college jacket to distinguish them from the crowd. Moreover, it's also a politically correct statement. The rainbow flag printed on the jacket is in support of gay rights, first introduced during a San Francisco parade in 1978, and each color symbolizes something beautiful: red for life, orange for health, yellow for the sun, green for nature, blue for harmony, and violet for the spirit. Jorid uses up her fresh morning energy to curse the too tight jacket, which clings to her body. It feels neither harmonious nor healthy. The jacket's small size is yet another reminder that the campaign secretary is getting too old for camp on Utøya.

This morning, Jorid takes the first boat over to Utstranda on the mainland. She and the others set up a party tent, a table, a PC, and a petty cash box. It always gets hectic when VIPs and the press come to visit. Today will likely turn out to be chaotic. Parking spaces are few because of the rain and mud. The top two levels of the parking structure can't be used. "Oh no, not another car" has been a frequently used phrase in the party tent the last few days. Hence it's all the more important that drivers surrender their car keys so that the crew can strategically park the cars in the cramped space that's available. An organizational slipup has led to there being too few people with a driver's license among the crew on the mainland, so Jorid has ended up with many more parking assignments. She takes shelter under the tent and plays with the ID bracelets while they wait for the crew on the MS *Thorbjørn* to come over with breakfast.

Jorid has a red and white bracelet labeled "crew." A bracelet without that label means that a camp participant has paid 1,000 Norwegian kroner for three meals a day. A blue plastic bracelet costs 700 Norwegian kroner and provides one meal a day, that meal being dinner. Journalists and photographers get green plastic bracelets and sparkling water at the information house. Lecturers have white plastic bracelets. Then there are all the party members who come on day trips and get bracelets that vary from neon green to orange, depending on what day of the week it is. Finally, there's a separate category for police officers, government ministers, and political leaders. They don't need red, white, or blue bracelets. Nor do they need to register. Jorid keeps herself fairly warm under the tight purple jacket while the others trample around her to keep themselves warm. Out there on the lake they see the MS *Thorbjørn* approaching with bread, cold cuts, and some spreads on board. It'll have to be the cheese and ham for Jorid. She doesn't understand how people can bear to eat that crap chocolate spread Nugatti.

Hildegunn Fallang rubs the sleep out of her eyes. She stayed up late in the red party tent that the Oppland County camp had set up on the island at the bottom of the forest, next to the trail called E6. Ingrid Endrerud did something they actually were not allowed to do: she fetched a narrow conference table with folding legs from the little hall. Party members placed the table amid the new camp chairs Morten Djupdal had purchased. The battery-driven Clas Ohlson lamp hanging from the ceiling was also acquired for the occasion. Coziness is a primary goal on Utøya, while rules may often be bent according to the occasion. The county friends talked about everything and nothing and ate a variety of chocolate spreads for supper—even though the fridge contained real mayonnaise, turkey ham, and blue cheese in a tube. The only dent in Hildegunn's happiness was the frogs hopping around just outside the tent. She saw that they were small and knew that they couldn't do any harm, but she has a surreal fear of the slimy creatures.

Hildegunn takes out her earphones, sticks her head out of the opening in the blue tent, and sees a friend put on soccer boots in the rain. The campaign song from the 2005 election, "Red," is playing over the PA system. The girl from Hadeland is tired, cold, and hungry, but her opening statement that Friday morning is: "That's so nice. They're even playing 'Red.'" Henning Kvitne's song brings forth good feelings, as the 2005 campaign was their first. "Red for the heart that beats / Who has not only himself in his thoughts / Red for the strong warm hands / That help also those they don't know." Hildegunn wears shorts, a T-shirt, shin pads, and studded shoes; she grabs a slice of bread and jogs down to the soccer field.

A girl with long dark hair wakes up a little groggily in her military green three-man tent. Some experienced party leaders have no qualms about sleeping indoors because they've earned the right. Not so Ingrid Marie Vaag Endrerud. She's of the opinion that if one is staying on Utøya, one should sleep in a tent. Admittedly she has the luxury of sleeping alone in the tent on a thick blue inflatable mattress, but she doesn't act important because of that. On the contrary, she is feeling pretty small now. Due to a lack of players, the cheerleader from the town of Gjøvik has to play in the soccer match. Soccer doesn't come to her naturally.

Ingrid is taking drama in school. She shouts more loudly and frequently than anybody on the cheerleading squad. She can't play soccer, but she can cheer best. The AUF leader pulls out black thermal undergarments with red seams, blue denim shorts, and a thick woolen sweater from a bag. For a moment Ingrid contemplates wearing sneakers, but she's so bad at playing soccer that no one will notice that she's not properly equipped. Ingrid puts on her reddish blue rubber boots and a yellow raincoat and goes out of the tent. She's already late for the soccer match.

In the Oppland camp the obvious topic of conversation is yesterday's Datarock concert. Party members danced for over an hour in front of the outdoor stage to hits like "Computer Camp," "Life Is a Musical," and "Fa-Fa-Fa." An avid fan from Gjøvik dressed up in Datarock's signature red jogging suit. Some of the girls thought he was a member of the band and asked whether he could autograph their breasts. The eighteen-year-old had no choice but to say yes. As the concert drew to a close, one girl managed to drown out the music with, "Can I get a hug?" All the youngsters, or at least as many as there was room for, were allowed to come up on stage to join the band from Bergen. The vocalist, Fredrik Saro, then urged everyone to hug each other. "Together, Datarock and AUF shall save the world," he cried out and got wild cheers in response. The musicians would hardly say the same thing at a Young Conservatives Camp. When a British magazine recently asked the band members what they liked best about Norway, the answer was succinct: "Our extensive social welfare system." For a lot of Norwegians, and for everyone in front of the stage at Utøya, the welfare state is synonymous with the Labor Party. When the music started up again, the band members moved up against the load-bearing wall at the back of the stage. They finished with the theme song from a popular teen movie in the 1980s: "I've had the time of my life / No, I never felt this way before / Yes, I swear it's the truth / And I owe it all to you." Many felt that this was the best concert ever on Utøya. "Insanely great" and "awesome" were some of the words bandied about.

After the concert, the Datarock guys hung out with the youngsters at the cafeteria building, selling red suits and signing autographs. Several campers got the Bergen band to sign autographs on the back of their Utøya ID bracelets. Jorid noted the hysteria in the distance, along with her friends Hanne Hestø Ness and Lene Maria Bergum, who worked at the night cafe. She was more than satisfied that the band members were obviously stone cold sober, unlike the warm-up band. They had just as

much fun in the cafe as in the main hall, where karaoke was being per-
formed. There's a widespread misconception that it's impossible to sing
and dance while making junk food. The kitchen crew has been running
smoothly since Tuesday, thanks to an inspiring chef, who also insisted
that everyone had to be polite to one other. The obedient crew took his
words literally and always said thank you. "Hamburger; thank you." "Order
received; thank you." "The french fries are done; thank you." "Thanks for
tonight; thank you."

Some girls from Østfold County seduced the karaoke enthusiasts with
the song "Let It Swing." The audience stood up and sang along. They were
almost as popular as the bold and hip-swiveling Eskil Pedersen, who's
always surprised that someone has signed him up to sing macho songs
like "Barbie Girl" and "Oops, I Did It Again." Not this year though. As the
newly elected AUF leader, he volunteered freely. In his opinion, he didn't
sing Britney Spears's hit song "Hit Me Baby One More Time" in a raun-
chy manner. Eskil flirted with the audience, blowing many kisses to them.
"Oh, baby, baby. My loneliness is killing me." But no one made a bigger
impression than the three Oppland guys who danced to the catchy song
"Mambo No. 5." Their vocal skills were so-so, and none of them knew the
lyrics, but what an impressive dance performance it was! The young girls
with too much makeup screamed in front of the stage in the main hall
as if they were at their first Justin Bieber concert. Not all the girls are on
Utøya for the political workshops. And not all the guys either. So no one
was shocked when one of the fifteen-year-old girls stopped in the middle
of her dancing, pointed to one of the guys, and cried out, "He's mine!"

Ingrid, Morten, and Hildegunn spent the rest of the evening in the red
party tent at the campground. The high point was when one of the young
and popular dance guys from Oppland came to the tent after karaoke.
Hildegunn and Ingrid asked him whether the other two had been
swarmed by the girls. The answer was a smile and a nod pointing to the
steps in front of the cafeteria building. Morten told him to go and take
a picture with his mobile phone camera, so he left but soon came back
with the results. Hildegunn and Ingrid felt like old gossipmongers, sitting on their camp chairs and grinning at the images of the girls flirting
with the guys by the steps to the cafeteria. Or was it the other way round?
That's how Utøya should be: you fall in love, frequently and deeply. With
people and also with the island. And preferably with politics. Ingrid
crawled into bed at two in the morning. It was three when Hildegunn

rationally but reluctantly left the others and lay down exhausted on the cot in the tent she had borrowed from Morten. "We're supposed to play a soccer match tomorrow," she said before leaving.

Ingrid Endrerud doesn't like to play soccer, but she's sacrificing herself for the common good. Last year the Oppland County team won the soccer tournament that is played among the various county teams on the island. This year they're having problems even forming a team. They have had to join forces with their rival county, Hedmark. Inland, as the team has been dubbed, has a colorful team song. "We've come out of the barn; swimming lessons have we learned in Lake Mjøsa; we're tough, we can swear—go Inland!" Many of the youngsters have put on rubber boots, as Ingrid has done. Someone suggested that they should play mud rugby instead.

Hildegunn has to play at the back in the middle of a puddle. Ingrid is playing midfield and has understood that the point is to run up and down, a strategy that the eighteen-year-old masters surprisingly well. Soccer matches on Utøya are not like other soccer matches. Even the non-sporty types find it rewarding to run after a leather ball here. The competition is dead serious, but the game is unpretentious and inclusive. Cheerleaders scream themselves hoarse, and friendly curses are shouted. The North and South Trøndelag teams are not only rivals on the field but also argue on the sidelines about who has initiated the phrase "Beer and beatings, moonshine and fucking, South Trøndelag, South Trøndelag, yeah, yeah, yeah!" North Trøndelag members insist that they are the ones who're best at moonshine and beatings. Hedmark and Oppland cooperate today. There are fewer egoistic players. Ingrid doesn't score, but she centered the ball to a player who passed to the guy who kicked the ball into the goal. Innlandet Island wins 7–0 over Hordaland County and qualifies for the semifinals.

Morten is rudely awakened by jubilant cheers from the soccer pitch. When party members in Oppland want a bed indoors at Utøya, they send an application to county secretary Morten Djupdal. To whom does the county secretary himself apply? He applies to Morten Djupdal. And here he is, indoors in bed, as he hears Ingrid's laughter coming from one of the rooms in the barn. In the application to himself he justified his request for an indoor bed on the grounds of "headaches because of insomnia." People who're easily offended ethically could argue that everyone has trouble sleeping on Utøya, but Morten would rather not get bogged down in bureaucratic details. "I guess the soccer match went well," he thinks as he gets out of bed.

The previous year has progressed slowly for him as county secretary. Recruitment had been nonexistent, and the county board lost enthusiasm in the course of the spring to the point that it was sometimes just him and the Oppland party leader around the conference table. Many members declined to join the summer camp, and Morten was so distraught over the situation that at the end he just sat in his office and wept. He arrived on Utøya totally burned out on Tuesday, which was actually his last day as county secretary, and had spent the last few days sleeping in the warm bed in the barn. He puts on a black AUF hoodie and thinks that he should go up to the Oppland campsite. The campers there are almost certainly demotivated by the crappy weather and are wondering whether to go home. Morten is also the county's delegation leader at this year's summer camp. His task is to help keep the party members' spirits up: "Remember how nice it was yesterday! There'll be good weather tomorrow, just wait and see."

In order to prevent the muddy pitch from being irreparably damaged, the matches are canceled for the rest of the day. The soccer players look like hell on the pitch in the fog. They have to shower quickly before the former prime minister, Gro Harlem Brundtland, arrives. Hildegunn has never liked to wash herself in the common showers; with three hundred girls going through the showers in the course of the day, it can get quite muddy and gritty, so she's one of those who puts on swimwear and dives into the lake from the Nakenodden promontory. It is cold but not that cold. In any case, it's just as cold in the showers. Afterward, she puts on loose black chinos, a gray AUF hoodie, and an Aztec yellow raincoat. The dark green rubber boots she has on were borrowed from her mother. Outside the tent the rain is still coming down in buckets.

Thursday was just idyllic. At the amphitheater, in front of hundreds of youngsters on the sunny, grassy slope, Foreign Minister Jonas Gahr Støre discussed the Middle East conflict with Sidsel Wold from the Norwegian Broadcasting Corporation (NRK), Norwegian People's Aid's Kirsten Belck-Olsen, and Eskil Pedersen. The youngsters liked the foreign minister's message that Israeli occupation must end and that the Palestinians should have their own state, and he got a lot of extra cheers when he demanded that the West Bank barrier be demolished. There was just as much applause when the foreign minister made a backhanded comment about Barack Obama, who had declared that Americans would not accept UN recognition of the Palestinian state: "The United States has said it would veto [recognition]; that's its business." AUF has long been a supporter of the international economic boycott of Israel. New this year is that the youth organization advocates a unilateral Norwegian trade embargo. Eskil believes that the drastic measure must be interpreted in light of the widespread frustration among party members that Israel continues to violate human rights. Negotiations and discussions continue while the plight of the Palestinians worsens day by day. AUF wants to have a more activist Middle East policy than that of the Labor Party and the Norwegian government.

Enthusiastic boys and girls got up from the ground, shook off the grass, put their hands to their hot faces, and regretted that they had ignored their mothers' advice to put on sunblock. Stine Renate Håheim had sat at the bottom of the slope, close to the trees, and half her face got sunburned. She had come straight to Utøya after a two-week stay in Athens, where about four hundred activists from around the world were waiting for permission to travel to Palestine with medical supplies. That Norwegian members of parliament get involved in controversial projects such as Ship to Gaza isn't the norm, but neither is the twenty-seven-year-old from Nord-Aurdal municipality. She was exasperated by the fact that the foreign minister, earlier in the summer, would not answer the question of whether the blockade violated international law. She also supports the youth organization in calling for a unilateral Norwegian trade boycott of Israel. The former AUF central committee member responsible for the Middle East arrived on Utøya tired but excited, with a new sense of idealism and commitment. Sidsel Wold and Kirsten Belck-Olsen, whom she has met several times in Palestine, are two of the toughest women she knows.

After the debate, Støre strutted up to the tent area. In the northern Norway camp, the foreign minister was greeted by waving AUF flags and banners. The youngsters wouldn't talk to him about the High North policy, as one might assume, but rather about the famine in the Horn of Africa. They had taken the initiative to start a fund-raiser. Party members wanted the foreign minister to be the first to put money into the donation box. "If you have some money, that is." Støre had 200 Norwegian kroner. While the photographers' cameras flashed against the lights and the television cameras zoomed in on the donation box, he said to the national media, "Typical AUF." It's July, the vacation period and carefree days. The youngsters are on a secure island with full facilities in the north of Lake Tyri, far from the hustle and bustle of the city. Yet their thoughts are with those who have nothing. It's beautiful. Some may argue that they're far removed from reality. Naive, romantic, and idealistic. But the island is a place on earth where you don't shun clichés—you actively seek them out. On Utøya, socialism is always on the wing, even if the sun don't shine, as it says in the AUF song.

After lunch, or what is called dinner on Utøya, Støre played for AUF Oslo against South Trøndelag in a soccer match. He changed to shorts, soccer boots, and a T-shirt. The soccer boots were impressive since he had come directly from the family cabin. Everyone on the Oslo team was supposed to wear T-shirts with an advertisement for AUF's newly launched website, jeg.stemmer.no. Johanne Butenschøn Lindheim picked out a size XXL from the cardboard box. The leader of AUF Oslo looked at her in surprise and smiled, "Aren't you just a medium?" True enough, but Johanne liked to have a little more room. The film team requested that she go through the session again so that it could get better pictures. For Johanne the repetition was bearable, but then she began to worry that the camera was getting on people's nerves.

The South Trøndelag players already got a psychological advantage during their warm-up when they ran back and forth on the field and sang to underline the fact that there was nothing wrong with their condition. Furthermore, their supporters' chants from the sidelines were louder and more creative. The members of one group held each other around the shoulders, rocked side to side, and sang, "It's my day today, my God what a wonderful day." NRK was filming the match but was lured away by free waffles and soft drinks. Photo enthusiast Tore Sinding Bekkedal picked up NRK's camera and started to film the dribbling and tackling. The Oslo team had lost one of its most powerful weapons in the battle to psych out its opponents. Eskil had previously made the mistake of cheering too loudly for one particular team or cursing at the referee. This could be interpreted as partiality on the side of the AUF leadership. Hence he now preferred to shout diplomatic encouragements from the sidelines such as, "Come on everybody!"

If the foreign minister were to be tackled in such a way that the result was a torn ligament, it would first of all be unfortunate for Støre, but there was no ignoring the fact that it would give the press photographers a fresh new angle to the news coverage from Utøya. Eskil's other concern was short-lived and hypothetical, though no less a scoop for the journalists. Before the match someone had joked that Trond Giske (the industry minister and Støre's party rival) would show up unannounced and play for South Trøndelag. It would have been a legendary Utøya match; moreover, no political commentator with the right instincts would refrain from using the match as a metaphor for the battle of the Labor Party's two crown princes. Neither Støre's reinforcement of the team nor the new T-shirts helped, although the foreign minister almost scored once.

Cooling down in Lake Tyri seemed like a good consolation prize for Johanne. She wondered whether she should bathe in her undergarments, but she kept the soccer jersey on. There was, after all, a movie camera close by. The hot and sweaty gang from Oslo took running jumps from the pebble beach in Bolsjevika Bay into the water. The lake was surprisingly cool and the stony bottom was uncomfortably rough, but Johanne nevertheless felt a sense of joy right then and there. Furthermore, the carefree and playful splashing made for interesting scenes for the film documentary. The youngsters from Oslo came up together from the water. Dripping wet, walking barefooted on the gravel, and carrying soccer boots in their hands, they moved up the hill toward the campground. Johanne changed to her favorite dress and put on makeup in the tent before she hung up the wet suit and sports bra on a stick. The sun felt warm, worries started fading, and that Utøya feeling finally came. But the first person to see Johanne in the beautiful blue dress made a backhanded compliment: "Westside Lady." Comments about her affiliation and dress are usually meant jokingly, but when they are repeated often enough, if one knows the strength of "eastside romanticism" in the labor movement, it's not easy to be completely unaffected.

Jonas Gahr Støre left Utøya inspired by the youths. He noticed during the visit that with Eskil as the leader, AUF has been freshly energized. The foreign minister left Lake Tyri with a sense of belonging in a meaningful community. AUF members returned the compliment by insisting that the foreign minister had helped to make the perfect Utøya day. There wasn't a cloud in the sky, not a breath of wind in the air, only the sun reflected on Lake Tyri. Eskil couldn't recall a nicer, warmer, and more summery day on Utøya. Sun, swimming, soccer, Middle East, Datarock, karaoke, hookahs, and intimate conversations long into the night.

Socialism with Wings

Fellowship is real but also imagined. It's designed to consolidate party loyalty, strengthen the fighting spirit, and mold future leaders. "It's now more than ever! For if unity frays and dies, our enemies await / And they will split our group. / And our flames will turn to ashes and embers," according to a popular workers' song. Every community creates its own exclusive narrative where those who don't fit in are ignored. Hence there are few who care that a twelve-hectare site in Hole municipality once symbolized all that the labor movement has fought against—the monarchy, large-scale farmers, the bourgeoisie. The island of Utøya was owned by the king when it was mentioned in written sources for the first time in 1577. Over the centuries it was, along with two other islands to its north—Geitøya and Storøya—used as grazing land by farmers from Sundvollen on the mainland. Hence the name Udøen, the island that lies furthest out from Sundvollen. In the 1890s Utøya was purchased by an authoritarian, conservative man. Jens Kristian Meinich Bratlie's pet cause was the battle against socialism. Utøya was the unmarried, sturdy, and combative man's private vacation paradise. Therefore it's paradoxical that he chose to sell the island to a branch of the main trade union, the Oslo Trade Union Confederation. The organization paid 28,000 Norwegian kroner and intended to use Utøya as a holiday camp for the children of the unemployed. A mess-up with the concession led to this plan not really being offered until 1938, just two years before the Nazis occupied the island. In 1950 Utøya was donated to the AUF in connection with the labor youth organization's fiftieth anniversary.

The story of Utøya is parallel to a power shift in Norwegian history from the official state's enlightened despotism to the era of Einar Gerhardsen, where AUF's purpose was to contribute ideologically trained recruits who could administer the new, egalitarian Norway. The method was simple: morning gymnastics, folk songs around the campfire, and splashing by the waterside. Learning through play isn't a pedagogical strategy that Rudolf Steiner patented. There's no Norwegian island that has shaped the political landscape of Norway more than Utøya. They say that the Labor Party headquarters isn't really located in Youngstorget

Square in Oslo, where there's only room for bosses. It's located on Utøya, a forty-minute drive from Youngstorget Square.

From a distant height Utøya looks just like any island, but every nook, path, and building has a name, anecdotes, and a character. From the mainland it's about half a kilometer to the stone pier on the east side of Utøya, where there's a swimming ban because of power lines under the water. The current ferry, MS *Thorbjørn*, was built at Oskarshamn Shipyard in 1948, and *Rasmus*, as it was then called, was owned by the Swedish Navy until the 1990s. AUF's new acquisition, to the tune of 250,000 Swedish kroner, was inaugurated by Justice Minister Gerd-Liv Valla in the summer of 1997. "I think it has just as much capacity as the man it's named after," said a contented Valla. The man was then prime minister Thorbjørn Jagland, who had formed his first government the previous autumn. The ferry can take up to fifty passengers if its certification is upheld.

From the ferry berth by the pier a gravel path leads to stone stairs and up to the white information house. Above the entrance hangs a red "Utøya" sign, constructed of wooden debris. Old AUF party members would call the information house the main house because it has been there for as long as the island has been in the party's possession. Young party members will argue that it's a slightly odd designation for the little white house since the cafeteria building in the middle of the island is where all the relevant activities are conducted. The oldest part of the information house stems from the 1860s. When the labor movement took over Utøya, the main house then had two spacious living rooms, a smaller room, and a kitchen on the ground floor. Upstairs there were four rooms with closets, and one of the rooms had a door to a verandah facing south. The basement was large and bright. Now the information house has been properly modernized and has the island's only television.

To the right of the information house are the red barn and granary and the amphitheater where political meetings are held with hundreds of party members sitting on the grassy slope. To the left of the path leading up to the information house is a volleyball court, where the surface is known for causing ankle sprains. At the end of the soccer pitch against the water on the north side is a promontory called Stoltenberget, named after two prominent Norwegian politicians after they generously donated the profits from their book, *Conversations*, to the island in summer 2010. When the party members thanked Thorvald and Jens Stoltenberg for the generous donation of 270,000 Norwegian kroner by naming the promontory after them, the daily *Dagbladet* joked that the young politicians should name the rock ledge next to it after Justice Minister Knut Storberget. Stoltenberget is located on a bay called Bolsjevika, a frequently used swimming and barbecue spot for the youngsters.

Continuing west past the information house up the hill to the center of the island, you will come to LO Peak, where there are three small, spartanly furnished guest cabins. Behind the peak lies the green-painted cafeteria building, which has the little and main halls, dining hall, kitchen, and kiosk, as well as the media room and the *Planet Utøya* newsletter editing room. At present the cafeteria building is used for conference activities, but when it was first built in the 1930s, it housed dormitories. The campground is on the large, usually greenish-brown lawn in front of the cafeteria building, down the slope to the south, where party members pitch their tents according to their county of origin. The T-shaped lavatory block is east of the cafeteria building, and northeast of the campground. There are common toilets, but the shower facility is separated by gender. From seven o'clock in the morning there's heated water in the pipes. Some objecting voices claim that the water stays hot only until about five minutes past seven.

Outside the kiosk at the entrance to the cafeteria building, among the Isabella vanilla ice cream, Turkish Pepper sweets, and coffee deals for 100 Norwegian kroner hangs a postcard in English: "Utøya. Welcome to the island. The Nordic paradise." On the window someone has pasted up a faded clipping from the *Ringerike* newspaper with the headline, "Trout weighing 7.5 kilos caught in Lake Tyri." There is, of course, a wheelchair ramp up to the platform in front of the kiosk. By the entrance stand black garbage bins for plastic, paper, and other waste. The youngsters will put anything that can't be sorted into the last type: "Polystyrene cups, smelly socks, and old underwear," says a white sign beside the bin. On the wall hangs an old white garbage bin from Drammen Ice Cream on which someone has hung a green and white sticker with the words "Prejudice leads to stupidity." All the buildings on Utøya are spartan. You have to be a labor politician to appreciate their charm.

The fabled Lovers' Lane, where many a youngster got his or her most memorable kiss, goes all along the western shore of the island, from Bolsjevika Bay in the north to the Nakenodden promontory in the south. When the stunt reporter Alex Rosén was a guest on the island in 1994, he was determined to be a part of all the local traditions. He stripped off his clothes and threw himself enthusiastically into the lake. No one had the heart to tell him that nude bathing was something in which party members traditionally participated only on the first night on the island and preferably without an overly large audience.

On the south side lies the red-painted schoolhouse, which was built in the 1940s out of materials the Germans had used for roadwork on the mainland during the war. A green swing stands close by, but it hasn't been used for some years. Norwegian People's Aid is located at the schoolhouse. Beside the first-aid tent, where the health workers drink coffee and talk about why everything is much better now compared to the old days while they patch up bruises and cool down sports injuries, there are three *lavvus* (a type of tepee) for them to sleep in.

The island isn't big. You can walk at a leisurely pace from north to south in under ten minutes. The main gravel road is the E6. The road goes in a circle from the information house up to the cafeteria building, then through the campground and woods to the schoolhouse and back along the east side toward the back of the information house. Most of the youngsters prefer to go along Lovers' Lane.

It's not just the buildings that have survived from the old days. The program follows a strict routine. On Friday one of the top Labor Party politicians comes; on Saturday the prime minister comes or, God forbid, just a party leader. There are concerts with well-known artists performing; there are barbecues at Bolsjevika and plenty of leftovers for supper. Dinner is served at one o'clock, as though the Utøya youths have more in common with the hard-working farmers from the 1700s than cosmopolitan intellectuals from the continent. Other rules and traditions are more up to date. If you have allergies, you may be exempted from sleeping in a tent. In the spirit of gender equality volleyball and soccer teams must have as many boys as girls. The island has an annual budget of around 2 million Norwegian kroner, but most of the work is done by volunteers; for example, in the summer camp around one hundred party members at any one time are a part of the work crew. However, the toilets in the outhouses are now emptied by professionals. The reason for this decision was based on lessons learned from harsh experience. Hedda Foss Five and Sindre Fossum Beyer emptied the toilets in 1994. The result of their amateurish efforts was that the barrel cracked open and all the yellowish brown contents spilled out. Beyer, who later became a prominent adviser to Jens Stoltenberg, augmented the spillage with her own vomit.

Rival party youth organizations are green with envy about AUF's summer camp. In 2008 AUF leader Martin Henriksen welcomed 750 party members to Utøya, where there were political workshops, concerts, and campfires. At the same time the Progress Party (FrP) held a camp in Strømstad in Sweden. A record 120 participants got to know one other in the course of one Caribbean-themed evening at the local water park. The foremost politicians in Norway come to Utøya, where they leave their historical imprint. Thorbjørn Jagland was on his first Pentecostal camp in 1974. There he heard former prime minister Einar Gerhardsen talk about the Spanish Civil War, while another former prime minister, Trygve Bratteli, gave an account of what it was like to be an inmate of a concentration camp. It was also here, around the campfire, that Jagland met his wife, Hanne Grotjord. Utøya has the prettiest girls and the handsomest guys. Females are overrepresented among the 9,500 party members. Precisely because of that fact, a big contingent of sixteen- and seventeen-year-old boys comes to the summer camp, which then has the effect of evening out the gender distribution. Everyone falls in love at least a dozen times during the camp, so long as one isn't stuffy or very busy. "There're so many to choose from," a still single AUF leader said to the *Dagsavisen* newspaper before the 2011 summer camp.

Lovers' Lane is usually quite busy after suppertime. If the interactions get a little too saucy, people sitting by the waterside the next day may read about it in the camp newspaper, *Planet Utøya*. One year former AUF leader Jens Stoltenberg was raffled off in an auction. The prize was a romantic stroll with him along Lovers' Lane. The lucky winner was the future culture minister, Turid Birkeland. She took a walk with the party's then crown prince along the shore but came back a little disappointed and unkissed, albeit full of facts about Norway's membership in NATO. If someone is observed creeping out of the wrong tent in the morning, which has happened a few times in the camp's history, it becomes headline news in the camp newsletter. And even if you've slept alone one night, on your own thin mattress, the *Planet Utøya* newsletter may still say that you crawled out of Don Juan's steamy, narrow, one-man tent the day before, with suspiciously tangled hair and a sheepish grin. The camp newsletter has more risqué personal ads than the *Dagbladet* newspaper, but people argue vehemently about whether the ones from Utøya are pure fantasy. The inside jokes are crude and not infrequently have a titillating, flirtatious undertone.

The camp lives up to its reputation as "Love Island" and "Norway's best pickup place" with speed-dating events. The main hall teems with two hundred boys and girls in red conference chairs facing each other, row by row. Some quick questions about hobbies, family trees, and favorite colors—"Where're you from?"; "Do you do sports?"; "What kind of music do you listen to?"—plus some footsie under the table, and then it's on to the next potential mate. The girls are seated while the guys move around. Two minutes for each person. You don't need more to initiate Utøya's most popular activity. Many think this is harmless, innocent fun, but the Labor Party knows the importance of creating sustainable dynasties. The wisecracking leader of the Norwegian Confederation of Trade Unions (LO), Konrad Nordahl, claimed that the AUF was "a marriage bureau." It should be noted that to be named "Norway's best pickup place" by *Dagbladet* has its disadvantages. Some people who go to the summer camp are neither members of the AUF nor particularly interested in the famine in Africa. The most notorious skirt chasers are exposed through their names and ages being printed in *Planet Utøya* as a warning to the rookies.

Parents are often reluctant to send fifteen-year-olds to camps or music festivals. This isn't the case here. Many even accept the fact that their son or daughter would prefer to skip the family vacation to Izmir in favor of the short week on Utøya. At the Roskilde Festival, there's a lot of crazy stuff going on, while on Utøya the youths are in the company of adults, hired guards, and Norwegian People's Aid, who'll heal all wounds, both real and imagined. And best of all, the camp is free of alcopop, Ringnes beer, and Liebfraumilch wine, despite the fact that it has a liquor license. Jens Stoltenberg managed, in his time, to smuggle alcohol onto the island, and there have been episodes of both drugs and fist fights, but the climate has changed in recent years. The earnest generation is imbued with strong moral values. There's no one singing abusive songs any longer: "We'll geld Carl I. Hagen with a long and rusty knife" or the classic "We'll fill our bathtub with Young Conservatives' blood." Or almost none. Furthermore, the registration process on the mainland has become more thorough. Many foreign visitors, especially those from Eastern Europe, suffer a big blow after being forced to empty their bags. The registration booth could end up looking like a medium-sized liquor store. Winners of the soccer tournament are now bathed in the kind of "champagne" that children are served on New Year's Eve. Every parent must just love this combination of safety, indulgence, and seriousness. The only thing parents need to worry about is that the youngsters might eat Nugatti Air, Nugatti Crisp, or Nugatti Max chocolate spread for breakfast four days in a row.

Utøya is a place for fellowship, singing, love, political discussions, and major political controversies. In 1991 there was a scandal when it appeared that some people on Utøya had asked the Ministry of Defense for help in transporting two NRK buses over to the island. The TV channel wanted to broadcast live from the island, but Utøya's own boat was too small. When the AUF, under the leadership of Turid Birkeland, made a request to the engineering regiment at the Hvalsmoen military camp, it got a flat refusal. Birkeland was told that the task could not be carried out without retaining soldiers who were going on leave. But there's always an alternative. Via the political leadership of the ministry, it was determined that the task could be carried out by an American engineering corps of the NATO forces that were on exercise in Norway at the time. Defense Minister Johan Jorgen Holst's personal secretary at the time, Frode Berge, happened to be a member of the central committee of the AUF.

Twenty-eight soldiers built an armored ferry that transported the buses to the island. "That's the way we want the military to be used," said a proud AUF leader. The debate raged for days. Members of the opposition demanded Holst's head on a platter—or at least his secretary's. They thought that this was yet another example of the Labor Party's arrogance and misuse of political power. The chairman of the Progress Party's youth wing, Jan Erik Fåne, sent a letter to NRK's current affairs manager, Egil Sundar, and asked him to cover his party's youth camp in Grimstad in August of that year. In appreciation of the Americans' rescue operation, it's only reasonable that the party members have named the old outhouse in the woods after the organization that has actually caused the AUF much torment. The green oblong wooden building with three red doors behind the cafeteria building is called the NATO toilets.

The AUF is part of the establishment, but the youth organization's mandate is to be a corrective force. Say no to the EU when Labor says yes. Say no to oil drilling in Lofoten and Vesterålen when Labor says yes. Say yes to a unilateral Norwegian trade boycott of Israel when Labor says no. The AUF has power and veto power at the same time. The Labor Party expects its representatives to be accountable and realpolitik to be set aside, while in the AUF it's idealism, visions, and dreams that rule. In the AUF, a multicultural Norway, feminism, gay rights, and global engagement are more than just empty words. Labor has struggled to recruit politicians from minority backgrounds to the leadership, despite the fact that the party's youth organization is the country's most multicultural. At the camp on Utøya in the summer of 2011 all the world's religions are represented, with almost as many nations as the membership of the UN—Bosnia, Kurdistan, Pakistan, India, Chechnya, Somalia, Turkey, Ghana, and Sweden, to name but a few. Multicultural Norway originated as a kind of novelty for the elder generation of Labor in the 1970s, but for party members diversity, cultural tolerance, and broadmindedness have been an integral part of what they grew up with—a natural way of being and just the way it should be. For some Labor Party members immigration and asylum policies are a purely theoretical discussion about amending some legislative clauses, but for many party members they are deeply personal and emotional issues.

Hence AUF members can be relentless in their criticism when they see that adult politicians talk as if they were still living in the 1950s. When Labor politician Libe Rieber-Mohn, after a series of brutal rapes in Oslo in spring 2011, suggested that newly arrived asylum seekers should undergo a psychological examination, the AUF leader in Oslo, Håvard Vedehus, gave a scathing response: "A typical Progress Party initiative." He also clearly chose sides in the discussion on religious headwear in court. "You won't change a judge's background, attitudes, or opinions by taking off the headwear—it's like believing that Raymond will cheer for Lyn soccer club when he tears off his Vålerenga club jersey. I think this is naive," Vedehus said on the podium in the People's House in Oslo during the Labor Party congress in spring 2011. In the audience was an Indian Norwegian, Prableen Kaur. She started wearing a turban at age twelve, for which she had to endure innumerable abusive epithets and years of bullying. The Romsås girl wore a turban, against parental advice, because she saw it as a symbol of equality and solidarity. For her it wasn't about religion but about women's rights. Turbans shouldn't be reserved for male Sikhs. Jonas Gahr Støre, the head of the integration committee, persuaded the congress to ban religious headwear for prosecutors and judges. In the audience, an eighteen-year-old girl saw her dream for her career crushed, and she wept.

In the spring of 2011 Eskil Pedersen had a decisive confrontation with FrP politicians Christian Tybring-Gjedde and Per Willy Amundsen, who claimed that immigrant boys were more hot-headed than Norwegian boys and that Muslims had a worse work ethic than others. "This not only borders on racism, it is racism," wrote the AUF leader in an article. He further wrote: "The extreme right is gaining ground in Europe, and the FrP is playing with a potentially and historically extremely dangerous fire." The AUF took the step of charging Tybring-Gjedde with violation of the penal code provisions for racism, which prohibit discriminatory or hateful statements based on national or ethnic origin.

On Wednesday, July 20, 2011, Eskil unveiled a plaque on Utøya in honor of party members who had fallen in the Spanish Civil War. Seventy-five years ago Gunnar Skjeseth, Martin Schei, Torbjørn Engebretsen, and Odd Olsen fought against Franco's totalitarian ideology. "There's much to be proud of in our history. One of the things we can be most proud of is the fight against fascism," he said in front of hundreds of party members. At the bottom of the plaque, which hangs on a tree opposite the cafeteria building's main square, is an excerpt from Nordahl Grieg's poem "To Youth," written during the Spanish Civil War: "War is contempt for life; peace nurtures it. Use all your might; death will lose."

The Spanish Civil War is a little-known chapter in European history. The war divided Norway in the 1930s. The conservative parties in Norway rallied to Franco, while the socialists and Communists supported the leftist government. The Labor Party was almost riven apart by internal discord. The government of Johan Nygaardsvold aligned itself with the major powers in not interfering in the conflict, primarily to protect Norwegian dried fish exports. Norwegians were forbidden to enlist for military service in the Spanish Civil War. Nevertheless, hundreds enlisted, among them several party members. In recent years there has been a growing interest in the war, largely due to the publication of *A Thousand Days*, a book that depicts Norway's and the Norwegians' role in the civil war. One of the authors is Jo Stein Moen, a former central committee member and deputy chairman of the AUF. At the summer camp of 2009, a few months before the book was published, Jo Stein gave a lecture on Spain at the schoolhouse, focusing on the AUF members' role in the civil war. In late autumn 2010 he sent a suggestion to the leadership: "As Spain in the years 1936 to 1939 was the first time and the first place that some people actually put up resistance against the rise of fascism and AUF members traveled down there voluntarily—as soldiers, health workers, and reporters—a plaque in honor of those who fell would be an appropriate gesture."

Eskil got help from Jo Stein Moen to write the speech he gave on July 20. In front of the plaque he talked about the idealism that made some young people enlist in a war in another country and who were killed in the name of tolerance. They were young like those in the audience, party members like them, and one of them even went from a course on Utøya organized by the trade union straight to the trenches. Eskil was close to tears several times, and it surprised him. Even though it was all about the past and about people he didn't know. But it was precisely the historical distance that made his eyes tear up and his voice crack: "A word of gratitude for the sacrifices they made so that youths in Norway today can live a carefree, prosperous life, far removed from war, fascism, and dictators."

Eskil had joined the AUF as a fifteen-year-old. This was his twelfth year on Utøya but his first summer as AUF leader. The hope was that this would be the best camp ever—that it would have the best weather, the best alcohol-free parties, and the best media coverage. Gro, Jens, and Jonas would make sure of the last part. The capital's newspapers, NRK, and TV2 had taken the bait every single day. The headline in the local daily that day, Friday, July 22, was "It's grand with the big guns." It sounded like war reportage, but it was actually the headline for the newspaper's story on Jonas Gahr Støre's visit to Utøya the day before. It could just as well have been about war since the topic had been the Middle East, but it wasn't. It was about some of Norway's most famous politicians. Yesterday, Thursday, Jonas Gahr Støre had visited; Saturday, Jens Stoltenberg would come; and today, Friday, Gro Harlem Brundtland was coming. It didn't get any grander than that. "Brundtland is the feminist of all feminists," says Christina Nessa from Bergen to the newspaper before adding: "It's so grand with the big guns! The fact that Støre, Stoltenberg, and Brundtland come to the camp says something about the impact that Utøya has." The newspaper has also talked to the Oslo politician Khamshajiny Gunaratnam. She's the store manager in a tent booth called "Trade Ministry," located next to "Waffle Stand," which sells sweaters, T-shirts, pens, and badges with the redesigned AUF logo. "Here's where the youths receive valuable lessons in social democratic values," the twenty-three-year-old says to the local newspaper. Especially for first timers—that is, AUF members who are on Utøya for the first time—the gray tracksuit is popular. The nostalgic ones prefer T-shirts with the revolutionary slogan from 1789, "Liberté, égalité, fraternité." Liberty, Equality, Fraternity.

Before coming to the camp, a slightly nervous Eskil had conferred with former AUF leaders. It is, after all, a long way from working in a hamburger joint in Skien to giving the opening speech on Utøya, although the transition has been gradual. The former leaders reassured him that there was no reason to be anxious before the opening speech. They assured him that the campers were the most appreciative audience any politician could wish for. Anything he said would be met with wildly enthusiastic applause. Yet he had sat up until the wee hours of Wednesday morning with his advisers and rejected drafts, honed the text, and cut the speech down to an appropriate length. He had returned very early on Wednesday morning to the party office in order to ensure that all the main points were in place: make party members proud of Utøya and gear them up for the election campaign; challenge the party leadership; strongly condemn the Progress Party's immigration policy; and clearly confront the Conservative Party's attempts to steal the social democrats' rhetoric. The Conservatives' new slogan, "People, not billions," must be a typo, the speech says. It should actually be "People *with* billions."

After a brief interview with a journalist from the financial newspaper *Dagens Næringsliv*, where the photographer took a picture of him by the Aker River to give the impression of his being on the island, Eskil had left Youngstorget Square and driven out of the city in the direction of Hønefoss. The speech was ready and his mood was improving, but one factor was beyond his control: the weather. For the outsider the choice of venue for the speech may seem a trifling matter. The experienced speaker knows, however, that there's a difference between the acoustics indoors and outdoors. He or she knows it's easier to keep the audience's attention within the four walls, floor, and ceiling of a room. Unlike most AUF leaders giving their inaugural speech on Utøya, Eskil has chosen to tempt fate. He wants to hold his speech outdoors. But he had prepared an alternative introduction in case of rain: "I see that it's Erna Solberg who has arranged for the weather here on Utøya today. But my dears, we have a very clear message for Erna Solberg and the rest of the Conservatives: It will take more than a little rain to stop the AUF and electoral victory for Labor in this fall's election!" By the time Eskil and his entourage had arrived at the ferry berth at Utstranda on the mainland half an hour before the opening speech was supposed to be given, rain drops had started falling on the car's windscreen.

"Welcome to the absolute highlight of the year! Welcome to the biggest political youth summer camp! Welcome to the country's most beautiful island! Welcome to the AUF summer camp on Utøya 2011!" Eskil Pedersen called out from the amphitheater stage on Wednesday, July 20. Over five hundred AUF members sat on the grassy green slope and screamed until their vocal chords were sore and clapped until their hands turned red. They applauded when Eskil said that young people were interested in more than just cheap alcohol and gasoline. They applauded when he said that the AUF would eradicate poverty and create a new, just world. They applauded when he attacked the Progress Party's view of multicultural Norway: "Our message to the FrP is very clear: Those who mess with our friends with immigrant backgrounds will not be left in peace!" And they applauded when he talked about the cold, selfish bidding policies of the Conservative Party. But they applauded most of all when Eskil talked about the summer camp: "Utøya really is a summer dream. To those of you who're here for the first time, look forward to the days ahead—nothing is like the first Utøya camp."

The cheers he got in response could almost rival those for the revolutionaries outside the Bastille in Paris on July 14, 1789. The party members were not affected by mass psychosis; the youngsters were just convinced that at that moment in time the greatest people living on earth were gathered on this little green isle. Eskil ended his speech with an overt flirtation that also confirmed their worldview: "You're the best that Norwegian youth has to offer. You're beautiful. You're knowledgeable. You're enthusiastic. You're impatient. And you're at the AUF summer camp on Utøya. It doesn't get any better than that."

3

And Then He Fell Out with Everyone

A few hours ago a young paperboy had gone around at dawn and tossed newspapers on the doormats in the Skøyen neighborhood of west Oslo. Now the doors are opening at short, regular intervals. One woman emerges, bends down in a blue dressing gown and picks up *Aftenposten*, takes it with her into the kitchen, and reads the first section while she eats a cumin cheese sandwich and drinks freshly squeezed juice. She reads about how lower interest rates and a longer repayment period will save Greece and keep the euro zone intact. The front page confirms that there's not much happening in Norway. The financial crisis in southern Europe is the dominant news. The news in Norway on July 22, 2011, is about the new semester starting soon and a Christian center in Vestfold County that has ambitions of becoming Europe's largest.

It's a normal day in the Skøyen neighborhood. The weather is gray on the west side of the city. Each and every person has his or her own plans for the day—someone is taking the bus into his office at the Ministry of Justice; others follow their children to kindergarten; some are returning from their vacation; many will start theirs; most will rent a family movie and eat tacos for supper, while a few will go downtown to chat up girls. If there's one event that can unify Norwegians this Friday, it's the after-noon's decisive stage in the Tour de France. Yesterday Luxembourg's Andy Schleck won convincingly in the tough stage up to the Col du Galibier, 2,645 meters above sea level. The Norwegian cyclists took it easy and came in thirty-six minutes behind the winner. Today the winner will be decided from among the four favorites: Andy Schleck, Frank Schleck, Thomas Voekler, and Cadel Evans.

A young man wakes up in his mother's first-floor apartment at 18 Hoffs-veien Street just before eight. He doesn't really stand out with his light hair, blue eyes, round and slightly plump face, stained teeth from ciga-rettes and snuff, muscular upper body, and height of around 183 centi-meters. In fact he often seems anonymous in the company of others. Neighbors find the man polite, kind, and intelligent, but lately they have seen little of him. The thirty-two-year-old has no plans to watch Thor Hushovd and Edvald Boasson Hagen, the Norwegians in the Tour de

France, in the afternoon. Nor will he spend the day with his sixty-four-year-old mother, who, in a few hours, will take the tram to run some errands in the city center and buy shrimp for their dinner together in the evening. At eight o'clock, the young man makes himself breakfast at the kitchen counter. He also makes two packed lunches with the same bread toppings—cheese and ham—and drinks a protein shake. Of late he has been drinking four a day to increase his muscle mass.

He has told his mother that he's writing a history book about Norway and Europe in English. He has also said that for it to be as complete as possible, he'll have to start from 600 BC. When mother and son have discussed politics at the dinner table, she has found him uncomfortably intense; plus he has also dismissed her as a "small-time Marxist" and "feminist." The young man has talked about an impending civil war. He has increasingly shut himself up in his room, and in the last year he has become more and more strict and strange. The mother hasn't been allowed to sneeze in her own apartment. He has often complained about the food and that there are too many spiders in his room. He has refused to get up in the morning. He has kept bags of dietary supplements and backpacks filled with rocks in his room. Several times he has worn black and green clothes, which he calls survival gear. He has also been wearing a red uniform jacket with insignias. In April he told his mother that he was going to become a farmer. He had rented a farm with 9.1 hectares of arable land. The mother was happy that her son had finally found something to do and looked forward to visiting him on the farm, but it was never convenient to do so.

Two rented cars are parked outside the apartment in Skøyen. The night before, he parked a Volkswagen Crafter van outside Olsens Enke garden center on Sigurd Iversen Street, a few hundred meters from his mother's apartment. Then he went back to the farm he has been renting since April. The farm, Vålstua by the Glomma River, is an idyllic place with a farmhouse, barn, outbuildings, and flowerbeds. From there he fetched a gray Fiat Dublo. It was late before he came back from the farm in Rena, but now both cars are parked within walking distance of the apartment on Hoffsveien, in a quiet and child-friendly Norwegian neighborhood. Right in front of the block, on the other side of the road, is the Coop Mega supermarket. A little down the road in the direction of the highway are the Volvat veterinary clinic and the GymClub training studio. Inside the van is a bomb made from about 1.5 tons of fertilizer mixed with diesel.

The young man was born at Aker Hospital in Oslo on Tuesday, February 13, 1979. His diplomat father already had three children aged nine to fourteen from before, while his mother, a nurse, had a six-year-old daughter with a Swedish man. During the young man's first year the family lived in London, where his father worked at the Norwegian Embassy. His parents divorced in 1980, when he was one year old. The mother took custody of the boy and settled in Nedre Silkestrå, the newly built Oslo Housing and Savings Society (OBOS) housing, not so far from Hoffsvein, while his father moved to Paris as a member of the Norwegian OECD delegation. His father was mostly abroad when the thirty-two-year-old was a boy, so they didn't have much contact except during the summers, when the young man visited his father and stepmother in France. He had an average middle-class upbringing, and he himself thought he was in the company of responsible people. But the mother didn't have an easy time raising the boy and a daughter as a single parent. She had to work long hours to be able to afford to live on Oslo's west side, and the children were often home alone until late at night. In 1983 she went as far as to ask for help from the Norwegian Child Welfare Services for him and his half-sister, who was six years older. A psychologist examined the passive and timid boy and concluded that he had been a victim of neglect. The psychologist reported that if the conditions of his upbringing did not change, things could go wrong. Child Welfare Services took no action despite his father's having fought for custody after the report. Those were different times with different standards. The boy stayed with his mother and started to go to the Vigeland Park nursery.

He attended Smestad Elementary School. The resource-rich school is prestigious, not least because among its former pupils one can count the crown prince and princess, Haakon Magnus and Märtha Louise. Here it's important to have the proper logo on your jacket, and your dad's pockets should be deep. With a single mother who didn't earn a high income, it wasn't easy to live up to the standards of the school. He was moderately good in school, went around in his own head, could be dorky, but could also focus when he had decided to carry something out. He was teased because he lived alone with his mother. At Ris Middle School, where he started in 1992, it was tagging and sports that occupied him. During that time he got up at six every day to train before school started. He kept his anonymity there too, in a school characterized by distinctive social class signifiers. But he got some short-lived attention when he was accused of vandalism and responded by hitting a teacher in the chest. The yearbook from the ninth grade says: "Before, Anders was part of the gang, but then he fell out with everyone. Anders's goal is to have a perfect body, but we have to say that it's a long way away." In 1994 Child Welfare Services got involved again after he was arrested three times for tagging. They held discussions with the family, but the case was closed without any measures being taken.

In 1995 there was a break in communications between father and son. The young man himself blamed this on the fact that he listened to hip-hop music and dressed in sagging pants and a hoodie, all of which the more bourgeois father disliked. When, at the age of sixteen, he and a friend from the graffiti milieu were caught tagging and had to pay a sizable fine, there were rumors that one of them had snitched to the authorities. He was ostracized by his classmates and beaten up. He responded by escalating his training regimen before and after school. He ate raw eggs for lunch and did push-ups before he went out. He longed for some social redress, and it would come in the form of money. "Get rich or die trying," was the way he put it some years later.

Hartvig Nissen School was abandoned in favor of Oslo Commerce School after the young man's first year of high school, but the change in environment did not do much for his motivation, and he dropped out before the final school year was over in order to devote himself to politics. The companies he started, such as those in telephone sales and advertising boards, were forcibly dissolved or closed down. The advertising company, called "Media Group," went bankrupt in 2007. Although the firm that he established failed financially, the part of him that was socially engaged benefited from the company's sojourn at Nedre Slottsgate in Oslo. His company shared a lunchroom with a law firm that represented Ole Nicolai Kvisler, who was suspected of killing Benjamin Hermansen, a fifteen-year-old boy from the Holmlia suburb, in 2001. The young advertising entrepreneur took note of the defense efforts of Geir Lippestad, the lawyer for the right-wing extremist.

Neo-Nazism flourished in the Oslo suburbs of Ris and Bøler in the mid-1990s, with slogans such as "White Pride" and "Norway for Norwegians." Through his gang, Boot Boys, Kvisler fought against immigrants, Jews, and miscegenation, and just a few weeks before he stabbed Benjamin, he was supposed to have warned an acquaintance of his that something historic and memorable was about to happen. Joe Erling Jahr, his sidekick during the racially motivated killing in Holmlia, just before midnight on January 26, 2001, was called "Hollow" in the neo-Nazi community because of a sunken chest that was used as an ashtray at parties. Jahr's childhood had been difficult. Even though his mother could be away from home for months at a time, Child Welfare Services did not intervene. He was twelve years old when the police first knocked on the door. Veronica Andreassen, Kvisler's girlfriend and the third defendant in the case, had an equally troubled childhood, with divorce, fights, and domestic violence. She started doing drugs at age thirteen and ended up in foster care two years later. Compared with Jahr's and Andreassen's family background, Kvisler had had a harmonious adolescence, but all three were loners, and on at least one and perhaps more occasions they had felt threatened by immigrant gangs. They got protection from the neo-Nazis.

In Oslo forty thousand people, with Crown Prince Haakon and Crown Princess Mette-Marit at the helm, marched in a torchlight parade to show their revulsion for the murder of Benjamin Hermansen on a cold winter's day, February 1, 2001. Prime Minister Jens Stoltenberg addressed the issue of everyday racism from the stage at Youngstorget Square: "Today all Norwegians must look inside themselves. Are prejudice and intolerance going to gain a permanent foothold in us?" he asked. The thirty-two-year-old on Hoffsveien dislikes immigrants but has never sought out Viking Vest, the skinhead gang on Oslo's west side. According to him, the Holmlia killing is the only example in Norway where a white Norwegian man has killed a dark-skinned man. He claims, however, that Muslims have killed between one hundred and two hundred Norwegians in the last twenty years. But the media have deliberately hushed these killings up.

A friend from his youth came from a Muslim background. They had a close friendship. They tagged, listened to hip-hop, and were rebellious and anti-authoritarian. According to him, when he decided to break away from the milieu after the episodes with the police, a bitter rivalry developed between the two youths. Today he says that the friend was hateful and bitter and backstabbed him. The friend, who knew people in the Norwegian-Pakistani gangster milieu, is supposed to have threatened him with violence. He was witness to what he now calls "a low-intensity jihad": Pakistanis came to the western edge of the subway line from Furuset or Holmlia and raped, robbed, and beat up white Norwegians. His Muslim friend had allegedly developed a hatred for all things Norwegian and wanted him to convert to Islam. The breach not only led to his losing his habitual milieu, but it also caused him to seek out pure Norwegian values. He moved away from the leftist tagging milieu to the other extreme and joined the Progress Party's youth wing (FPU), where he eventually became a deputy at the party's Oslo West branch. His fellow party members did not see him as an impressionable character but rather as an outgoing, confident, and sociable guy who wasn't afraid to voice his opinions.

FPU offered him an ideological community, but it wasn't bold enough. The party members turned out to be politically correct career politicians who let polls and PR agencies decide policy. He lived with insights that he could not share with the others. He maintained a calculatedly pleasant exterior to gain benefits while his thinking became increasingly dystopian. He had realized something that the others had not: there was a secret Muslim invasion of Europe, and no one was trying to stop it. No one but him. Before, he was part of the gang, and then he fell out with everyone. In 2007 he canceled his membership in the FPU.

In scattered discussion groups online he found like-minded people, but he had no power to act. In 2010 in a post on the immigrant-hostile website document.no, he argued with politically correct Norway and all those who believed that just possessing a Norwegian passport entitled one to be called Norwegian. "Sorry, but it doesn't work anymore. Many are increasingly immune to your control techniques due to the massive inflation of rhetoric. I think the majority of Norwegians require the full cultural assimilation (European culture) of the immigrants for them to be considered as true Norwegians," he wrote. The target of the post was Gro Harlem Brundtland, who he believed was responsible for the dilution of Norwegian culture. In the post he gave the former Norwegian prime minister (who was known as the Nation's Mother) the new title of "the Nation's Murderer."

In Ingvar Ambjørnsen's novels about the neurotic dreamer Elling, Gro is the symbol of everything that the loner admires and misses. She's determined, authoritative, caring, courageous, and wise. Elling is convinced that all is safe and well in Norway as long as Gro is in power. For the thirty-two-year-old on Hoffsveien, these very same qualities are a reason for hatred. They have feminized the country and feminized him. Feminism has diminished the manhood that is needed to protect society from immigrants, crime, and pornography. Feminism has made Norwegians soft, cowardly, and conformist. The ideal social norm that he seeks stems from the gender stereotypes of the 1950s, when mom looked after the kids at home, cooked a proper dinner, and aired the bedsheets twice a day. The streets were safer then. The schools were better. Nobody divorced, married immigrants, or was homosexual. The man was the boss. Dad could smoke cigarettes, drink at the office, and pinch secretaries' bottoms without being accused of sexual harassment. Everyone was well dressed, pure, and God-fearing, and no one swore.

He blames society and the feminist revolution for the fact that children today will grow up in female-dominated, fatherless homes. Child benefits, public housing, and other support mechanisms have not only made it affordable for a woman to be a single mother, but the welfare and consumer society has also made it possible for women to shift the responsibility for their children's upbringing to the kindergarten, school, and television. He calls such developments "cultural suicide." He directs his hatred toward these social trends, which have affected his parents and which in turn have affected him. He was left to himself; he has become feminized; he stands as a warning to people of what can happen to children who grow up in a dysfunctional family. Social contempt and self-loathing go hand in hand.

In 2006 he moved back in with his mother on Hoffsveien to save money. Over the past five years she has washed his clothes regularly. She has shopped for groceries and cooked for him. She has cleaned, vacuumed, and tidied his room. In the meantime the thirty-two-year-old has acquired ten different credit cards to finance his large-scale projects. He has also joined the Oslo Gun Club, rented a farm, and bought fertilizer. He has stepped up his exercise regime at the Elixia training studio in Sjølyst, Oslo. For a while he stayed home and played World of Warcraft and Call of Duty: Modern Warfare 2. In the latter game you can simulate a terrorist attack and shoot civilians. His mother is worried about his isolation and thinks he's obsessed with the virtual world. Furthermore, he has gone around with a mask indoors and gotten angry about trivial matters. Friends and acquaintances think he's suppressing his homosexuality. In reality he's been preparing himself to become a martyr to save his people from ethnic cleansing. The civil war has begun. You are either a nationalist or an internationalist. He believes it's not possible to be both.

The young man on 18 Hoffsveien Street is scrupulous with his hygiene and vain about his looks. For him the body is a temple. He believes it's important to look one's best every day and especially so this Friday. He has made the effort to enhance his appearance before the mission by going to the solarium, pumping iron, and shaving and putting on makeup. Although he went to the hip celebrity hangout Skaugum, by Solli Square, after he came back from the farm in Rena at about eleven in the evening, it's not a hung-over man who's making preparations at the apartment. At Skaugum he ordered a sweet raspberry drink that the bartender served with a slice of lime. He drank the Bacardi Razz at leisure in the back patio of the bar, in the midst of a loud, inebriated crowd comprised of the cultural, economic, and political elite. The bar's motto on its website is "Our philosophy embraces the informal, and we are open to all who are open to us."

The thirty-two-year-old put on a brown polo shirt, brown sweater, and brown pants. He's delayed. The mail program for doing a mass mailing of documents, which he installed on the PC in the morning, took longer than planned. The plan was to be in the city center by 10:00 a.m. He doesn't leave his mother's apartment until half past ten. He opens the door at Hoffsveien, gets into the Fiat, and drives into Oslo. The last thing he says before he leaves is: "I'm just going to the Elkjøp electronics store to buy something for the computer. We'll eat dinner together when I get home." His mother was planning to serve spaghetti with meat sauce that afternoon.

He parks the rented car by Hammersborg Square. The parking spaces slope down from Grubbegata Street toward Møllergata Street, interspersed by shrubs, parking ticket dispensers, and bike racks. The cars have to park crosswise, coming in from each one-way street so that they are standing bumper to bumper. One street runs past the turquoise OBOS building while the other goes past a building with the address of 39 Møllergata, where it says "Norwegian Police Federation" on the façade. At the top of Hammersborg Square, next to Grubbegata, is Margareta Church, where one can "attend services, drink coffee, read Swedish newspapers and books, or meet other Swedes." At the bottom of the square, on Møllergata, stands St. Edmund's Church, a red brick building in the Gothic style for those who prefer the services, food, and newspapers in English.

Today, a Friday in the middle of the vacation period, the parking lot is relatively empty. He drives down from Grubbegata and finds a spot about half way along, in front of the building at 39 Møllergata that for many years housed the *Dagsavisen* newspaper office. He gets out of the Fiat and locks it with an electronic key. He then goes over to Oslo Cathedral, where he hails a taxi at Stortorget Square, and it takes him back to Hoffsveien and the van by the garden center.

A stone's throw away from the cathedral, in the prime minister's office, hangs a painting titled *The Way to Soria Moria*. When government negotiations among the Labor Party, the Center Party, and the Socialist Left Party were concluded after the elections in 2005, the three party leaders were presented with the painting by the artist herself, who was an enthusiastic supporter of the new Norwegian coalition. Jens Stoltenberg has held two New Year's speeches in front of this painting, the last one in 2007. In May 2011 the artist, a former apprentice of the artist Jakob Weidemann, packed up her painting equipment and four cats and moved from her studio by the Glomma River in Skarnes to the famous Languedoc-Roussillon wine district in France. There the sixty-year-old artist currently paints Expressionist-style flowers and lives the sophisticated, carefree French life. Last weekend the Norwegian cyclists Hushovd and Boasson Hagen cycled past there. By her side in the garden is her husband, who's a retired economist and diplomat. He hasn't talked to his son for sixteen years.

4

Casual Friday

A few blocks up Grubbegata in the OBOS building's characteristic head office on Hammersborg Square, a young and competent executive officer sits with a throbbing headache. He'd had at least one drink too many last night. He and his friends hadn't seen each other for a while, and that's when time flies by with anecdotes and embellished reminiscences, lubricated successively and alternately with beer, gin and tonic, champagne, and shots of whiskey. There aren't any juicy scandals to be embarrassed about, but the twenty-five-year-old knows that he'll soon call up one of the friends to hear how it went with the woman he tried chatting up at the trendy bar, Skaugum.

Eivind Dahl Thoresen has a summer job in the legal department of the building society. In the spring he wrote his master's thesis on bankruptcy regulations, and in the fall he was scheduled to complete his law studies in Amsterdam. It's purely coincidental that he ended up in OBOS, but the work period from June 20 to July 31 suited his vacation plans well. So far the work has been challenging, but much of it was about housing cooperative regulations and the Planning and Building Act. If someone has done what isn't permitted—extended too far or built an overly large terrace—what kind of sanctions can the housing cooperative board impose? Small, trivial matters that the cooperative's founder, Labor Party politician and carpenter Martin Strandli, did not envision would overshadow the dream of affordable housing based on solidarity for Oslo citizens in general. "Housing for all the people" was Strandli's motto. No one has had greater influence on urban space in the capital than Strandli and OBOS, from the blocks built in Etterstad in the early 1930s to the development of suburbs such as Lambertseter after the war. The current OBOS isn't as purely social democratic as in the time of Gerhardsen. Now the building society owns office buildings, shopping centers, and a hotel chain and builds apartments for the wealthy in Fornebu. Outside the main office building, the Nils Aas statue, *A New Challenge*, looms in stainless steel.

If there's anything Eivind has learned from his trainee jobs in other companies and during the past few weeks, it's that people can argue about the most trivial matters. And often such arguments escalate into small-scale wars. A boy kicks a soccer ball into a neighbor's yard. The neighbor then confiscates the ball. The boy starts to cry, and his father goes over to the neighbor, who refuses to give the ball back, and the whole thing ends in a fistfight. Eivind doesn't know which aspects of the law he'll be working with, so it's okay not to take things too seriously in the meantime. The former Skeid soccer club player had to choose among law, economics, and physical therapy. His buddies thought he should become a lawyer as he's so infuriating to argue with.

It's peaceful and quiet in the office today, and that suits the law student perfectly. He and a colleague are the only ones in the department. There're no urgent tasks, and most of them can be postponed to next week. Eivind sits in front of his PC in the impersonal and spartanly furnished office, nibbling cashew nuts and eating chocolates while trying to look professional. He dispensed with breakfast in the morning and instead bought some food for his hangover at the corner supermarket by the roundabout at Bislett Stadium before he got on the tram going to the city center. By the side of his desk is a packed sports bag. The consequences of drinking one too many pints are not only side effects, but also ripple effects. Eivind had set aside some time in the morning to pack sensibly for a trip to Stavanger this weekend, but his splitting headache laid that plan to rest. Instead he had to fill the bag with items for every contingency: a nice white shirt for going out to restaurants, a black raincoat for outdoor activities, underwear and socks for all-weather use, and a John Grisham paperback for the flight. Then he put on a pair of dark denim shorts and a white polo shirt and ran out of the apartment on Underhaugsveien Street. The dress code at the OBOS office is far from strict. Moreover, today might just be an extra casual Friday.

Eivind goes down to the cafeteria and picks up a couple of sandwiches before he settles down at the table where his only departmental colleague of the day is sitting. The topic of conversation between the two cycling fans is a given: the imminent 109-kilometer-long nineteenth stage of the Tour de France, which runs from Modane to Alpe d'Huez. They don't talk much about the four favorites. They are mostly occupied with the power performance of Hushovd and Boasson Hagen. The editor of *Dag-savisen*, Lars West Johnsen, has gone as far as to claim today that Thor Hushovd is the best Norwegian sportsman ever. It's a daring and contrarian thing to say in a country that is mainly occupied with winter sports.

The road from Modane to Sardinia is shorter than first presumed, at least around the lunch table at Hammersborg Square. Eivind's colleague hasn't been on the Italian island himself but knows enough about it to recommend to Eivind which attractions to explore, delicacies to devour, and Cannonau wine to sip in a civilized manner. In a week's time Eivind and his girlfriend will be traveling to the Mediterranean as soon as he has finished his summer job with OBOS.

Every morning Andreas Olsen walks across Hammersborg Square on the way from his apartment at the bottom of Grünerløkka to the office on 8 Apotekergata, vis-à-vis the supermarket in the VG newspaper building. The publishers Schibsted and Cappelen Damm are also located in this quarter. "OLSEN" is written in capital letters over the entrance to the Oslo trade union offices. Carl Marius Olsen used to run Oslo's leading coach-man business and had the honor of driving Norway's new royal family from Vippetangen to the castle on November 25, 1905. Some of the court coachman's forty horses were stabled on Apotekergata. In the building and backyard he had stalls, coach equipment, sleighs, hay, and straw, as well as sheep- and bearskins with which to warm the seats. Given the fact that the coachmen were quite prone to going on strike, especially when the first taxis appeared in the city in 1908, it's noteworthy that the Norwegian Confederation of Trade Unions' most powerful union is located here today.

One of Andreas's tasks at the trade union is to scrutinize the news to find issues that management should consider. He has read the national newspapers but has not found anything that undermines the impression that it's a peaceful, uncomplicated summer's day in the capital. The daily *Dagbladet* has devoted the front page to the Norwegian singer Gabrielle, whose single, "Call Me," has topped the charts but who doesn't want people to call her anyway. A new study reveals that people from the Trøndelag region of Norway argue mostly about sex and that elderly people argue about the remote control. The daily VG is advising people to put up with the rain as it'll be sunny in the coming week. The *Dagsavisen* daily's front page appeals more to the socially engaged with an article about our inability or unwillingness to help the famine-stricken Horn of Africa. Five million Norwegians have given a total of 3 million kroner to aid organizations—that is, well over half a kroner per person. The aid organizations—Church Aid, Save the Children, and the Norwegian Refugee Council—show some understanding for the low figures and blame it on the summer vacation period.

Normally there are twenty-five employees working in the Apoteker-gata office, but today there are just two from management, a secretary, and information officer Andreas Olsen. Hence, the thirty-six-year-old from Tonsenhagen in Oslo can read the newspapers in peace in the morning. The Middle East isn't at the top of the agenda for the trade union before the election, but Andreas is particularly interested in the reports on the foreign minister's visit to Utøya. vg has angled yesterday's Middle East debate as a contest between the "no crown prince," Trond Giske, and the "yes crown prince," Jonas Gahr Støre, with regard to Norway's joining the European Union. Olsen has spent a combined total of eleven weeks at summer camp on the island on Lake Tyri. The former county secretary and central committee member of auf received his membership in the organization for his eighteenth birthday and was on Utøya as recently as seven years ago. His wife, Marianne, is also a longstanding auf member. The couple had plans to take their four-year-old son to Utøya for their first visit in years to give him a taste of their youthful paradise. Earlier in the week, however, they decided not to go because the weather forecast was so miserable. A soaking wet camp in pouring rain doesn't sound much like paradise, even for a four-year-old.

Instead Andreas is spending this Friday almost utterly alone in the office. He flicks through the union's campaign pamphlets: "The city council took their jobs!" says one under a picture of gardeners Anne Kristine Sandborg and Thor Truls Lie. They are two of the eighty-nine employees of the city's Parks and Recreation Department who were given notice this spring that their jobs would be put out to tender after the department had used its own gardeners for 136 years. Another pamphlet, written in English, Urdu, Somali, and Tamil, encourages the people of Oslo to vote. A picture shows Mary Khayumbi, a deputy in Ullern Trade Union; Fauzia Hussain, the head of the Planning and Building Services Trade Union; and Farideh Keshavarz, a member of the Oslo Public Transport Workers Union in front of City Hall. The text criticizes the conservatives' zeal regarding privatization over the past fifteen years, so the three proud, photogenic women don't give the impression of being politically impartial: "Vote Labor, Socialist, or Left-Wing!" Andreas Olsen will soon submit the text to management and an agency for approval and translation. Then he will greet the weekend with a broad, warm smile. The information officer leans back in his chair, rests the back of his head on his clasped hands, and stretches his legs out on the table while he considers whether

to buy flowers for his wife on the way home from the office in the afternoon. She certainly deserves flowers.

Oda Faremo Lindholm cobbles together a salad in the canteen on the
fifth floor of the YMCA building on Grubbegata. For the vegetarian it's a
daily challenge to find something tasty to eat among all the pork and
chicken dishes. She takes the salad with her up to the seventh floor, where
the *Dagsavisen*'s culture section is located. The summer intern, who, in
addition to holding the newspaper job, is writing a master's thesis on
currency regulations in Norway's Central Bank after World War II, is a
little stressed. She's almost done writing about Joddski, the rap musician
from Bodø, but there is an unexpected hitch in her plans when he comes
late to the scheduled interview. Half an hour more or less is normally not
the end of the world, but the plan was to be done quickly so that she
could walk out the door at three-thirtyish and get a head start to the
weekend. In the end Jørgen Nordeng, as the musician was originally
called, was so delayed at the Internasjonalen Club in the People's Theater
building that she had to call to track him down.

When Oda listened to the tape of the interview, she had to acknowl-
edge that he didn't say anything sensational. It's a standard interview for
Monday's launch of Joddski's second solo album. When the ex-rapper,
known from his previous band, Tungtvann, and as a participant in the
TV show *Det store korslaget* (The Battle of the Choirs), starts talking about
how small Bodø's music scene is and how reggae, hard-core, and elec-
tronica musicians played together in the 1990s, the conversation starts to
digress. The music journalist and the interviewee go off topic and talk
instead about mutual acquaintances. The music scene is small in Bodø,
but it's not big in Norway either. The digression was pleasant. But as a
consequence the article is taking longer to write, and Oda has to work
longer hours at the office.

Hanne Gro Lille-Mæhlum sits in a crisp uniform at the reception area
in S-Block, where the Ministry of Labor, Ministry of Health and Care
Services, and Government Service Center are located. The uniform is
comprised of a light blue short-sleeved shirt tucked into a navy blue skirt
reaching to just below the knees, nylon stockings, and black flat shoes.
Around her neck she has an orange patterned scarf. The thirty-three-year-
old is doing a master's in sociology and started working in late May. The
S-Block was completed the same year that Hanne Gro was born—that
is, 1978. The building was erected on the site of the old prison associated

with the police station at 19 Møllergata, and the remains of the prison wall can still be seen at the reception area. Two former prime ministers of Norway, Einar Gerhardsen and Trygve Bratteli, and key Labor Party leaders and members of the resistance were imprisoned here during the war. Einar Gerhardsen and Trygve Bratteli were later sent to the Sachsenhausen concentration camp in Germany. When Germany capitulated in 1945, Vidkun Quisling stood on the steps under the clock that adorns the façade facing Youngstorget Square and surrendered himself to the Norwegian police. The S-Block shares the same reception area as that of 19 Møllergata, where, among others, staff of the Government Service Center have their offices.

On this day one could be misled into thinking that the "S" in front of the block stands for "summer serenity." No ministers on the job, not many meetings, few visitors to register and sign out. A few times Hanne Gro has gone over to the High Rise Building, which houses the office of the prime minister to get coffee in the lunch room. Fresh-roasted coffee, which can be transformed into cappuccinos or lattes, is a fringe benefit that she's never had at previous jobs.

After lunch the reception guards took a tour of the government buildings to familiarize themselves with emergency exits and evacuation procedures. On the tour the guards discussed how they could best protect themselves against harm while evacuating employees in the ministries during a potential emergency. The discussion ended with someone jokingly pointing out that it wouldn't take long for the firefighters to come to the rescue since the main fire station in Oslo was located next to the S-Block, just a few meters away. "Yes, there's not much chance of their driving to the wrong place," he joked.

Hanne Gro reads on the Internet about the Prince concert that she'll be attending on Sunday with a childhood friend from Brumunddal. The ticket costs 850 Norwegian kroner, but she thinks she can indulge a little since she has worked practically full time the whole summer. According to the work schedule Hanne Gro is supposed to be on duty at seven o'clock Monday morning. She ventures to call the desk manager to see if she can change to a later shift and is told that it should be no problem. There's nothing in her email inbox except a pollen count alert for Saturday, July 23. She is looking forward to the end of the summer's grass pollen season.

She browses through the daily *Klassekampen*, which she always brings in the bag with her to work in case she doesn't find someone to eat lunch with. In today's issue there's an article saying that the AUF leader, Eskil Pedersen, thinks the Labor Party should sacrifice the mayoral seats in some municipalities rather than cooperate with the Progress Party, as party secretary Raymond Johansen has proposed. "Cooperating will send an unimaginably negative signal," said the leader. The headline on the front page concerns Norwegian complacency. Professor Nina Witoszek thinks Norwegians are more concerned about the poor summer weather than the financial crisis in Europe, while Iver B. Neumann, the head researcher of the Norwegian Institute of International Affairs (NUPI), claims that Norwegians view the rest of the world as one big holiday resort where one can visit for a short while and throw a lot of money around. He has spent his life trying to argue that the world is bigger than Norway but has realized that Norwegians are not particularly receptive to such arguments. "I think there is currently a lot of bragging among Norwegian politicians. But it's not due to the politicians that things are going well in Norway. It's due to pure luck in our having found oil; a skilled business class; and an easily managed, homogenous society," Professor Janne Haaland Matlary says.

Hanne Gro puts away *Klassekampen* and kicks off her black standard-issue shoes. She has clammy feet and reminds herself that she should air them before going across Einar Gerhardsen Square to the High Rise later in the day.

5

Gro Day

Wearing white summer pants and white sneakers was a mistake. The red hooded raincoat barely shields her from the insistent rain. Only she knows what's inside the brown bag. It's certainly not black sunglasses, as she has them on. Even when it's raining. On the mainland Gro Harlem Brundtland is welcomed by excited party members who're also wearing red raincoats. Red is the color of Utøya.

It was getting embarrassing. No one was aware that she'd arrived, neither the AUF welcoming committee nor the press. They only saw a beige Toyota and then a young girl who stepped out. "Is it Gro?" asked one of the central committee members who had come over to greet her. In a red raincoat. "No," replied Jorid Nordmelan. "It's just Julie." Julie Brundtland Løvseth is certainly Gro's grandchild, and Jorid thinks it strange that she came alone, but she didn't see any other passengers in the car. The photographers lowered their cameras, and the journalists continued disparaging their colleagues. As Julie walked slowly toward the registration booth, Jorid saw a head of fair hair barely protruding above the roof of the car, looking around confusedly. "Huh, that's Gro," said the central committee member as she ran toward the car and shouted a little desperately, "Hand me an umbrella!"

Gro is escorted on board the green deck of the ferry MS *Thorbjørn*, and she finds her own way into the cabin and settles down on a bench near the window. "I can't remember having been here in such bad weather," Gro says before reconsidering and adding, "Well, maybe once before." Her first visit to the island was in 1945. The time span says something about the amount of rain that's pouring down over Lake Tyri a little before 11:00 a.m. on Friday, July 22.

On the pier the seventy-two-year-old is received by Eskil Pedersen and others in the party leadership. The youths have brought along umbrellas, and they compete with each other to hold them over her. It's not that far to walk up to the hall where she will talk about her life in politics, but Gro and Eskil are being driven up there in a black car. Meanwhile, the youngsters are streaming toward the main hall. The most social democratically romantic among them choose a spot along the wall under the black and brown poster from the Norwegian Building Industry Workers' Union, on which is written in red letters, "Tomorrow is built through solidarity." Some stop by the kiosk. Some have to fill their stomachs before eating a meal of meatballs, gravy, cranberry jam, mashed potatoes, and vegetables later in the day. Many people buy waffles from the red-and-white striped tent as they didn't manage to eat breakfast. On the wall of the cafeteria building hangs a white paper plate with letters written with marker pen: "Waffles contain 80 percent happiness and 20 percent love. What are you waiting for?" While they wait for Gro, the youngsters listen to Snorre Haller's welcoming speech from the LO and to Renate Tårnes playing the song "Idyll" from the band Postgirobygget. "There was beer, intoxicating words; it was summer, it was sunny, there were hearts on fire, calm waters, everything on earth." A fitting picture, minus the alcohol, of course, and the sun and calm waters.

Two girls from Namsos municipality have overslept. Hanne Hestø Ness and Lene Maria Bergum were born on the same day at the same hospital. They have been in the same class from elementary school to high school. They tend to celebrate their birthdays together, the last one having been their nineteenth. Hanne and Lene Maria and twenty-eight other youngsters from the county traveled down by bus from Trondheim to Lake Tyri. The bus had a flat tire and had to change the engine oil, but the ambience was still great. The gang arrived at seven o'clock and pitched a green four-man tent in the rain. Hanne took an idyllic picture of Lene Maria in front of the campground after she had changed into typical Utøya attire: a light, flowery summer dress and rubber boots. She has a work crew lanyard around her neck and a coffee cup in her hand. She is smiling at her best friend.

The Namsos girls' tent consists of two twin rooms divided by an awning. The plan was that they should have separate rooms, but Lene Maria's thick, inflatable double mattress did not fit into her part, so it was set on grass under the awning. On the very first night the air went out of Hanne's single mattress. Since it can often get cold at night on Utøya, it made sense to share the double mattress. The tent was then used as a walk-in closet. The improvised arrangement, due to unforeseen circumstances, led to widespread envy at the camp when the clouds dispersed on Wednesday. Hanne and Lene Maria pulled the mattress out of the tent and used it as a sun lounger. There they lay during the day, tanned themselves, and read *Planet Utøya* and novels—for Hanne it was Lars Saabye Christensen's novel *Lead*.

Hanne and Lene Maria had been spending the evenings at Utøya working at the night cafe, except for the previous evening, when they got an hour off to attend the Datarock concert. When they came back to the tent at half past three, there was still activity in the North Trøndelag county campsite. The offer to sit down for five minutes was rejected with a winsome smile. The work at the night cafe is instructive and fun but tiring. It's therefore no surprise that the Namsos girls overslept this Friday morning. Hanne and Lene Maria just managed to get a quick wash in the lavatory block before they had to run up to the main hall where Gro was holding her speech.

Tore Sinding Bekkedal is rudely awakened in the navy blue two-man tent at the Oslo campsite. It's not uncommon for young people to oversleep at Utøya. Many go to bed when others wake up. In Tore's case it's not due to staying up all night. He went to bed at half past one in the morning, after sitting around the hookah by the stage and learning the Arabic word for "good." Still Tore wakes up rather stressed out by the applause from the main hall this morning. Utøya's unofficial photographer has been asked to take pictures of the "Mother of the Nation," Gro Harlem Brundtland, for the Scanpix photo agency since it's undermanned during the vacation period. It's an honorable and important job for a young hobbyist photographer and certainly one for which he shouldn't be late. Tore puts on the typical black-and-white Hawaiian shirt and runs up to the cafeteria building, where the Canon 5D camera is kept in the basement. He also takes along the new wide-angle lens he bought before coming to the camp. Heading into the cafeteria building, he stops by the kiosk and buys a microwaved pizza.

In Emma Martinovic's green two-man tent it's not standard camping gear that's in the suitcase neatly placed in the corner. She and her friend have packed as if they were going for a weekend in Paris—the prettiest dresses, high heels, hair straighteners, lots of makeup, music speakers, and two cameras in case one doesn't work. The girls from Kristiansand have looked forward to the Utøya camp for several months now. On board the MS *Thorbjørn*, the eighteen-year-old county party leader was so excited that she was trembling. Emma has already managed to take numerous photos with the camera and mobile phone: Team Agder playing a soccer match, hookah smoking, card games in the tent, the Datarock concert, karaoke evenings, lunches, Eskil's opening speech, camaraderie around the grill, and even the sun and the AUF flag. Memories for life. Now she lies in the green tent, feeling slightly unwell, but she manages to get up in time to go listen to Gro. A small puddle has formed under the inflatable mattress, so she packs up her clothing and accessories in the black trolley suitcase before she puts on a hoodie. She quickly puts on makeup and opens the tent door. The shoes that her mother bought for her in Germany are lying there, soaking wet and dirty. The Kristiansand girl doesn't have time for trivial matters. She puts them on and negotiates her way through the hundred meters of mud and puddles up to the cafeteria building. Emma is annoyed with herself for coming to Utøya without a raincoat and rubber boots; she brought only canvas shoes and high heels with her.

Ten youngsters have been allowed to speak for three minutes each after Gro's speech. Ingrid Endrerud is just about to subdue the panic attack she got when she was interrupted while cheering at the volleyball match with the message that Gro is coming at 11:00 a.m. and not 2:00 p.m. as she'd originally thought. The eighteen-year-old stood below the information house, drenched to the skin, not having written a word of her speech. She ran to the tent; fetched clean, dry clothes; and went to one of the storage rooms at the inner part of the little hall. She took a chance that no one would come in, took off her soaking wet clothes, and hung them to dry on the chairs before she went into the little hall and started to write the speech. She's not nervous. The youths in the main hall are usually an appreciative audience. Nevertheless, it's good to know what you're going to say before going to the podium. It has to be something about the famine, she thinks, and she will finish off with a quote.

Gro maneuvers among hundreds of sneakers, rubber boots, crocs, and sandals; past wet coats that are hung up to dry on the available hooks and doors; and over the small, dirty puddles on the linoleum floor. Johanne Butenschøn Lindheim left her boots back in Oslo, so she has placed her new Converse sneakers, purchased in Nicaragua, strategically in the hallway so they wouldn't be trodden on. But that was before someone realized they had to make a path for the main guest and threw the shoes carelessly against the wall. Johanne's white shoes are no longer white. Furthermore, it won't be easy to find them again.

Cries of "Gro, Gro, Gro" rise in the main hall. The youngsters are impatient, but the Mother of the Nation first has to be made welcome by the AUF leader. In 1991, when unemployment reached record high levels in Norway, AUF members marched in the Oslo May Day parade under the banner "Gro—where the hell are the jobs?" The Buskerud AUF started a campaign to bring unemployment down to 2 percent with the slogan "Press Gro to less than two." The South Trøndelag county faction demanded the prime minister's resignation. At a seminar on Utøya in spring 1992 the county leader claimed that full employment was no longer the Labor Party's number one objective. "I simply will not accept this," said an angry Norwegian prime minister. Such conflicts are a thing of the past now, at least for today's AUF members. Norway's first female prime minister is a heroine without any blemishes.

"We're all very fond of Gro. But we also have enormously great respect for Gro. We're proud that you chose Utøya as your soapbox in Norway this summer," says Eskil and gets a resounding round of applause. The youngsters in the hall are like most young people. They sit or lie close to each other, drink from Coke bottles or snack on chocolate, smelling of sweat, cheap perfume, and superficially washed bodies. The hall is packed. It's impossible to change one's position. Legs fall asleep under stiff bottoms. Even though it may look like it, they're not enjoying movie night with lovers and friends. They're listening to something that many of their peers back home in Mandal, Hamar, or Tromsø find dead boring: politics. Politics and history.

Eskil believes Gro is the greatest political figure we have in Norway today. She's a role model for everyone on the island but especially for the girls. Through her political work she has paved the way for girls in politics, he says, before concluding, "I think that all those sitting here can really thank you for something much greater, something more important. The policy you have implemented on gender equality, whether it's day care or maternity leave, has, in fact, made it possible not only for children to go to kindergarten, but also for girls to not have to choose between having children or working. This policy has contributed to the fact that Norway now has one of the highest birthrates in Europe. Some of those sitting here can perhaps safely say, "We wouldn't have been born if you hadn't done what you've done. We thank you for life." Eskil gets thunderous applause on his way down from the stage, as Gro gets roaring cheers on her way up. It sounds more like a cup final at Ullevaal Stadium, filled with soccer fans rather than a political rally.

Gro talks about the first time she was here, in 1945. It was five years before the island was donated to the AUF and when the Danish foreign minister had had a little too much to drink. "I was here with my father at the Pentecostal camp. Yes, that's what it was then—a Pentecostal camp, not a summer camp. Even then there were young people from other parts of Scandinavia here too. I remember one man, Hækkerup. He drank several beers. More beers than my dad. I noticed that the adults were not entirely sober. And how did I notice that? Because I was put to bed at 8:00 p.m. in the schoolhouse. I just had to put up with it and do as my father said. I was six years old. It was sunny and gorgeous outside. After half an hour, some girls came and knocked on the window, saying, "You know what, we think it's too cruel of your father to lock you inside on a sunny summer evening. Now we're going to sneak you out!" It was one of the first offenses I committed here," she says to widespread laughter and applause. The young people know they are witnesses to a significant part of Norwegian history, as Jagland realized in the 1970s, when he was on Utøya listening to Gerhardsen and Bratteli talk about the war. Gro also talks about the war, the fight against Nazism, the Cold War, the Gerhardsen era, and the fight for women's rights. "Gro is on the podium, and I'm weak in the knees. Fabulous lady! #utoya," Renate Tårnes tweets.

Gro tells the girls in the audience to watch out for misogynistic control techniques. She was called "the Loudmouth of Bygdøy" during the election campaign in 1977. Four years later, when she became Norway's first female prime minister, the Conservatives' slogan was, 'Get rid of her.' They used the fact that I was a woman against me. But something like that doesn't ever happen today," she says sarcastically and gets some laughter. Violence against women, both verbal and physical, is just as prevalent in 2011. Hence on Utøya the youngsters are not only taught ways to expose unscrupulous speech and debating techniques, but in the afternoon they can also strengthen their self-defense skills. The course starts at five. The Friday night movie is the American action comedy *Kick-Ass*, which is in line with the self-defense theme. The Utøya program says that the movie is "ideal for people who are keen to learn self-defense. However, the AUF does not in any way condone the violence depicted and would like to remind everyone that this is a pacifist summer camp."

Hadia Tajik is sitting in the main hall. She has come to Utøya expressly to hear Gro's speech. When she hears the former prime minister say "Everything is connected to everything else," the young member of parliament starts to grin. She sends a text message to a friend: "Now I've heard her say it—live!" "Lucky bastard," was the response. The twenty-eight-year-old sitting in the audience listening to Gro is one of the most prominent symbols of the new Norway. She's a journalist, feminist, and politician, as well as well educated, resourceful, career-driven, and multicultural. Her parents emigrated from Pakistan to Norway over thirty years ago. Her father's family hailed from Tajikistan and Afghanistan, while her mother's came from Iran, Turkey, and Afghanistan. Hadia grew up in Bjørheimsbygd in Rogaland County. As a child she often spoke Urdu, Persian, and Norwegian all in one sentence. She's Muslim but attended a Lutheran kindergarten and went to the gospel hall. She's a modern example of the concept that everything is connected to everything else—in a way it's a distinctly Buddhist approach to life.

Matti Brox comes into the cafeteria building in a slightly groggy state just as Gro is nearing the end of her speech. Since it's completely packed in the main hall, the sixteen-year-old finds a seat along the wall in the corridor. The alarm rang two hours ago. Nine in the morning seemed unreasonably early then, considering how late he had been up last night. The conversation was silly and vague around the hookah. The first stirrings of serious controversy appeared when the Oslo gang had to choose between grape or peach flavor. The evening featured everything that the novice party member had expected of the summer camp at Utøya: concerts, karaoke, strolls along Lovers' Lane, intimate conversations by the pump room. He even played some guitar. Some Pink Floyd and one of Led Zeppelin's classic songs: "Yes, there are two paths you can go by, but in the long run, there's still time to change the road you're on." Matti has a repertoire of amusing comments and often makes others laugh. As is the case even now, in the corridor outside the main hall, against the wall, as he sits beside other youngsters who didn't get a seat inside. He is harshly shushed by the others.

Gro steps down from the stage to thunderous applause. To deserve such cheers one has to have saved the fatherland, as was pointed out when Nansen arrived back in Kristiania after the conquest of Greenland. Preferably saved it twice. July 22, 2011, is undoubtedly right up there with June 7, 1905 (dissolution of the union between Norway and Sweden) and May 8, 1945 (liberation from German occupation).

And now youth takes the stage. Ingrid Endrerud talks about the famine in the south. "I've been to war and experienced extreme weather. All at the same time. Here on Utøya. War against Hordaland County in the mud. Extreme weather with buckets of rain. It's not like that for people in many other places around the world. . . . So I'm a little hungry, and there's a rumbling in my stomach. But for me it's just a matter of walk-ing over to the waffle booth. . . . And on this side we have a kitchen full of food. In the worst case I can trudge down to the Oppland campsite and make myself some sandwiches there. . . . Currently we are witnessing the most severe drought in fifty years. The thing that frustrates me most is why it takes so long to come to their aid. Why do we not have a UN pot that is ready to be used? Why do we have to start from scratch every time?" the eighteen-year-old asks, and she ends with a quote: "Our goal is to save the world—if it's too painful and difficult, we might as well lie down and die."

Ingrid is applauded. The young people in the audience can relate to her description of their privileged lives, where war, weapons, insecurity, and hunger are almost unknown to them. On the way down she gets a pat on the shoulder from the county leader of Hordaland, Tore Eikeland, one of the rising political stars of the youth organization. He's adept at rhetorical turns of phrase and applause-winning jokes. Only Eikeland is capable of sneaking in references to light-fingered parish priests in a speech about EU postal legislation. When he speaks in the plenary ses-sion, it's not certain that everyone understands all the time what he's talking about, but everyone is left with renewed affirmation that he's going to go far in the organization and, indeed, probably all the way to the top.

This year, for the first time, he is working as a journalist for *Planet Utøya*. Before coming to the island, he was considering introducing the AUF's very own fashion column in the gossipy newsletter. Instead a pop-ular innovation this year has been a page with stupid or revealing status updates and a layout that looks like a real Facebook page. During each status update the editor sent a message to the enthusiastic and extremely active Facebook queen from the Rogaland Labor Party, who has added all the AUF members as friends, even though she doesn't really know them: "Thumbs up for Facebook Likes!" There's teasing and joking around, but it's done with love. The adult politician thinks it's great with all these engaged AUF members, and the AUF members think it's great that the Rogaland politician is so engaged in cake baking and gender equality.

Gro makes notes while the youngsters speak and answers their ques-tions at the end. Ingrid thinks that the former prime minister really didn't answer her questions. Instead she feels she's being criticized because Gro got hung up with her quote. The Mother of the Nation doesn't want people to lie down and die if things get difficult. Something is at least something, and it's far better than nothing. It's a case of the pragmatist versus the idealist, and that isn't so unusual a confrontation when AUF members meet with representatives from the parent party. Ingrid thinks that the question was badly answered until she discovers that her stomach is growling irritably. The only thing she has eaten today is an apple while writing the speech in the little hall.

The youngsters go out to the courtyard in front of the cafeteria building and start queuing up for food. If you are unlucky and end up at the back of the line, the wait can take up to an hour. The queue is the only reason why some campers sign up for the work crew, as they get served dinner first. Moreover, there's dessert, usually jelly, caramel, or chocolate pudding and canned fruit for vegans and allergy sufferers. The dining hall can't accommodate everyone, so many people have to eat dinner in a tent or in the courtyard. But not today. The rain has made the camp administration magnanimous. The youngsters are allowed to find a place anywhere in the cafeteria building, and they don't need to remove their shoes. The seats around the tables fill up quickly. Many people have to sit on the floor. Yesterday light summer food was served—chicken thighs, lettuce, rice, and béarnaise sauce. Today's menu is tailored to the chilly weather—mashed potatoes and meatballs in brown sauce. Muslims are served halal meatballs, while vegetarians can have fried rice with onions, an American vegetable mix, and lentils. The meals can be washed down with yellow or red juice. The three who are serving one line are having fun repeating Ina Libak's familiar phrase: "Remember" (from the server dishing out the meatballs), "you are" (from the one doling out the mashed potatoes), and "amazing" (from the one putting the vegetables on the plate). Ina Libak is a twenty-one-year-old party member from Akershus known for her winning, gentle nature, and nothing makes for a better ambience on Utøya than to hear her say, "Remember, you are amazing." The menu is the same every year, but this time it seems to Hildegunn Fallang that the food tastes extra good. An empty stomach since breakfast and soccer matches in the mud and the miserable, wet, and cold weather work up an appetite.

After the youngsters have left the cafeteria building to go meet Gro at the campground or to relax in the tents, Ingrid sits in front of the piano in the little hall to prepare for choir practice later in the afternoon. They will be singing, "We are the world, we are the children, we are the ones who make a brighter day, so let's start giving." On Wednesday ten people came to choir practice at five o'clock. On Thursday only three showed up. They had a very fine session anyway, in the sun, on the field down by the volleyball court, as the band Datarock had taken over the little hall for its backstage room. The singers were enthusiastic and the atmosphere was good, except for those damned slimy frogs everywhere that paralyzed the eighteen-year-old. A girl picked up a frog and said, "Oh, so nice." Ingrid had no musical instruments with her, but using an iPod and three song-books, they selected a handful of songs for the performance, all depend-ing on how many people showed up for practice. Other than the opti-mistic but serious "We are the World," the playful and sing-along-friendly song "Smart," by DeLillos and Ida Maria, is a top candidate: "Yes, you're darn smart / For you everything is possible / You create things, 100 per-cent natural / You're the man / For you everything is possible."

Ingrid has mobilized quite effectively for the afternoon practice at five, but it's already clear that the spectators are not going to witness a poly-phonic extravaganza on the outdoor stage on Saturday. A former leader of the choir has suggested that they can perform "To Youth," but Ingrid doesn't think much of it, especially not as a choir song. "The Internatio-nale" has more pep and tempo when sung a cappella: "For too long we've endured exploitation, / Too long we've been the vulture's prey. / Farewell to days of condemnation! / The red dawn brings a bright new day!" Ingrid has chosen three genres: a traditional work song, a modern pop song, and a political song. The last type will probably be a song by Bob Dylan. While two young boys in the work crew wash the floor of the little hall, Ingrid Endrerud plays and sings an inspiring protest song from 1963: "How many deaths will it take till he knows that too many people have died."

When the youngsters on Utøya are cold and wet and want to go home, as is the case when the weather is miserable, Morten Djupdal's job as del-egation leader and county secretary is to come up with a motivational pep talk: "Remember how nice it was yesterday." "There will be good weather tomorrow." "There's no such thing as bad weather, only bad tents." As a matter of course Morten trudges around in slippers instead of rub-ber boots since he has come to the conclusion that he's going to get just as wet anyway, even with boots. But he belongs to Utøya's upper class. He's indoors and they're outdoors, a fact that the party members from

Oppland County are quick to point out when he comes up with super-ficial, facile phrases. "Come on, you sly fox; you sleep indoors!" Truth be told, it makes no difference to Morten. He is tired, lethargic, and trudges around in his own world. When the AUF secretary general pointed out to him that there were too few people attending the political workshops, his response was that people should be allowed to do as they please.

Morten is credible giving pep talks, but he has also gotten wrinkled fingers and feet from all the rain. Therefore he is planning to go to his uncle and aunt's in Hønefoss to take a hot shower. Since the truth can be misconstrued sometimes and lead to an outbreak of the bad weather blues, he asks around the Oppland campsite whether anyone would be interested in going with him to Hønefoss to shop for food. At one time or another before going home on Sunday, they'll need a refill of bread and spread, but there's no real hurry. No, it seems no one wants to leave the red party tent. "Buy more chocolate spread," someone shouts. "We'll see," says the county secretary, who actually has no intention of buying more sugary sweet spread. The deputy of the Oppland Labor Party has been visiting for the day, and Morten makes arrangements with him to take the same boat over to the mainland at 4:00 p.m. Utøya isn't big and neither is the social setting, so in a matter of minutes a rumor spreads that there's a man from the Oppland campsite going over to the main-land. Three youngsters come over and ask Morten if they can come along. "No more than two," says Morten, who's still hoping that someone from his home county will reconsider.

After dinner, according to tradition, Gro makes a visit to the camp-ground. Eskil walks beside her and holds the umbrella. Her white sneak-ers have been replaced with more suitable footwear for trampling around in the mud. She has borrowed high green rubber boots from Bano Rashid. The eighteen-year-old and the Mother of the Nation have the same shoe size. The girl can hardly imagine a greater privilege than lending Gro her boots. She calls home to her mother in Nesodden to tell her about it. "Remember to get her autograph on them," the mother says to her excited daughter.

"What is it with Gro?" wonders the TV2 reporter Finn-Ove Hågensen in front of Bano's tent. "I feel that she has done everything for women. That's what we say. It's thanks to Gro and our grandmothers. Gro for-ever!" a gleeful and boisterous girl says. Hågensen's article headline is "Gromania on Utøya." Bano and six others in the Akershus campsite have been chosen to have a conversation with Gro. The young girls wonder what it's going to take to be heard and to be taken seriously. "Be yourself, do what you believe in," Bano says.

TV2 also stops in front of the three-man tent of Matti Brox and his buddy. When they pitched the tent on Tuesday, they hadn't noticed that it was right over a depression in the ground. For the young and well trained who stay up all night and need little sleep, it's not a problem to lie on rugged terrain. This morning, however, is a different story. That was no fun at all. The tent did not keep off the rain. All the water collected under the green tent. Consequently they had to move the tent one and a half meters up toward the road. It was a time-consuming affair that caused the pillows, sleeping bags, and luggage to become thoroughly soaked. Now there's a pond where the tent once stood. The TV2 reporter asks the Oslo boys how's it going and gets a "Thank you, great atmosphere" in response. To exemplify the "great atmosphere" Matti and his buddy improvise a scene: one of them takes off all his clothes except for his underwear, jumps into the pond, and swims merrily around while the other one takes out a bottle of shampoo and washes his hair to a cheerful little tune. Matti is convinced that the pictures will be on the news tonight.

The NRK follows Gro around with a camera and microphone. When it comes time for the state channel to interview Gro, the reporter asks her how it is to be back on Utøya. "It's always very nice," she replies, "as well as inspiring and engaging. I'm always very glad to be here." "Do you see any potential in some of these young people?" the NRK reporter asks. "There's potential in everyone who's here; otherwise they wouldn't be here," Gro replies. The party members on Utøya are the crème de la crème of the country's young politicians and are the most committed and dedicated in the Labor Party youth organization. Everybody becomes something or other, but not all become career politicians. In fact few of the participants at summer camps do so. They become journalists, information consultants, bankers, bureaucrats in the ministries, tour guides in Italy, or advisers in the Finance Sector Union of Norway. Not all on Utøya become politicians, but all the leaders of the Labor Party have been to summer camp on Utøya. It was there they were trained and where they developed useful contacts through networking. The road from Utøya leads to all manner of occupations, but it usually leads to promising careers. It's never a disadvantage to specify your AUF party membership in your cv. It probably means that you are well spoken. It means that your social interests and engagement are broad and deep. You will be an asset to an employer.

Jorid Nordmelan doesn't go along on Gro's tour around the campground. She wants to relax for a few hours before going back to the mainland to move cars around in the mud. Kristine Hallingstad, a central committee member in the AUF who is working on the mainland together with Jorid, reminisces about Wednesday's speed dating. They did not participate, God forbid, but were responsible for arranging the event. After the regular program they organized "Blind Love": the audience can see the dream boy and dream girl sitting on chairs behind a wall but not the three boys and girls who have been chosen to compete for them. They're given ten multiple-choice questions each. For example: What king of dress style do you like best on a girlfriend? (A) Track suit, faded sweater. (B) Stylish designer wear. (C) Stark naked. (Naturally the mood in the room was greatest when the answer was C.) The one of the three who was the poorest in guessing the dream girl's and dream boy's preferences was knocked out. Then it was the turn of the dream boy and girl to ask the two remaining participants questions. The dream girl had a creative variant: "If I meet Bruce Springsteen, am I allowed to be unfaithful then?" One boy answered yes, albeit on condition that the same should apply to him and the currently sexiest woman in the world, Jessica Alba. There's giggling in the audience. The other boy replied no, but on the other hand, he could go along on the date with "the Boss." That wouldn't be construed as adultery, would it? There's even more giggling and laughter in the hall. Jorid and Kristine are still grinning. Jorid thinks speed dating is kind of awkward to participate in but fun to organize. They are both embarrassed and a little thrilled that they have now become famous on the island and been anointed with the exuberant nickname of "the Love Makers."

While Gro eats lunch with the AUF leadership in the information house, Tore Sinding Bekkedal has a chat about photography with the press professionals from the capital. Because of the Scanpix job, he feels enough like a press photographer to help himself to the free baguettes. Tore is also going to record a video greeting from Gro to the youngsters afterward that will be posted on YouTube. He considers asking an acquaintance in the NRK if he can get a ride to Oslo. Tore is a technician at the Frikanalen TV channel and has a deadline on August 1. The plan was to

work from Utøya, but it was impossible because of the bad Internet connection. Therefore he should go home. However, before Tore got around
to asking for a ride, someone else took the seat he wanted.

Gro leaves the island a little before three on Friday afternoon. She takes
the MS *Thorbjørn* over to the mainland with her granddaughter. Hadia
Tajik is also on board. They get into their cars at Utstranda on the mainland and drive toward Sollihøgda, along the E16 motorway to Sandvika,
before they turn onto the highway going to Oslo. The guests from Utøya
notice that the traffic coming in the opposite direction on the E18 is at a
standstill. A twenty-year-old delivery driver in a Peugeot full of TVs bound
for Drammen lost control of his vehicle after driving over a puddle just
after the Frognerkilen Sailing Club and ran into the crash barrier. "Now
it's all going to hell," Mohamed, the driver, thought before the car went
into a tailspin. The accident was causing delays for motorists heading
south to their villas in Asker or cabins in southern Norway. "Clearing-up
work is taking a long time, and there are huge traffic jams," the entry in
the police log says.

6

Four Hundred Years after the Battle of Vienna

"The time for dialogue is over. We gave peace a chance. The time for armed resistance is here. The Knights Templar will, on behalf of the free people of Europe, declare war against all Marxist and multicultural regimes in Western Europe."

He is back in the apartment on 18 Hoffsveien. The Fiat is parked on Hammersborg Square in downtown Oslo. The van stands here on the street in Skøyen, among people who go into the Mega Coop supermarket to buy a bread roll, Italian salad, and orange juice for a late lunch. The thirty-two-year-old sits in front of the computer and puts the final touches on a work he has called *2083*.

He rationalizes that even though what he is going to do is brutal, it is necessary in order to spread his ideological message. His victims will carry that message. The bomb explosion will make his name and draw the public's attention to his life's work, *2083*. The justification lies here in the document in black and white. The way he sees it, it's the worldview emerging from these pages that has forced him to carry out the crimes. He has given up on the power of the word, the word's ability to influence people and get them to change their perceptions. Yet he has written and collated fifteen hundred pages of words in the global language, English, to ensure that the words are read by as many as possible.

2083: A European Declaration of Independence. For almost a decade he has been developing the ideological foundation in the declaration of independence in his own words. In the last three years he has intensified his research and writing. All together he estimates that he has used 317,000 euros to finance the writing of the fifteen-hundred-page compendium. He has been forced to sell off personal belongings, including a Versace Rosenthal dinnerware set worth 5,000 euros, in order to finish the project. If it's correct, 317,000 euros is a considerable sum, especially for a person who in 2010 earned 1,236 Norwegian kroner. Therefore it's all the more important that he distribute *2083* to patriots all over the world through a spectacular marketing campaign. *2083* is his gift to mankind. In 2083 the Western cultural Marxist regime will fall, and the resistance movement, of which he is a part, will seize power. It's a divination worthy of Nostradamus, but at the same time it's also a convenient year. At that time the author would be 104 years old if he were to live that long.

He is the leader of the Norwegian branch of the Knights Templar. It's a military order, a martyr organization, and a court that allegedly was founded in London in April 2002 after lying dormant for a thousand years. At the inaugural meeting there were nine members present—from Greece, France, and other European countries—and the organization now has eighty cells all over Europe. They are armed and prepared to carry out crusader wars against jihadism. A member who executes a traitor will be decorated with medals and insignias. One hundred traitors killed merits an award of a medal with one silver sword and two silver stars. The organization members have code names. His mentor is called Richard the Lion Heart. It was on commission from the Knights Templar that the thirty-two-year-old from Skøyen has written the compendium to inspire and incite potential supporters.

Indications are that the Knights Templar organization exists only in his head, but there are several groups in Europe inspired by the Knights Templar, and they are prepared for confrontation. A former member of the right-wing English Defense League, Paul Ray, calls himself "Lionheart" and his organization, the Ancient Order of the Knights Templar. Its blog says that the knights are God's army on earth and that "it is time you came out of the shadows and helped your fellow countrymen; the time of peace and security has passed."

He claims that he has written half of the compendium himself. The rest has been copied from various websites. The first half of 2083 creates a total worldview that is inspired by anti-feminist, Christian, conservative, right-wing populist, and Islamophobic ideas, while the second half is a user manual on how patriots should prepare themselves for an attack on the cultural Marxist enemy. Long passages are copied from the 1995 manifesto of the American letter-bomb terrorist Theodore Kaczynski, otherwise known as the Unabomber. He has substituted the word "black" in the Unabomber's text with "Muslim."

The Norwegian blogger Fjordman is the main inspiration behind the manifesto of the thirty-two-year-old. Thirty-nine of his articles are reproduced verbatim in 2083. They are ideological soul mates, but Fjordman didn't want to meet him in person despite repeated requests via email. However, they meet in cyberspace, where other rules of contact apply. In November 2009, in the wake of the minaret ban in Switzerland, they traded comments on the document.no website. The topic was how long it would take before Europe was embroiled in a civil war. The author of 2083 thinks they have to put up with the Islamization of the continent for a while—say between twenty and seventy years. Fjordman thinks that the EU will disintegrate within twenty years and that there will be a full civil war in at least one West European country before then: "This is history's greatest betrayal, and it is inconceivable that our press corps, who're supposed to be critical of power, including the country's largest newspaper VG, do not write a single word about it. The fact is that Western leaders are engaged in a demographic and legislative war against the white majority population in Western countries to break them down in favor of an authoritarian, post-democratic world order with themselves at the top. The EU is already well on the way."

Fjordman's worldview has Old Testament overtones. The prophet has divided the universe into good (English Defense League) and evil (Norwegian Stoltenberg government), where the future of civilization is at stake. He encourages his disciples to take action before it's too late. Doing nothing will lead straight to doomsday. Fjordman believes that we must use "appropriate means to maintain our own security and to ensure our national survival." Just a few weeks ago he posted an item in which he advocated that "Islam and all those who practice it must be totally and physically removed from the Western world." He leaves it to his followers to find the means that will be appropriate to remove them.

In addition, the thirty-two-year-old leans heavily on known critics of Islam such as Robert Spencer, Bat Ye'or, Daniel Pipes, Ayaan Hirsi Ali, and Bruce Bawer. The common thread among these writers is that they all argue that Europe is in crisis, threatened by Islam, and must be saved. A confrontation between Islamic and Western values is inevitable, alleges Hirsi Ali in her book *Nomad*. We are already at war. The Muslims' uncritical stance regarding the Qur'an "is a direct threat to world peace." Islam isn't just a belief but "a violent way of life." In wartime, which is now, "internal feuds among atheists, agnostics, Christians, and Jews only serve to weaken the West." So while we prepare and gird ourselves to fight the enemy without, the Christians must awaken. According to Hirsi Ali, Christendom, headed by the Pope, must take up the fight against Islamization. Christian society has to make sure that Muslims adopt a modern lifestyle: "Teach them hygiene, discipline, a work ethic, and what you believe in."

The root of the continent's problem is a lack of national confidence. Europeans have become apathetic, lazy, and lacking in motivation for battle. Hence we have become easy prey for Muslims, who want to take over the continent and turn it into Eurabia. The helpless regimes in Western Europe have teamed up with the establishment to propagate a multicultural ideology. These are traitors and betrayers. The ideologue Bat Ye'or—a pseudonym used by the Anglo-Egyptian Jew Gisèle Littman—believes that this Euro-Arabian pact was sealed in the wake of the oil crisis in 1973 so that Western Europe and the Arab countries in alliance could undermine Americanization and Israeli domination. This is a version of George Orwell's dystopian scenario of *1984*, where "Eurasia" has become a new superpower extending from Portugal in the west to the Bering Strait in the east, after the Soviet Union has taken over continental Europe and implemented neo-bolshevism. The new breed that arises is a bastard with Mongolian traits.

Bat Ye'or claims that the Arab countries imposed certain conditions, which the European countries accepted, in order to call off the oil embargo in 1973: import workers from Muslim countries and accept family reunions; allow Muslims to practice their religion unobstructed; make sure schools teach how the West has a cultural debt to Islam; support wholeheartedly the demands set by the Arab League in the Palestinian conflict. Hence she believes that the Europeans have already become second-class citizens in their own homeland. When Norwegians refuel at an Esso station, they contribute, in effect, to the undermining of their culture—even if oil isn't what we most lack in Norway. Switzerland, which introduced the minaret ban in 2009, and France, which banned the full veil in 2011, are the deal breakers. Palestinians will soon be living in clover, thanks to this agreement from 1973.

These theories float around in an open, democratic network and not its murky underworld. Supporters of the Eurabia theory, such as Bruce Bawer and Ayaan Hirsi Ali, have been praised in Norway's main newspapers. A *Dagbladet* reviewer named *Nomad* the year's best book in 2010. Even relatively responsible Norwegian politicians have talked about "Islamization" and "creeping Islamization" and have stated that we have nothing to learn from Arabian culture and that immigration undermines Norwegian values.

In his book *Letter from America: Europe in Peril* former member of parliament Hallgrim Berg pays tribute to Oriana Fallaci, Bat Ye'or, and Fjordman for their penetrating analysis of the Muslim conquest of Europe. He says he warned against such tendencies in 1991 but regrets that he did not have access to the same incriminating documents that Bat Ye'or had. Berg supports the theory that EU bureaucrats in Brussels want to consolidate Europe, Arabic north Africa, and the Middle East into a single cultural, political, and economic entity. According to Berg, it sounds like a conspiracy, but it isn't.

The Statistics Bureau of Norway has estimated that the proportion of Muslims in Norway in 2060 is going to be 7 percent. Fjordman, Berg, and the thirty-two-year-old from Skøyen don't believe in such statistics. Only they and very few others have torn away the veil of Maya that masks reality. They have seen through the brainwashing carried out by the state. They know that Muslims are going to become the majority of Norway's population in 2060.

The author of 2083 takes the Eurabia theory to its logical conclusion: patriots and freedom fighters who want to avoid capitulation must participate in an armed resistance struggle. He says that today's power elite must be replaced by a patriotic governing body through a coup. Muslims in Europe must be deported back to their native countries. Those who don't leave voluntarily will be executed. There is a list of five thousand Norwegians categorized as A and B traitors. They will be exterminated using a large-scale anthrax campaign. A-category traitors are top politicians, business leaders, and media figures such as Foreign Minister Jonas Gahr Støre and former prime minister Gro Harlem Brundtland. B-category traitors are writers, academics, and public figures who have influence without formal positions of power, such as the social anthropologist Thomas Hylland Eriksen and the journalist Marte Michelet. These traitors don't necessarily have to have a positive view on the future of a multicultural Norway. They are, by virtue of their positions, representatives of a multicultural, politically correct, and cultural Marxist hegemony.

This mindset is not original. Replace "cultural Marxism" and "Muslims" with "bolshevism" and "Jews" and you have a familiar hate rhetoric from 1930s Europe. Decisiveness and the will to act, however, are rare in modern times. Terrorists usually attack symbolic buildings, such as the World Trade Center in New York in 2001, or random victims, such as those on the underground in London in 2005. Political assassinations are normally directed against individual leaders or other powerful persons. Loners carry out school massacres and direct their hatred against their peer-bullies, popular girls (whom they blame for their misery), or teachers before they turn the gun against themselves. The author of 2083, through his actions, seeks a mix of terrorist attacks, targeted political assassinations, and the outcast's revenge. The Declaration of Independence is a recipe for creating the first Islamophobic mass murderer.

The compendium includes secret codes, cryptic messages, and obscure references to symbolic figures, events, and years. The year 1492 is crucial. That year the Christian Spaniards reconquered Granada from the Muslim Moors. The conquest was the beginning of the expansionist era on the Iberian Peninsula but also the end of the multicultural heyday. Queen Isabella gave 150,000 Spanish Jews the choice of either conversion to Christianity or expulsion. The Jews fled to Constantinople. Sultan Beyazid II, known as "the Just," ridiculed Ferdinand II and Isabella I for the folly of expelling such a resourceful group of people. Beyazid sent the Ottoman fleet to evacuate the refugees from southern Spain to the city now known as Istanbul and imposed the death penalty for those who discriminated against Jews. Three years later the sultan gave refuge to the Muslim Moors who had been expelled from Spain.

The man in front of the PC on Hoffsveien in Skøyen hasn't been inspired by the sultan. The 2083 author applauded Ferdinand and Isabella's ethnic cleansing and expansionism. In August 1492, funded by the royal couple, the adventurer Christopher Columbus sailed with three ships—the *Santa Maria*, *Nina*, and *Pinta*—in search of an alternative route to India to acquire spices for Spain. On October 12 he arrived at the Bahamas, and on December 6 he reached Haiti. The Western conquest of America started in 1492, and thus the year is also the starting point of Europe's heyday—imperialism, colonialism, slavery, the Renaissance, Voltaire, Mozart, van Gogh, and Kipling. The year 2083 will be a new starting point and a new era of European glory. That's when "all multiculturalist category A and B traitors will be executed" and Muslims will be expelled from Europe for the third time. The first time was in 1492, and the second time was after the Battle of Vienna in 1683: "Islam will be thrown out of Europe within seventy years for a third time, of that you can be certain. You may judge me today, but history will judge you."

The year 1683 is also mythological in the compendium. It was then that the triumphal march of the Ottomans through Western Europe came to a halt. A battle on September 12 marked the end of a two-month-long siege of Vienna. The grand vizier, Kara Mustafa, succumbed to the

German-Polish army led by King Jan III Sobieski. One of the city's bakers celebrated the victory by creating a butter dough pastry shaped like a crescent, like the one on the Ottoman flag. One Austrian princess, Marie Antoinette, introduced the "croissant" a few years later in France when she became the country's queen. He has written in the compendium that after 2083—that is, exactly four hundred years after the Battle of Vienna—September 12 will be celebrated as a new independence day in Europe.

The overall ideological platform likewise stems from the Battle of Vienna. "We have chosen the Vienna School of Thought as the ideological foundation," he posted on the document.no website. In recent years he has worked to further develop and promote the "Vienna School," as he calls it. The school exists only inside his head and on paper, but he considers Fjordman, Bat Ye'or, and Spencer as adherents. He sums up the doctrine of the Vienna School in certain keywords: pro-cultural conservatism, anti-Islam, anti-racist, anti-totalitarian, pro-Israel, pro-Christian, anti-Eurabia. In the document in front of him on his PC he equates the Vienna School with "crusader nationalism" and adds further pros and antis: pro-patriarchy, anti-matriarchy, anti-feminism, and anti-pacifism. These ideas can be found on the Gates of Vienna website, where Fjordman is an active contributor.

Faith-based terrorists are concerned about the long term. Osama bin Laden wanted to restore the caliphate, which ended when the Ottoman Empire finally collapsed in 1924. He divided history into three phases. The first phase was the heyday of Islam, the second was Western colonial oppression in the twentieth century, and the third began on September 11, 2001, and proclaimed the resurrection of the caliphate. Here history is dialectical, like a cosmic battle between good and evil forces, with a wavering divine authority as a spectator. Moral legitimacy is derived from religion and history. The chosen will restore balance by making right what has been wronged. The mission is natural and inevitable. For bin Laden the attack on the West and Christianity was a calling and a duty. The author of 2083 is just as dedicated in his crusade against Islam. Both see the battle in a fourteen-hundred-year perspective.

But the past is ahistorical and symbolic. The crusader is taken out of his time frame and placed in the battle against the Turks in the 1600s or is writing a blog in 2011. He calls himself Sigurd the Crusader and considers himself a perfect knight. His mentor is Richard the Lionheart. History for him is a smorgasbord from which he helps himself to the tastiest dishes and ignores the rest. Norwegian king Sigurd I Magnusson departed from Bergen in 1108 with six thousand men and sixty ships. The destination was the Holy City, Jerusalem, and the objective was to drive the Muslims out of the city. The Pope had encouraged the crusaders with demagogic speeches in which Muslims were portrayed as the devil incarnate. But Sigurd and his men learned something else in the course of the voyage. They didn't stay in Jerusalem long before they traveled further to Constantinople, today's Istanbul, which was then ruled by the Byzantine emperor Alexios I. There Sigurd saw that the emperor surrounded himself with Jews and Muslims. They were advisers and members of the court. They were allowed to practice their religion in peace. The ships and the Norwegian army stayed in Constantinople, except for a hundred men. And Sigurd came home a far more knowledgeable and tolerant king.

King Richard the Lionheart led the Third Crusade in 1187. He was also ordered by Pope Gregory VIII to recapture Jerusalem and kill the infidels. But Saladin's army put up a stronger resistance than expected. Richard was forced to negotiate a truce. At the negotiating table he met Saladin's brother, al-Adil. He was a learned man without the demonic forces conferred on the Muslims by the Pope. Richard the Lionheart received medication for his illness and it worked. Muslims, it turned out, were more scientifically advanced than Europeans. Richard even offered his sister, Joan, as part of the peace agreement. Both the English and the Norwegian kings were Christian fundamentalists before they left, but they returned with a more nuanced picture of the enemy. The Knights Templar consulted Arab doctors as they realized that Arab knowledge of science was superior to their own. Muslims were more advanced in mathematics, astronomy, navigation, and agriculture. They cultivated sugar, a commodity that was as valuable as gold in Europe. Many members of the Knights Templar decided to stay in Jerusalem. They would not draw their swords against a reality that was merely in the Pope's head.

The thirty-two-year-old from Skøyen regards himself as the most perfect knight since World War II. By crushing cultural Marxism and multiculturalism, he will become Europe's greatest hero. His own people are committing demographic suicide. He wants to save the indigenous Norwegian people because he loves them and they will—in the long term— love him. The Knights Templar organization will take over Europe, and he will become the Regent of Norway under the name of Sigurd the Crusader II. He will start a program to breed white, blond, indigenous

Norwegian people, and immigrants will be sent into reservations or expelled from the country. He, and only he, the chosen one, shall decide who shall live and who shall die.

July 22. The date could probably be another manifestation of symbol fetishism. On that day in 1099 the French knight Godfrey of Bouillon was crowned king of Jerusalem on the Temple Mount, an event during the First Crusade that gave rise to the Knights Templar mythology. Mehmet II's Ottoman army was defeated by the Hungarian Christian king at the Battle of Belgrade on this date in 1456. The systematic deportation of Jews in the Warsaw ghetto began on this date in 1942. July 22 is also the feast day of the penitent Mary Magdalene, but the irony of fate is hardly that fickle. The date has been chosen for a more prosaic reason. It is the date when the bomb was ready.

He looks over the fifteen-hundred-page document one last time. It's written in the Word docx format. Misspelled words are underlined with thin red lines. It's a culmination of many years of work and brooding. He writes that "Time is running out. . . . This is going to be an all-or-nothing scenario." He also says that he's run out of money and that if he doesn't succeed, he will be heavily in debt. Also if he fails, he will start a private security firm operating in conflict zones to generate the most money in the shortest possible time. He concludes with, "If you want something done, then do it yourself." American researchers have found that terrorists' language use changes as words turn into actions. The writing becomes less personal and emotional and more aggressive and hostile. The sentences often become shorter and more bombastic. The use of the word "I" disappears or occurs less frequently, as depression is about to transform into an all-or-nothing scenario.

His last sentences are different. The words are personal and emotional, verging on the hysterical, with LOLs and smiley faces, and he still maintains the first person "I" form. The text speaks to an imagined community of lone wolves or "radical losers," as Hans Magnus Enzensberger calls rootless individuals who seek out groups with totalitarian doomsday tendencies. His email address book contains 1,003 gmail, hotmail, and yahoo addresses from over thirty countries, mainly through his contacts on Facebook. He has found the email addresses of high-profile anti-immigrant politicians and extreme-right supporters in Europe on the Internet. There will be 250 people receiving the compendium in the UK alone. 2083 will be sent to each and every listing in his email address book. He clicks "Send."

It takes a long time to send out the Word 2007 document even though he'd installed the fastest modem on the market in the morning. The document contains hundreds of thousands of characters, numerous graphs, and illustrations. At the end of the document he has pasted in photographs of himself. He poses for an imagined world stage, under the floodlights, where CNN, the BBC, and the NRK reschedule their regular programs to talk about him. He wears a Masonic costume, protective clothing, and an elite soldier's uniform. In the picture where he poses with weapons there's a label on the upper-left arm of the uniform that says, "Marxist Hunter." Taken out of context, it could look as if he were on his way to a macabre costume party. In one of the pictures he looks like an ordinary man from Oslo's west side: a brown coat over a dark blue suit and a light gray dotted tie with a silver pin. The sweaty, uncut blond haircut undermines the refined overall impression. The two narrow tufts of hair on his chin look like the remnants of an aborted shave. According to the cover letter he sent out with the document, he urged email recipients to distribute 2083 to as many people as possible. He ends with, "Sincere and patriotic regards, Andrew Berwick, London, England, 2011."

One of the recipients of the email is the former member of parliament from the Progress Party, Jan Simonsen from Rogaland County. He sees that it's sent to hundreds of names and thinks that it's probably spam mail. Simonsen doesn't know that the document he has just deleted contains detailed descriptions of an impending terrorist attack in Norway. The parliament's youngest representative from the Progress Party, Mette Hanekamhaug, also receives the email on her hotmail address. The twenty-four-year-old thinks the message is spam and deletes it. Between 2:00 and 2:30 p.m. 1,003 emails are sent from the apartment on Hoffsveien. They go to potential sympathizers in Finland, Denmark, the Netherlands, Belgium, and many other countries.

The thirty-two-year-old leaves the apartment and goes to the garden center on Sigurd Iversen Street, where the Volkswagen Crafter rental van is parked. He changes to a homemade uniform in the back of the van: a black NATO sweater with stuck-on police insignia. He himself has scanned and printed the police insignia on a printer in the Czech Republic. He tucks a pair of black pants with reflectors into black shoes. Over the sweater he wears something that looks like a bulletproof vest. He puts the Glock into the holster on his thigh. He passes the cable from the earplugs to the iPod underneath the vest. He has been shopping on eBay,

Amazon, and other foreign websites. Around his neck hang a Cross of St. George and a skull. If the neighbors saw him now, they would be surprised at his career change. The man in a police uniform starts the van and drives toward the government quarter in the city center. There department officials, bureaucrats, secretaries, and receptionists are just getting ready for the weekend.

7

No Entry

The sign at the entrance to the High Rise from Grubbegata says "No Entry." A thin chain and some lock bolts underscore the seriousness of the sign, but safety precautions in front of the building don't seem very intimidating. Oslo's first skyscraper houses the prime minister's office and the Ministry of Justice, among others. The government quarter is neither a physically closed nor heavily guarded area. In Grubbegata, Akersgata, and Møllergata through Nygaardsvold Square, Einar Gerhardsen Square, and Supreme Court Square thousands of people go to and fro in all directions to and from work every day. They meander unnoticed and effortlessly among busy department officials, personal secretaries, and receptionists. Norway's ministries are located here (with the exception of the Ministry of Defense, Ministry of the Environment, and Ministry of Foreign Affairs) in mastodon-like buildings with cryptic names such as "G-Block" and "R4."

The quarter is surrounded by the Deichman Library and Trinity Church on one side and the Supreme Court building at the opposite end toward Grensen. The iconic glass vg building is located on Akersgata next to r5, where, among other things, the Ministry of Culture bureaucrats eat lunch. On Grubbegata vis-à-vis the Ministry of Fisheries stands the much maligned ymca building, where the newspapers *Vårt Land* and *Dagsavisen* have their editorial offices. The parliament, Labor Party headquarters, Youngstorget Square, Norwegian Confederation of Trade Unions, and Domkirka Cathedral are just a stone's throw away. Power may be defined in many ways, but a person with ambition will find many a career opportunity in this intersection among government, law, trade unions, the press, and God.

The oldest building, somewhat Art Nouveau–inspired and in granite, was designed by Henrik Bull and first put to use in 1906, the year after Norway gained its independence. G-Block, as the building is called, houses the Ministry of Finance. On the wall facing the Supreme Court building one can see the Berlin-educated architect's national romantic aspirations: "Ja, vi elsker" (the Norwegian national anthem) and the notes to the anthem are inscribed on each gable. The building is listed as a national monument and is elegant in a pompous way, but it differs markedly from the modernist government buildings that are inspired by functionalism. On the façade of the Y-Block in the government quarter—the building is actually shaped like a Y—an artwork, *The Fishermen*, by Pablo Picasso and Carl Nesjar, is engraved into the façade facing Akersgata. Both the Y-Block and the High Rise were designed by the Le Corbusier-influenced Norwegian architect Erling Viksjø and are considered the culmination of postwar architecture and symbolic of the success of Norwegian social democracy. Le Corbusier called his vision of the good life in housing blocks "machines for living in." The working life's parallel must be "machines for working in." In the government quarter bureaucrats should be inspired to think logical, clear, and expansive thoughts.

After the al-Qaeda terrorist attack in the United States on September 11, 2001, it was recommended in a report that Grubbegata be closed to normal traffic. The American fear of terrorist attacks had come to Oslo. The street goes from Grensen past the Ministry of Fisheries, the High Rise, and the Ministry of Education in Y-Block. On Grubbegata are the Ministry of Petroleum and Energy, located in the R4 building vis-à-vis the High Rise, and the Ministry of Health in S-Block on the opposite side of Y-Block. In other words it's not just the prime minister's office that is vulnerable to attack. With Norwegian oil pipelines all over the globe the Ministry of Petroleum and Energy in R4 is an equally obvious terrorist target for those who're seeking to inflict harm on the nation. The National Police Directorate approved the proposal to close off the street in 2004, as did the government the following year. Since then the proposal has sporadically been taken up for discussion in the municipality, but delaying tactics by tenants in the neighborhood hindered any real progress. Now, however, everything should be in place. In September Grubbegata will be closed to civilian traffic. The street will be blocked off with submersible steel bollards in the south by the Ministry of Finance and in the north by the Deichman Library.

Oslo inhabitants ambling from Akersgata via Supreme Court Square and Grubbegata down toward Youngstorget Square—perhaps to meet friends at the clubs, Fyret or Internasjonalen—barely spare a thought for such bureaucratic technicalities. It's summer. It's far from sunny, but it'll be the weekend soon anyway. Setting up submersible steel bollards in front of buildings in natural concrete is certainly not a topic of conversation. It's more rewarding to discuss whether Norway has become a cycling nation, with or without artificial stimulants. People in the street have a sense of either relaxed idleness or determination. In the ministries the summer working hours are in force, so most of the staff goes out the door at precisely five to three. Some Japanese tourists have strayed from the main street, Karl Johansgate, in their hunt for interesting camera motifs. In *Dagsavisen*'s editorial offices the interns are staying in order to polish up items for the Saturday and Monday editions. The final space on the culture page is filled by a freelance journalist in Molde covering the end of the jazz festival. At Arne Garborg Square, which had to be partially covered over to make room for Y-Block, shift changes are taking place at the main fire station. It's siesta time in Norway's largest city. Anyone who can afford it—and there have been gradually more who can— has gone or is on the way to southern Europe or a cabin in southern Norway. Three thousand people work in the government quarter. Around 10 percent of them are in their offices on the Friday afternoon of July 22.

An Avis white van Volkswagen rental drives into Grubbegata from Grensen at thirteen minutes past three. The driver is focused. Three weeks ago he did a reconnaissance of the area, planned the driving route, and plotted it on his GPS. He stops outside the YMCA building and turns on the signal lights. As he puts on a helmet with visors, the unsuspecting receptionist sitting a few meters away prepares to start the weekend. The computer is turned off, the automatic answering machine is turned on, and the coffee cups are placed on the kitchen counter. He has considered the editorial offices as a legitimate target. The conservative Christian thirty-two-year-old would then have simultaneously struck the Christian bastions, *Vårt Land* and *Korsets Seier* (Cross Victory). The Socialist Left headquarters, Youngstorget, and the Blitz house have also been rejected for logistical reasons. Instead he must carry out Plan B.

After two minutes he turns his emergency lights on and drives further up Grubbegata, past a couple of pedestrians coming from the opposite direction on the wet pavement. They have to cross over to the opposite side at the corner of R4 because of roadwork. The driver of the Volkswagen van signals a left turn into an opening between the chains and the lock bolts, where the sign categorically states that there's no entry. There's a black car from the state security service already in the space where he intended to park the van to cause enough damage to the High Rise for the building to collapse. He backs the car into the space next to the main entrance at sixteen minutes past three. The reception guard sees him and contacts the guards' control room, located under the High Rise, to ask whether the visit has been registered. There are workmen going in and out of the building the whole time, so it's not surprising when a van parks outside the entrance. The reception guards are supposed to safeguard the inside of the building while the control room below ground has responsibility over the outdoor areas. The answer from the control room is that the visit has not been registered.

He opens the white door on the driver's side but remains sitting and lingers a few seconds. His pulse rate is rising. He fears that he will be exposed, that the fuse won't work properly, and that the bomb will go off prematurely. Will the reception guard come out to check? He has prepared for this for years. If you need something done, do it yourself. It feels like an eternity, but the clock shows that it's been only a minute. He lights the fuse, gets out of the car, and presses the electronic key to lock the van. The guard in the control room underground, who has been keeping an eye on him via the surveillance camera, calls up the reception guard to ask whether anyone has delivered an envelope or package. The answer is no.

The reception guard in S-Block has been talking with her friend about the Prince concert and checking the weather forecast. Now Hanne Gro Lille-Mæhlum mulls over what she and her partner will be watching on TV in the evening along with the taco dinner since the usual Friday programming is taking a break. Otherwise the afternoon has been spent saying "Have a good vacation, good weekend, and good summer" to colleagues leaving S-Block. Most of the staff have already left the building. One employee in the Ministry of Labor, who's actually supposed to be on vacation, has taken her husband and two children up to her office to print out tickets for Kristiansand Zoo. Coincidentally the husband is a journalist for the same newspaper she has folded up in front of her on the desk. She struggles a little to remember his name, which is both long and not traditionally Norwegian. Hanne Gro tries to joke that the journalist has given her the biggest challenge of the day. He replies that it's not important to him whether his name is spelled correctly. But for the reception guards it's important.

Now the employee walks out of the elevator without her partner. Hanne Gro asks about him and reminds her that guests should always be escorted out. Her tone is jocular yet firm. He walks out of the other elevator and delivers his visitor's badge with the long name. The family goes out to Einar Gerhardsen Square and turns the stroller down toward

Youngstorget Square. The visit to the building took longer than anticipated because the hot chocolate maker didn't work when her daughter wanted to have something to drink with the bun given her by an employee in the ministry. It is almost half past three. Hanne Gro checks the pollen forecast again. The thirty-three-year-old should stay for only another half hour at S-Block before she works the final shift at the High Rise, after which it's the weekend.

At *Dagsavisen*'s editorial offices on Grubbegata the atmosphere is both relaxed and strained. Someone has just come on shift to put together the Saturday and Monday editions of the newspaper, while others have eaten waffles in the canteen and are passively waiting for the official start of the weekend. A summer intern in the culture section is working on a press release about the group behind the petition against the multicultural center at Stiklestad; the group has called for demonstrations when Bushra Ishaq and Jonas Gahr Støre speak during the St. Olaf's Day celebration. "Stiklestad is sacred. Stiklestad is ours, not the Muslims," the group's coordinator, Eivind Lund Ager, says. The plan is to get social anthropologist Thomas Hylland Eriksen to shed light on Norway's thousand-year-old multicultural history and get him to explain precisely when Christianity became a distinct Norwegian invention. Ice cream is being served all around as a thank you and sendoff for the temporary culture editor. He will be taking a half-year sabbatical to write a report on the forced population exchange between the Greeks and Turks in 1922.

Editors in the debate section of the newspaper discuss how to follow up on Torgrim Eggen's report in today's edition on the decade that has passed since the terrorist attacks on the World Trade Center and the Pentagon. "Truth with a capital T died that day," Eggen writes. Although the events are extremely well documented, conspiracy theories abound on the Internet, starting with the morning of September 11. The hole at Ground Zero has become a witch's cauldron from which all manner of toads and phantoms crawl out. Eggen writes: "No matter what you think, and no matter how crazy the majority may think you are, there are always some out there who agree with you. They publish it. They create forums where you and those who are like-minded can exchange views, spread rumors, discuss recently published documents, and talk about skyscraper construction and the melting point of steel. People tend to prefer news with which they agree and that is more in sync with their worldview." The writers Åsne Seierstad, Aage Borchgrevink, and Kai Eide have also been asked to contribute to the 9/11 series, as have others associated with the periodicals *Civita* and *Minerva*. Oda Faremo Lindholm sits in front of her PC and writes about the Bodø musician Joddski's new album for Monday's edition. Joddski's songs are a mishmash of genres. She thinks that the musician's philosophy is based on a musical expression that is far removed from what most people would associate with his previous project, Tungtvann. "Where does all the chaos stem from?" asks Oda in the lead-in to her article. Joddski's second solo album is called *Adding Fuel to Fire*.

Party secretary Raymond Johansen is at his villa at the top of the so-called "Dollar Hill," a residential neighborhood in the Lindeberg suburb, which is known more for its apartment blocks. He's in shorts and a T-shirt and is talking with his adviser, Pål Martin Sand. From the window of the Labor Party office on Youngstorget Square Sand can actually see the government quarter, but now he has his back turned to it. They discuss how to handle the fact that Stoltenberg was given a boat valued at 380,000 Norwegian kroner as a present by the Norwegian Association of Trade Unions and the Labor Party for his fiftieth birthday on March 16, 2009. The boat is not listed as a gift in the parliamentary register. The prime minister's previous craft, a nineteen-foot Ibiza console boat, sank in 2007 during a storm while docked outside his cabin on the Hvaler Islands. On this day the issue is front-page news in the financial newspaper *Finansavisen*. A few floors below Sand, two musicians from Tromsø who have braved the weather sit drinking coffee at a table outside the trendy Internasjonalen Club.

The guard at the security control room in the High Rise sees via the surveillance camera that he gets out of the van but loses sight of him at Y-Block. The parking lot is not regulated, and Grubbegata is a municipal road. Anyway there is little that the guards can do without police authority. Nevertheless, the control room guard attempts to trace the registration number and calls up a guard from the R5 building. The standing instructions are that if security guards at the government quarter see something suspicious, they are not supposed to intervene but to call the police. If a car is wrongfully parked, they can have it towed away. That's about it. He walks with quick, long strides up Grubbegata on the left sidewalk toward the Deichman Library and Hammersborg Square. Just after passing the statue at Einar Gerhardsen Square, he looks back to make sure that no one has come out to check the van. The gun in his right hand is raised in front of his belly.

The final likelihood of being discovered is now. He could have been discovered when he bought chemicals from Poland. Due to the global shield initiative, which in the winter of 2010–2011 worked to prevent international trade in substances that could be used in terrorism, Norwegian customs issued a list in March that was sent to the Norwegian Police Security Service. His name was on the list. The Oslo police determined that his application in January for a gun permit was "poorly substantiated" and called him up to request better documentation. The farm he rented in Rena in April was used just two years ago by a gang of robbers to establish Norway's biggest hashish farm. He managed to buy six tons of fertilizer in May despite the fact that he lacked agricultural skills. In the meantime he had been spewing bile and vitriol against immigrants, the government, and modern society on extreme-right websites. If only one of these events had aroused suspicion, the security police would possibly have tracked down a budding terrorist.

Andreas Olsen normally walks up Ullevålsveien Street to fetch his son from kindergarten, but now it's vacation time. Instead he will be walking from Akersgata via the Deichman Library down to Grubbegata on the way to his apartment at the bottom of the borough of Grünerløkka. He stops by the vg building on Akersgata and buys a bouquet of yellow tulips and chocolates. His wife has been staying home alone with their kid all week, so she deserves something extra nice. Andreas is rushing home to watch the final stage of the Tour de France, so he takes the route that he thinks is the shortest—that is, from Akersgata via the Deichman Library. Outside Jostein Rønsen's architectural offices on 14 Grubbegata Andreas spots a lone armed policeman wearing a helmet, visor, and armored clothing. "That's curious," he thinks, as police officers in Norway don't normally carry weapons. It's a sleepy, idle afternoon in a city in vacation mode. What could have happened that requires the presence of a well-armed policeman? And why is he alone? The man walks with a determined gait, as if he's on an errand, but Andreas has a faster pace. For a short while Andreas is walking almost side by side with him. Just two or three meters separate them. Andreas is 1.77 meters tall. Yet he sees the man as shorter, probably because he's coming up Grubbegata while Andreas is going downhill from the Deichman Library. When the policeman turns down toward the parking lot on Hammersborg Square at eighteen minutes past three, Andreas catches sight of the gun in his hand. Then Andreas hears the sound of a car being unlocked electronically on the steep parking lot, and he sees the lights flash on the small gray van with the green license plates.

Andreas doesn't know that the man dressed in a police uniform hates trade unions. He doesn't know that in 2003 the man regarded the Norwegian Union of Municipal and General Employees as a greater enemy than the Labor Party. "We'll start by weakening the Municipal Union (which the Progressive Party hates above all). It'll be weakened sufficiently in ten years' time. The battle has begun," he wrote on the party's youth wing debate forum in a how-to guide to weaken the left's influence in Norwegian society. The Norwegian Confederation of Trade Unions was in fourth place on his list. The government and political parties in parliament were not mentioned. Andreas also doesn't know that he should be thankful he isn't wearing the backpack with the trade union logo that he always uses to carry documents home from the office and wet clothes home from the kindergarten. Apropos of daily routines, today Andreas is dressed in jeans and a plain T-shirt. Information officers often wear T-shirts with the red and white trade union logo. Andreas doesn't know who he passed at the corner of Grubbegata and Hammersborg Square, but—more important—the man dressed in a police uniform also doesn't know that he has passed an AUF member who joined the youth organization in 1992 to fight the then growing racist and neo-Nazi groups.

Eivind Thoresen, who is working this summer in the turquoise OBOS building on Hammersborg Square, leaves from the employees' exit with a bag over his shoulder and his mobile phone held tightly to his ear. The last few working hours have not been productive. The twenty-five-year-old has been following the Tour de France on his PC while talking to his girlfriend on the phone. They are going on a weekend trip to Stavanger with another couple. They agreed on the phone to meet outside her office on Akersgata. She advised him to take the fastest route between Hammersborg Square and Akersgata, via Einar Gerhardsen Square. Eivind grew up in the Oslo suburb of Nordstrand but has studied in Bergen since he was nineteen. He thinks it odd that he has actually never crossed the square before. The plan was to leave the office early. The other departmental colleague left at half past two, commenting on his way out, "There's nothing to do here." Eivind thought about leaving as well and waiting at a cafe with a Coke while his girlfriend got ready. And then the pace started to pick up considerably on the Tour de France.

It's drizzling. Eivind wonders whether he should take the umbrella or raincoat out of his bag, but the air is so warm that he decides against it. Moreover, it's not that easy trying to open a bag while walking and talking on the phone. Eivind has called up a childhood friend to get updates on the Tour de France while walking to Akersgata. The friend, Espen Tobiasson, is on vacation and sits glued to the TV in the Oslo suburb of Lambertseter. Eivind doesn't notice anything unusual when he crosses the fairly empty parking lot by Hammersborg Square toward Grubbegata. He is occupied with watching his step so as not to collide with lampposts while he listens to Espen's commentary on the cyclists Thomas Voekler, Cadel Evans, and the Schleck brothers. Eivind ambles down Grubbegata, takes a look at the clock on his phone, and realizes that he has to get a move on.

There are few cars in the parking lot. Andreas Olsen notices that the uniformed man gets into a civilian car with green license plates. He takes off his helmet and visor before turning on the ignition. The driver doesn't drive down to Møllergata and then right toward the old police station at No. 19 by Youngstorget Square, which would have been legal and natural. Nor does he drive down and around the parking lot and up past the OBOS building toward Grubbegata, which would have been just as legal and natural. The man in the police uniform drives down toward the Church of England and then left against the flow of traffic into Møllergata, a one-way street. He drives past the Norwegian Directorate of Immigration and the Chili Lavpris grocery store, where the special offers are advertised in Vietnamese. Next to the entrance stands a red traffic sign with a white stripe across it. He passes Krist Park, where kids are playing soccer and climbing jungle gyms and where the fitness specialist Chr. Mobech and Møllergata school are located.

He has to turn to the side of the road several times in order to let oncoming traffic get past. The Royal Persian restaurant, the Free Evangelical Assembly, and Mitsu Sushi and Baguette are soon behind him, as well as the Pine Specialist and Vietnam House, which will officially open in August. He stops where Møllergata meets Rostedtgate and Hausmannsgate Streets, a corner that is an exotic cityscape. Here one can choose among Chicken Tikka for 19.90 kroner, oriental travel agencies, and Rosted Thai Massage. The driver turns on his signal lights and waits for the traffic light to turn green. Right in front of him there's a faded pink façade with "Love Thy Neighbor / Fight for Civil Rights" in black lettering. When the traffic light turns green, he turns down Hausmannsgata and out of sight of the former AUF member.

The odd behavior of the police officer makes Andreas suspicious. The weapon, the civilian car, his driving in the wrong direction into the one-way street. Before the thirty-six-year-old walks further on, holding tulips and a bag of chocolates in one hand, he notes down the Fiat's license plate as a text message on his mobile phone and saves it as a draft: "VH 24605." Then Andreas takes out his iPod, puts on earphones, and starts listening to his favorite playlist of over one thousand songs.

It's merely by chance that Oda Faremo Lindholm, Eivind Thoresen, Andreas Olsen, and Hanne Gro Lille-Mæhlum find themselves in the city center a little before half past three. They have plans for the afternoon that won't be realized. They have ongoing tasks or conversations that will be interrupted. They will be exposed to something about which, initially, they'll have no clue. When they do grasp what it's about, it'll be difficult for them to get their heads around it. This can't be happening, not in Oslo and not in Norway. Lindholm, Thoresen, and Lille-Mæhlum will be directly affected. That goes without saying, given their proximity to the van parked outside the High Rise. Then there are all those who would have been affected but were outside the radius of the explosion. It could have been anyone—a father, a lover, a colleague, a police officer, a lawyer.

Geir Lippestad from the suburb of Hauketo and a committee member in the Nordstrand Labor Party is sailing in Oslo Fjord on board a thirty-six-footer with the ambitious name *Good Life*. He and his family have been vacationing for two weeks along the Swedish coast. They concluded their vacation the day before, with all seven kids, plus boyfriends and girlfriends. While his wife Signe drove the car from the cabin in Bohus-Malmön, Sweden, to the house in Nordstrand, Oslo, Geir Lippestad was supposed to sail the boat home with the two youngest children, a three-year-old and an eleven-year-old. Now they are heading in the direction of Frognerkilen, where the boat will moor. The kids sing. Just before half past three on Friday afternoon, the lawyer and the *Good Life* are somewhere between Nesodden and Aker Brygge in Oslo.

Norway's new police commissioner, fifty-one-year-old Øystein Mæland from Smestad in Oslo, is at home. He has just concluded his three-week vacation. He is looking forward to start his new job as the commander of twelve thousand police officers. It's going to be demanding. Prime Minister Stoltenberg's friend and best man, a former chief of the Labor

Party Youth in Oslo and a previous deputy minister, has no police experience. He is hoping that the media will stop focusing on his homosexuality and the fact that he and his partner got their one-and-a-half-year old son through a surrogate mother in California. They're expecting a second child in the fall. Just before half past three he cleans his kitchen counter with a cloth.

The wall clock in the Ministry of Justice stopped working between 3:25 and 3:26 p.m. According to the Geological Institute, it stopped at 3:24:18 p.m. The clock dial on the wall above the entrance to 19 Møllergata is crushed between the IV and VII roman numerals. It has taken about seven minutes for the seventy-four-centimeter-long fuse to burn down to the 950-kilogram fertilizer package. The NORSAR seismic station at Løten in Norway registered the blast at almost 1 on the Richter scale at 3:25:22 p.m. The blast also registered on the Richter scale in Sweden, 160 kilometers away. When the bomb went off in Oslo, the shock wave traveled through the air toward the seismic station in Värmland, Sweden, at a rate of 4–5 kilometers per second. The time itself varied, but it's of secondary importance. What matters is that time stood still.

8

The World's on Fire

There is a three-square-meter hole in the asphalt where the car bomb once stood. Below you can see the two floors of the underground garage. Steel plates in front of the entrance to the garage are peeled back. The foundation is vertically cracked. Both the reception lobby and the canteen next to it in the High Rise are blown apart. The remnants of cars are blown into the nearby buildings. Car parts land a hundred meters away. The abstract woman's torso in golden bronze beside the fountain at Einar Gerhardsen Square, by the sculptor Knut Steen as a tribute to the Roman goddess Aurora, the dawn, is peppered with metal shrapnel. A cloud of dust lies over the government quarter. The dry, violent crash is heard all over the capital city. Most people think it's thunder.

Eivind Thoresen has plenty of time. It feels like that. He hears a gigantic crash, and then everything goes into slow motion. The twenty-five-year-old sees flames rushing toward him from the right. He turns his upper body to the left to use his hand to protect his face. His bag, which hangs over his right shoulder, is thrown forward. The flames from the explosion cause burn marks on the hand and arm in front of his face. Small bits of shrapnel strike Eivind's bag. The pieces are rusty. They come from the van's undercarriage. The John Grisham pocket book in the bag is pierced through by shrapnel. A small piece of shrapnel strikes the button on the folded jeans and breaks it in two. The cell phone, with Espen still on the other end, is thrust down the sidewalk as the shock wave lifts the law student up and throws him three meters back toward the flower bed in front of S-Block. Espen thinks he has fallen down a flight of stairs.

This is not Oslo. It's Dresden in 1945, Phnom Penh in 1975, Sarajevo in 1995. That's how it feels. Norway's capital has turned into a war zone. Concrete buildings are covered with a grayish-black fetid smoke; streets, cars, and sidewalks are covered with broken glass; confidential papers fly about while alarms howl asynchronically in the background. People call for help. An overturned "No Entry" sign lies on the ground in front of the High Rise, and a black car has its wheels in the air. There is an overwhelming smell of burning. Water spurts out of leaking pipes. There's blood on the asphalt and flower beds. Most of the ground floor of the

High Rise is gone. The blast has blown out the thin walls, leaving only the pillars. The ground floor is similar to the one that was originally built in the late 1950s, when you could drive a car under the building. It was only in the 1970s that simple walls were built around the solid pillars. It's possible to see Akersgata through the High Rise from Grubbegata. Flames extend wildly skyward from under the helipad on the roof of the Ministry of Petroleum and Energy. The reception lobby in R4 no longer resembles one. The signal panel on the wall flashes "Abnormal operating status."

Cups and saucers from the kitchenettes are scattered and broken over the floor in the High Rise. Electrical wiring, ventilation fixtures, and water pipes hang down from the ceiling. Filing cabinets are overturned, strewing out kilos of the twenty-two tons of paper kept in the building. The air is filled with the stench of smoke, torn fiberboard, fiberglass, and asbestos dust. Employees are thrown against the bookshelves and come to feeling dazed. The anti-shatter film on the windows is supposed to prevent glass shards from becoming projectiles shooting into the room. Instead the pulverized windows, including the frames, turn into projectiles. A fifty-year-old senior adviser is pierced in the head by a twenty-five-centimeter-long piece of wood from a window sill. It goes in at the jaw, through the masseter muscle, and out via the temple.

The main staircase out to Grubbegata is unrecognizable. Window frames and sills are blown out and lie all over the railings. Each footstep crunches into metal, wood, and glass. Ceilings have collapsed. Potted plants are overturned. In the High Rise's reception area employees used to go past one of the most famous artworks of Hannah Ryggen, the textile artist, feminist, and anti-fascist,. *We Live on a Star* showed a naked man and woman embracing each other over a globe, and it was an expression of Ryggen's faith in people and love. Two naked infants, symbolizing innocence and life, were suspended over the globe and the adults' embrace. When the timid artist, who had recently lost her life partner, Hans Ryggen, attended the unveiling of the piece in 1958, along with the architect and two workers with tools and ladders, she began to weep profusely. Now the artwork is totally destroyed.

Hundreds of men and women in the government quarter have been exposed to the same event, but each experiences it individually and formulates his or her own particular narrative. In recalling the event, the government employees diverge in their narratives even down to the basic facts, such as how the explosion sounded. Not like a loud bang, more like a muffled, dry rumble. Like the pop of a champagne cork, except louder. Thunder. An earthquake. A gas explosion. Those on the inside elevators hear a distant, strangled sound before they come to a halt; the walls tremble, and everything turns black. Some don't remember the explosion but rather the silence just afterward, the smell of burned metal, and the sound of paper fluttering through the air.

The window at the clothing store Cubus on Storgata Street is shattered, and smoke gushes in. A twenty-three-year-old employee tries to close the doors, but people, in panic, seek refuge in the store. In another store on 8 Møllergata a heavy lamp falls from the ceiling and almost hits a customer. The maître d' standing outside the Mona Lisa restaurant in Grensen feels the shock wave from the explosion. The doors and windows of the restaurant implode. Just a few meters away from him a waiter at the restaurant next door is hit by glass from the second floor. He is lying on the ground with a bleeding head. When the maître d' sees people on the street running with a dust cloud behind them, he recalls the scenes from Manhattan ten years earlier.

Pål Martin Sand is standing in front of the window and talking on the phone to Labor Party secretary Raymond Johansen. He is standing with his back to the window that faces Youngstorget Square and doesn't see the wave from the blast coming toward him from the government quarter. Sand is flung against the wall while Johansen is still on the line. Sand gets up, tells the party secretary that he must hang up, and runs. Below at the Internasjonalen Club two Tromsø musicians are cut on the forehead, head, and arms from the glass showering down from the People's Theater building. Right beside them is a sixteen-year-old. She calls her father and tells him that she can't breathe. A glass shard is stuck in her throat.

Most of the damage is not caused by the explosion itself but by the blast wave that ricochets violently for a long while between buildings, like the fertilizer bomb of Timothy McVeigh's that destroyed a third of the Alfred P. Murrah Federal Building, damaged 324 other buildings, and killed 168 people in Oklahoma City in 1995. Invisible energy and gas molecules cause unimaginable damage to unimaginable places but behave logically and predictably. Like water, energy finds inroads through the labyrinthine city spaces, with a velocity exceeding that of sound. When the blast wave meets a building, they change direction. The wave ricochets among swaying government buildings, moving up Grubbegata toward the oвоs building and the Swedish church, where the street curves to the left, past a newly restored building from 1895, and the Fredensborg housing center (a program for homeless drug abusers) before they meet a wall of apartment blocks on Fredensborgveien, where number 14 bears most of the brunt. The photographer Fredrik Arff has his studio here. The window in the studio is of the old type, with double glazing. Because the blast wave weakens in its trajectory up Grubbegata, partly due to a loss of power in the open urban space over the Hammersborg tunnel, only the inner pane is cracked.

Eivind Thoresen gets up. He thinks that there must be many who have died here. He hears nothing but catches sight of an older man in glasses, a beige jacket, and a blue shirt. He was standing beside his car, waiting for his wife to come out of the High Rise on Einar Gerhardsen Square when the bomb went off. The bleeding forehead looks dramatic, but his right leg is harder hit. It looks to Eivind as if the foot is hanging by a thread. Again the scenes of destruction seem as though taken right out of a movie. There's panic, chaos, and smoke everywhere, but Eivind hears nothing because of the ringing in his ears. He realizes that the man is calling for help. His hearing gradually returns; he hears fire alarms and cries for help far, far away. Eivind wants to say to the man, "You must shout louder if you want someone to hear you."

It's not the right thing to say. The man obviously needs help. Eivind takes a step toward him and gets a curious glance in return. The glance says, "You can't help me. Look at yourself." Eivind is a polite young man and does as he's told. Then he sees the blood streaming from his left upper arm, just below the edge of his short-sleeved white shirt. It's strange that Eivind doesn't faint. And the same thought goes through his mind: "It's strange that I didn't faint." Eivind can't stand the sight of blood. He turns off the TV when there are surgery scenes. Drawing blood from him is a nightmare. Eivind presses his right hand over the wound and thinks that the problem is solved. "Now I've stopped the bleeding," he thinks. The pressure makes the pain even worse. The blood gushes more intensely and the flow becomes as long and thick as the stream from a water hose. He can't help anyone. He'll have to lie down. And wait. Eivind and the older man cry for help in chorus. The law student sees people running away. He sees that they see him, but still they run away. "Damn, if no one stops, we're going to die," Eivind Thoresen thinks.

Oda Faremo Lindholm registers the sound of the blast before she sees the shattered windows. The twenty-three-year-old remains sitting on the chair in front of the PC in the editorial offices while her colleagues hide under desks or run to the exit door. She can be a little cocky in a way, a consequence of years of effort to keep hasty decisions and "worst case" scenarios at bay. But then there was this inexplicable feeling that something wasn't right, that something was fundamentally wrong. As the sports journalists, foreign correspondents, culture reporters, photographers, and editors rushed to the stairs, the alarm sounded. Oda followed the others. It was only on the way down the stairs, heading toward the YMCA building exit on Møllergata, that her heart started to beat very fast. Everyone remained calm, except for one woman who sobbed and shouted in broken Norwegian, "This is a bomb!" Oda thought she probably had been traumatized in her homeland, where bombs and war were a part of daily life. "This is a bomb!" In the meantime she noted the damage to the building on the sixth floor, fifth floor, and fourth floor: the ceilings that have collapsed, the cables that are exposed, shattered glass doors in the offices. "This is a bomb!"

On the sidewalk on Møllergata Oda sees that something is seriously wrong. People stagger unsteadily out from offices and shops. One of them sits bleeding in front of the Glassmagasinet department store. Some girls have salvaged meat, salad, dressing, and pita bread from the dust, glass, and detritus that have fallen from the roof of the Beirut Kebab cafe. A man tries to get into the driver's seat of a car that is full of broken glass. Oda doesn't catch all of this; her only impression is of scattered groups staring at the government quarter. They were saying that a helicopter crashed on its way down to the helipad on top of the R4 building, but that rumor is put to rest when Oda goes up to Grubbegata and peeks around the corner toward Einar Gerhardsen Square. She isn't aware of everything that is happening on Møllergata because she can no longer concentrate on herself, her colleagues, or the wounded. It has just dawned on the newspaper journalist that her mother may be dead.

When Oda was little, she spent a lot of time in the government quarter. Her mother, Grete Faremo, worked in both the Ministry of Justice and Ministry of Petroleum and Energy. Even when she has worked in other ministries in other locations, Oda has always thought of the government quarter as her mother's workplace because of all the meetings that took place there. Oda is distraught when she calls her mother's number on the mobile phone. Answer the phone; answer it, answer it. She's no less panic-stricken when her mother answers on the first ring, even though one would think that would be good news. It almost never happens that her mother does so. Oda usually has to leave a message, to be called back when convenient. Therefore she's certain her mother is buried under the rubble. "Where are you? Are you alive?" That last question in particular is an unusual one to ask on a Friday afternoon, so the mother asks her daughter to breathe out. That, in reality, isn't easy to do for a twenty-three-year-old who's scared and crying. "A bomb has exploded in the government quarter," Oda says. "Okay, calm down," says the mother, who doesn't believe her daughter's hysteria is proportionate to the events that have caused it. "I'll check with my colleagues and call you back." "Huh? She's hanging up? Here I'm in the middle of bombed-out rubble and she hangs up?" Oda thinks and doesn't know whether to laugh or cry at the surrealistic situation in which she finds herself.

Oda sits on the sidewalk in the midst of what looks like the great doomsday conflagration, Armageddon, and waits for a new heaven in the form of a phone call. Actually she knows very well that her mother's workplace is on Grev Wedel Square. But she often has meetings at the prime minister's office and usually on Fridays with the ministers. Oda doesn't know that her mother spent the morning at a medal ceremony for Afghanistan war veterans at Fort Akershus and went straight home afterward to prepare for a vacation trip to Montenegro. All around Oda rumors run rampant about helicopters crash landing, attacks on the Cappelen Damm publisher, and assassinations of Norwegian war participants in Libya. She doesn't care much for the baseless yet plausible scenarios, despite the fact that she was for many years politically active in the Red Youth Party. She's still only anxious about her mother.

"Can I go now? Who'll finish today's edition of the newspaper? God, I forgot to send the Joddski article to the news desk." Oda wants to get home to her apartment, but the door keys are in the gray Helly Hansen raincoat in the office on the seventh floor of a building that no one is allowed to enter now. Her parents have an extra set of keys. Oda calls her father and tells him about the bomb and the now inaccessible keys. The father responds quietly but somewhat distractedly, "Oda, that's probably no big deal. Can't you just go up and grab the keys? You see, the timing is a little bad now—I'm watching the time trial at the Tour de France." "Huh? They're hanging up on me again. Do I have to stand here and wait until the time trial is over? Is that how it's supposed to be?" thinks Oda and hangs up.

Oda's mother calls up again. Finally. When her mother is afraid, she doesn't become hysterical, which would be the more natural reaction. She stays calm and focused and looks for solutions. "Oda, I think you're right. It could be a bomb," she says. She knows that there's also the risk that there may be a second bomb. The first one kills people and attracts emergency first responders and curious onlookers, while the second kills the first responders and curious onlookers. "Can you go home?" her mother asks. "No, my house key is in the building and dad's watching the Tour de France." "Can you go to Ketil's? He's home. Go to Ketil's." "I haven't told my boss." "Never mind; just get out of the city center." Oda has no idea what happened during the two minutes from the time her mother, Grete Faremo, Norway's defense minister, ended the first phone call with her daughter until she called now, but everything suggests that the minister was first informed of the terrorist bomb in the city center by her own daughter and that the minister in the brief interim had confirmed that the explosion was not an accident.

Eivind Thoresen's friend, Espen, in Lambertseter hears the clamor, noise, and cries for help through the mobile phone lying on the sidewalk by Einar Gerhardsen Square. His suspicion that something is seriously wrong is confirmed when the Tour de France broadcast is interrupted by breaking news of an explosion in Oslo. He has been texting and shouting to Eivind but getting no response. When the call is suddenly cut off, he is perplexed. He calls up Eivind's mother, who works at a nursery in the suburb of Nordstrand. Espen stammers, using key words enigmatically, mumbling and blustering rather than articulating anything that makes sense. The only thing the mother can make out of what Eivind's good friend is saying is "Tour de France."

Eivind was thirty meters from the car bomb when it went off. Because the bomb was located above the underground garage, the force of the explosion went downward before creating an air pressure funnel that rose upward. Fortuitously Eivind was shielded by this air funnel. Moreover, he managed to turn his back so that the clothes in the fitness bag over his right shoulder bore the brunt of the many flying projectiles. A black car used by state security guards also diverted some of the force of the blast away from Eivind. Nevertheless, he was thrown several meters backward onto Einar Gerhardsen Square and was severely injured in the head, legs, and arms. A few meters away from the law student, a fifty-six-year-old administrative secretary lies motionless. Eivind sees that many people are taking pictures of him with their mobile phone cameras. One stops right in front of him and videos the whole scene. He stands there for a long time.

There are two reception guard positions in S-Block. When Hanne Gro Lille-Mæhlum's colleague went on vacation at 2:00 p.m., she was asked whether she wanted to move over to the desk closest to the main entrance. She said no and was sitting at the inner desk. As a consequence when the bomb exploded, the thirty-three-year-old was shielded by a large, solid machine used for scanning mail. If she had moved over to the colleague's desk or if the machine had not been where it was, the reception guard's fate would have been different. Hanne Gro doesn't remember whether she was standing or sitting in the lobby. She doesn't remember the blast. She remembers only the sound of broken glass and everything going black.

Hanne Gro is trapped among the desk, chair, scanning machine, and window. She feels as if she's been run over and shrink-wrapped. Hanne Gro has been thrown diagonally across one of the doors in the lobby and ends up with a pane of glass on top of her. The glass pane, which still has stretch film covering it, is almost intact, but some shards have come loose. When she tries to move out of her unnatural position, her arm is cut, and the glass shards come dangerously close to her neck. Sparks are issuing from the ceiling. In the corner stands a huge potted plant that's still intact. She hears her own heart beating. Under the desk are the black shoes she took off because of her clammy feet. The mobile phone isn't where she left it. The tall black rubber boots and the black raincoat with white dots are still in the corner.

The reception guard is trapped with glass right up against her neck, and the blood is dripping onto the floor from the cut on her forehead. She listens for broadcast messages on the communications channel, but there's nothing. "Have I turned the volume down too low? Damn," thinks Hanne Gro. In her head she goes through the number of ministers who are in the buildings and of the many VIPs and other guests she knows about. She is worried that she has let in someone who's not supposed to be there. Maybe it's some nutcase who's angry with the labor minister and has decided to destroy the building they're in? But it's she who's been hit, not the ministers who happen to be outside the government quarter. Hanne Gro doesn't know what has happened, but nevertheless she thinks about all the hours she has spent in various reception lobbies, on the front lines, exposed to potential threats, without being harmed. Her job is to wait for something that preferably won't happen. But it had to happen sooner or later.

The workers in the ministries run through the lobby and out of the building. Someone stops and says that they have to get her out. "No, don't touch me," Hanne Gro says. She'll wait until the fire department arrives to cut her loose. The alarm panel is behind her. According to standard operating procedures for emergencies, the operations manager has to come here. A group stops in front of the entrance. "Hello, does anyone know what's happened?" Hanne Gro asks. She wants to know where the fires are but gets no answer. In an effort to appear professional she tries to calm the people around her by saying that the security guards will be coming soon to take charge of the situation. The security control room has video cameras, so they must see that she needs help.

The fire department is located on the other side of S-Block. How long can it take for the firefighters to get here? Hanne Gro feels weak and nauseous. The cuts are pulsating with blood. Blood is streaming from her forehead. She's losing her vision. "Will I die in this way?" Hanne Gro hears someone banging on the inside of a door. Someone else stops right by her and cries, "Oh my God." A senior adviser from Government Administration Services, who on his way down from his office on the third floor has passed ceiling parts and ventilation equipment on the floor, shattered windows, and stately photographs of former ministers that have fallen from the walls in the hallways, stops in front of the reception desk on the first floor. He asks how it's going. "I'm stuck fast and there's glass in my eye," Hanne Gro says. "We must try to get you loose now," the senior adviser says, with the emphasis on "must" and "now." He ponders for a few seconds before moving the chair and other materials and tilting the glass window pane. While he pries and lifts, Hanne Gro asks for the black rubber boots. They can protect her feet from sharp objects on the floor of the lobby. He suggests that they leave the boots behind. He lifts her up, placing his hands under her knees and neck, and she smells deodorant and hears the sound of his pounding heart. "Wait; I need to get my keys and communications radio," Hanne Gro says. "We don't have time for that now," the senior adviser responds.

Out on Einar Gerhardsen Square, Hanne Gro asks the senior adviser what has happened. She can see only a little through her left eye, right in front of her and down on the ground. "It looks like hell," he replies and jogs down toward Youngstorget Square with her in his arms. His heart beats faster and he breathes more heavily. Hanne Gro is worried that he will stumble and drop her, thus hurting both of them. In an attempt to calm him down, she says, "You don't have to run so fast; I'm okay." The senior adviser ignores her advice. He wants to get as far away as possible as fast as possible.

The glass in the window of Uno Tailors and Dry Cleaning on Youngsgate Street was blown in by the blast wave. On the premises is thirty-four-year-old Delshad Rasul. Experience with twenty years of war in Kurdistan and knowledge of first aid propels him to rush out of the dry cleaners' and run in the direction of the smoke that is rising above the roofs. On the way he snatches napkins and dishcloths from Kitchen and Bar on Møllergata. The area between R4 and the High Rise is reminiscent of a war zone in Iraq, he thinks, before he looks around to see who needs the most help. Outside S-Block he finds a young man who is injured. Beside him sits Harpreet Singh, who works at OBOS and who has run out of the turquoise building on Hammersborg Square. Arriving on Grubbegata, he was told to stay away because there could be another explosion. Firefighters who came out of the station told him the same thing. Harpreet runs down Grubbegata anyway, in the opposite direction to that of many others, until he comes to Eivind Thoresen, who lies severely injured outside S-Block. But Harpreet Singh knows only minimal first aid. The first thing he says to Eivind is, "You look like hell."

The myth is that we panic and act irrationally and selfishly in disaster situations. It's equally true that people keep a cool head, have a heightened sense of fraternity, and offer a helping hand. Researchers who interviewed terror victims in the subway attacks in London in 2005 say that the usual sullen annoyance and suspicion very quickly gave way to cooperation and compassion among the passengers. Faced with life or death decisions for oneself or others, one's senses are heightened, the blood pumps faster, and the performance bar is raised. We often answer correctly if the wrong answer leads to punishment. If soccer players in a penalty shootout know that scoring a goal means victory for their team, the success rate is 92 percent, while that rate is cut by half if scoring has no impact on the outcome of the match. Moreover, according to psychologist Pål Johan Karlsen, it is possible to increase the degree of rational behavior in chaotic situations if we already know about emergency preparedness. It helps, for instance, to know where the emergency exits in a building are. Harpreet and Delshad have differing levels of expertise in first aid, but both run to the government quarter to try to save lives despite being warned of the risks involved.

Delshad knows that the most important thing is to stop the bleeding. He breaks off a branch from the green tree next to the flowerbed. The branch can be used to make a tourniquet. Harpreet and Delshad also get a plank and borrow a policeman's Maglite flashlight. They fish out clothes for bandaging the wounds from Eivind's bag. The first garment Harpreet takes out is a white T-shirt that he uses to bandage Eivind's left arm. Delshad loses contact with Eivind several times. He is falling asleep, so Delshad slaps him in the face and talks more intensely to him, saying that Eivind is strong, that it's going to turn out all right, and that he promises to visit him in the hospital. The law student wonders whether he is still alive. "Yes, you're alive." Since he can't feel his legs, he wonders whether they are still there. Delshad and Harpreet calm him by again saying yes. Eivind has lost a liter and a half of blood. He feels hot, very hot. Then he feels freezing cold and starts to shiver. He thinks he's going to die because he has seen in movies that a rapidly fluctuating body temperature is the beginning of the end. Delshad spreads a blue G-Star jacket over him and holds his chin up so that the air passages are kept open. Eivind feels no pain, other than when Delshad and Harpreet give the flashlight and plank one more turn to put more pressure on the wound. A policewoman comes over and asks to borrow clothes to bandage wounds and cover the dead. "Help yourself. I don't think he will mind," Harpreet says.

The senior adviser puts Hanne Gro Lille-Mæhlum down on a chair next to the Deli de Luca convenience store on Torggata. Along the way she has been checked by an English-speaking doctor who said that her eyes seem to be uninjured. But the heavy bleeding from the cut above the eye has to be stanched. On Torggata she meets a fellow student and colleague from the reception desk. The colleague has blood on the white top she changed into after she went off guard duty because she has been helping an injured woman. The senior adviser fetches a glass of water and paper from the convenience store. Hanne Gro becomes skeptical when she sees that he has put on blue gloves. "What do you know about first aid?" she asks as he washes away the blood from her face and arm. She's worried about getting infected and doesn't touch the armrest of the chair.

The two reception guards discuss whether it's safe to be on Torggata. "We should probably get out of here as fast as possible," the colleague says. Hanne Gro agrees, but someone has to look after the High Rise, where, according to the guard shift schedule, she should be at a quarter to five. Above all, it's difficult for her to imagine going anywhere without shoes. Her colleague takes off her shoes and gives them to her. "You need them more than I do," she says. The shoes are black and white, with small blood stains. When Hanne Gro realizes that her colleague doesn't have an extra pair in her bag (as she'd assumed), she starts to protest. "No, I'm not going to take them," she says and gives the shoes back. The senior adviser lifts her up again and carries her toward Youngstorget Square, where roadblocks have been set up.

A newspaper photographer takes a picture of the senior adviser carrying Hanne Gro on Torggata. The photo became a symbol of the heroism shown in and around the government quarter after the explosion. It looks as if she's so injured that she can't walk on her own, but in fact she's being carried because she can't walk wearing only socks on the cobblestones strewn with broken glass. Hanne Gro thinks how embarrassing it would be to tell her superior that she had taken off her shoes before the blast. She thinks about the needlessness of a man having to use up energy to carry her just because she was airing her feet. And she thinks about how practical it would have been if she had put on uniform pants today (instead of a skirt). For all she knows, the images and videos taken today will be shown on newscasts across the country. Maybe even abroad.

Hanne Gro is placed on the fountain in the middle of the square, with blankets over and under her, next to the wounded and traumatized. Paramedics flock to the improvised field hospital, where they check, clean, and bandage wounds. "Yes, the weekend just started off with a bang," she says, and asks if they have sterile gloves on. She gets help to look up the phone numbers for her boyfriend and her father. The senior adviser calls Anders, her boyfriend, for her but gets only his voicemail. He leaves a message. "I'm sitting here with your girlfriend, and she's fine. But you can't call her now because she doesn't have her mobile phone. She'll try to call you from another phone some time later."

At the Emergency Medical Assistance Communications Center (AMK Center) a chaotic picture of the situation is painted. First, there are reports of an explosion in the XXL sports store, three blocks from the High Rise. The leader of the paramedics doesn't see any damage in the sports store.

By Glassmagasinet department store he sees bloodied faces, and in Grensen he's stopped by desperate people who surround the ambulance asking for help. He receives a voice message over the radio that the vg building is hit. This is confirmed when he comes to Akersgata and sees the broken window glass. He goes right and notices that the damage is more extensive there—that is, until he comes to Grubbegata. Despite difficulties in the communications network he manages to convey the following to the center: "The High Rise is the target. Requesting all available resources. Terror." The team leader's thoughts are not of just any war zone but the one in the Middle East. "It looks like Beirut," he tells those who are coordinating the emergency rescue operation from the amk Center.

The paramedics who come to the aid of Eivind Thoresen were summoned from Skøyen district. Speed limits were exceeded and a bus mirror was broken along the way. The ambulance had first come to Grensen before it was ordered to Youngstorget Square, but the driver is still at a loss as to where they are most needed. They're standing outside the Kitchen and Bar restaurant on Møllergata when a newspaper photographer comes running down from Einar Gerhardsen Square and says that a young man needs urgent medical assistance. Coincidentally the photographer knows one of the paramedics, Stian Eriksen, rather well. With his colleague Tore Lund, Stian runs over to Einar Gerhardsen Square. Stian, like the former soccer player lying on the sidewalk, is most anxious about the legs, so he cuts up the blood-spattered jeans. The paramedic says that he is impressed by Delshad's and Harpreet's efforts to help Eivind. They have more than likely saved Eivind's life.

Because the ground is more uneven than normal between Møllergata and Einar Gerhardsen Square, Stian and Tore consider using a stretcher without wheels. It shouldn't be too heavy a load. "You don't weigh more than seventy kilos, do you, Eivind?" Stian asks. "Well, now the stretcher is going to collapse," Eivind replies with a slight twinkle in his eye. His smile broadens considerably when he's finally lifted into the yellow ambulance and gets a shot of morphine.

Bus 37, going to and from Nydalen district, runs on one of the busiest bus routes in the capital. The resourceful paramedics have stopped the bus driver and asked whether the long red vehicle can be used as a makeshift ambulance to transport those with minor injuries to the emergency ward. The driver is forewarned that the seats are going to get messy, but he dismisses this concern, saying he's used to mess because he drives the night bus to Stovner suburb on weekends. The passengers on the bus get off on Akersgata. The elderly, gray-haired yet athletic bus driver fills the seats with the wounded before he again starts up the bus, drives through Grensen, and turns left by the cathedral toward the emergency ward. The ambulance drives in front of the bus to clear traffic. It becomes somewhat surrealistic in the bus when the automated voice over the loudspeaker announces all the stops at which the driver has no intention of stopping.

Journalists struggle to get a clearer picture of the situation in the government quarter. Photographers are snapping pictures randomly without really knowing in what context the images will be printed. Is it an accident or a terrorist attack? Some immediately think that the explosion was caused by an attack on the Cappelen Damm publishing firm on Akersgata. On June 20 the police had to be called when the publisher introduced Flemming Rose's book *The Tyranny of Silence*, which featured a facsimile of the Muhammad cartoons. There was a threat of demonstrations, the building was evacuated, and twenty police officers were dispatched, but it was just much ado about nothing. Have Muslim fundamentalists been more motivated this time around? Or perhaps it's an attack against Norway's biggest tabloid, *VG*?

Pablo Burgos is on Akersgata with his wife and two children. The Spanish tourist has a bloodied face and is limping. "I've never experienced ETA's rage and never thought I would be confronted with terror in little Norway," he tells a journalist. A twenty-five-year-old *VG* photographer, Sara Johannessen, is taking pictures of a fifty-year-old senior adviser in the Ministry of Justice with a piece of wood sticking out of his forehead; he was working overtime on a draft action plan about domestic violence. Just a few hours earlier Sara was on Utøya covering Gro's speech to the AUF youths. The plan was to stay there the whole evening.

Anders Mølster Galaasen is a sociology student and freelance journalist, as well as Hanne Gro's boyfriend. When Anders sees the unfamiliar mobile phone number flashing on his phone display, he thinks it is about an ad they posted on the website finn.no. But the couple has already found a new place to stay. The ad should have been removed. A text message pops up and reminds him that he has voicemail. Just to be sure, he calls up the voicemail. "Strange message," he thinks. However, it's not unusual that Hanne Gro has left her mobile phone at home. He listens to the message again, and it sounds no less strange the second time around.

Perhaps she has to work overtime? Anders is still trying to figure it out when a friend calls and asks if he has control over the situation. "What situation?" Anders asks. "Have you talked to Hanne?" What Anders thought was the sound of thunder in the dark sky was—if he is to believe his friend—a bomb explosion in the government quarter. "Yes. Or no.... But I've got a message on voicemail from a colleague of Hanne's. He says that she's fine. Now I understand what he meant."

Three years ago Anders wrote an article in the news magazine *Ny Tid* about how Norway's war on terror was different in Afghanistan than in Sri Lanka, and he speculated on whether it was due to Norway's peace-maker role in the latter. The article, with the highlighted keyword "Grub-begata," is titled "Rising Fear of Terrorism in Norway." Tore Bjørgo from the Police Academy and the Norwegian Institute of International Affairs told the news magazine that he didn't rule out the fact that there could be a terrorist attack in Norway in the near future, and he rattled off a few factors that made it probable: Norway's participation in Afghanistan, Iraq, and the Balkans and its peacemaker role and substantial oil produc-tion. In light of the increased risk of a terrorist attack in recent years the city council has therefore decided to close Grubbegata in the city center in order to "prevent possible car bomb attacks in the government quar-ter," as the journalist wrote. The city council was initially skeptical about the proposal before the Norwegian Directorate of Public Construction and Property, but the Conservative Party and the Progress Party changed the minds of the council members after pleas from the police and the prime minister's office. At the end Anders Mølster Galaasen questioned the city council leader, Erling Lae, on his evaluation of the risk of a ter-rorist attack in Oslo. "I think we should leave it to others to evaluate," he responded.

While Anders stares mesmerized at the images from the government quarter on the website vg.no, he calls up the unfamiliar number and gets to talk with his girlfriend. Hanne Gro says that she has some minor inju-ries but is otherwise unharmed. Soon she will be taken to the emergency ward. She'll call him from there. In the meantime, she says, he must call her father in Brumunddal and his mother. The images on TV will surely be distressing to them. When Hanne Gro sits up in order to take the next ambulance to the emergency ward, she looks upward to the People's The-ater façade, and her eyes stop at the Labor Party's white logo with a red rose beside it. Hanne Gro has hitherto thought only of her own building and the High Rise. When she was evacuated from S-Block, she couldn't see anything due to her eye injury. Now she gets a glimpse of the magnitude of the situation. "Is this a terrorist attack?" she asks. "Who could have come into the building with so much explosive? Where are my other colleagues?"

The prime minister was talking on the phone in the Inkognitogate office when he heard a faint rumbling in the background. His adviser, Sindre Fossum Beyer, was in the kitchen. The sound was faint. Must be thunder, he thought. Jens Stoltenberg continued undeterred in the conversation with the parliamentary president, Dag Terje Andersen, until Fossum Beyer came running into the office. The adviser had talked to someone at the party office who reported that there had been an explosion in the government quarter. Stoltenberg told him to check with security guards but wasn't too worried. He thought that in the worst case it was a gas leak that had led to a small explosion. The communications officer, Arvid Samland, called to ask whether Stoltenberg was unharmed. Stoltenberg thought it a strange question. The only hint of drama so far was the word "financial crisis," found in the speech he would give to the youngsters on Utøya tomorrow. Samland's trembling voice worried the prime minister. The communications officer's office is on the fifteenth floor of the High Rise. Although the office faces Akersgata and not Grubbegata, the window shattered, and Samland was thrown backward. He walked downstairs and described to the prime minister what he saw. In the background Stoltenberg could hear the sound of shoes treading on broken glass.

Rumor has it that there are two bombs, not just one. The guards lead Jens Stoltenberg down to a secure location next to the gym. From the small room in the basement, he calls his wife, Ingrid Schulerud, who is on the Hvaler Islands with their children, Axel and Catharina. Then he calls his father, former foreign minister Thorvald Stoltenberg. Samland and his colleague Arne Spildo have arrived at the building behind the palace with bloodied clothes and bandaged wounds. It is then that the enormity of the situation starts to dawn on the Norwegian prime minister. The two communications officers are severely injured even though they were not in close proximity to the explosion. The prime minister assumes that there must be many casualties in the government quarter, so he calls the justice minister, the health minister, the defense minister, and the foreign minister. He thinks, as do several others in those initial minutes, that it's a terrorist organization behind the bomb, but he says to himself that it's too early to tell. We know nothing yet. Therefore he is eager to get the justice minister back to Oslo so that they can hold a press conference. Getting the defense minister or the foreign minister may send the wrong message. The building on 18 Inkognitogata comprises 670 square meters, but the bunker in the basement is small and is soon crowded. The prime minister's staff takes up the space in the hallway and gym. The exercise bike has to be moved out.

The Peugeot is fully packed with clothes, wife, cat, and two daughters. The family was on the way north to the cabin in Østerdalen Valley. Justice Minister Knut Storberget's mobile phone was out of range for a while, but he finally received a voice message in Engerdal municipality. Knut and the others in the car listened to the message via the hands-free speaker. Communications officer Trond Øvstedal says that there has been an explosion. The Ministry of Justice building was one of the hardest hit—there were forty-five employees at work. Øvstedal called while he was on the seventh floor. In the background the family can hear sirens and alarms going off. They can hear glass splintering while the wounded communications officer makes his way through the debris in the building. Storberget turned off the road and told the family to go to the cabin without him. The forty-seven-year-old got off outside Sølenstua Camp Ground in North Østerdalen. Soon afterward the sheriff of Engerdal picked him up. The car is civilian but has blue emergency lights, so they could drive as fast as possible. It's a three- or four-hour drive in the car. Storberget calls up all the relevant state departments and institutions. Soon his iPhone has gone from 100 percent battery capacity down to 4.

Sveinung Sponheim had left his office on the seventh floor of 44 Grønlandsleiret and was on his way home to the Nordstrand suburb. The acting police chief in Oslo was looking forward to putting on training clothes and cycling for an hour toward Enebakk before starting the weekend by spending some quality time with his family. He is on Kongsveien Road, just off Solveien, when his mobile phone rings and someone tells him that there has been a bomb explosion in the government quarter. One person has been confirmed dead so far. Sponheim has neither heard nor seen anything, even though the road overlooks the whole of Oslo. He turns the car around and summons his staff on the phone. For better or worse it's right in the middle of a shift change for the police. Many of the officers are on their way out to start their vacation. Many have to cancel flight tickets or jump off trains. One officer runs over from the SATS training studio and shows up in athletic tights.

The health minister, Anne-Grete Strøm-Erichsen, is with her husband on an eleven-day Arctic cruise around Svalbard. She has just seen a polar bear eating a whale on an ice floe in the Arctic Ocean. The weather is gorgeous. Her state secretary calls on the ship's satellite phone to tell her people are on the way in rubber dinghies to escort her to land. The health minister is being summoned to Oslo. The governor of Svalbard commandeers a helicopter from Longyearbyen, but there's no place to land. She's hoisted up into the helicopter hovering twenty meters above the ship with the aid of straps under her arms.

Jonas Gahr Støre changes hooks on his fishing tackle outside the cabin in Kilsund village. Maybe there will be fresh fish for dinner. While the foreign minister is fixing his fishing gear in the rain, he receives a short text message from the Foreign Ministry: "Powerful explosion in the government quarter. Get online." On the PC in the cabin Støre sees images from the government quarter, and the enormity of the situation dawns on him. He yells to his son to say he must get over to the mainland. Wearing fishing clothes, he gets into the family car and drives by himself from Arendal to Oslo.

Fabian Stang, the mayor of Oslo, is driving in the same direction. He was in the grocery store close to his cabin outside Kragerø when he received a code red message (situation 01) from the head of the Emergency Response Unit (call sign: Delta), which carries out counter-terrorism operations. At first he thought it was a drill. "Strange timing," he thought. Soon after, Stang got a phone call confirming that it was real and not just a drill.

The smoke still hangs like a blanket over the capital, but the swirling fragments of paper documents have settled on the ground. Nevertheless, no one thinks that the terrorist attack in Norway on July 22, 2011, is over. The police fear there are more coming. Police officers on duty in the government quarter chase away curious onlookers and photographers, all the while shouting, "Run, run; get away from here. It was a bomb; there may be more bombs." It's possible that there may be another bomb in the government quarter. But there may also be a terrorist attack on the palace. Or the parliament building. Or is Oslo in the midst of a Mumbai scenario, where terrorists blew up a hotel before they went in and gunned down guests? Or the attack may just be a diversionary tactic. If so, what's going to happen next—and where? If the intention was to harm as many as possible in the government quarter, the timing could hardly have been more off. The summer vacation period means that only one in ten employees was at work on Friday afternoon. And why today, July 22? If the purpose was to spread fear, anxiety, and panic, the perpetrator has succeeded.

At Elvebakken High School by the river Andreas Olsen heard a faint rumbling in the background to the music to which he was listening. The disruption was not sufficient enough for him to stop and take off his earphones, probably because the explosion merged into one of the most intense, bass-heavy, and manic songs on his playlist: Prodigy's "The World's on Fire." "Too close, you're too close / Too close, too close to the wire / Too close, you're too close / Too close, your world's on fire." He continued homeward to his Grünerløkka apartment, carrying tulips and chocolates and thinking about the Tour de France, which he'd be watching on TV when he got home; the tapas dinner at a restaurant that he planned to suggest to Marianne; and the coming vacation week, which must be planned out. The family has rented a cabin on the Hvaler Islands through the Oslo Fjord Recreation Department, after which they'd be going to the Uppsala Reggae Festival. He has many funky Kingston albums to listen to over the weekend.

When Andreas gets home to the apartment, there's no cycle race on the TV2 channel but a news broadcast about an explosion in Oslo. Andreas thinks that it's related to Norway's involvement in the wars in Libya or Afghanistan. There is also something about a cop on Hammersborg Square. The gun, the civilian vehicle driving in the wrong direction down a one-way street. The illegal driving maneuver makes sense only if the intention was to get away from the crime scene. But the man Andreas saw through the car window was white-skinned. A right-wing terrorist? Andreas has been following the neo-Nazi movement closely for the past twenty years. For a while he was the anti-racism officer in AUF's county council and attended anti-racist demonstrations in eastern Norway. He knows that these extremist groups have been passive for a while and that acts of violence tend to start small and then escalate rather than start with a large-scale operation. Yet one never knows.

Andreas Olsen calls the emergency number, 112, and gives a description of the suspicious policeman he saw hurrying away from Grubbegata. Andreas thinks he's white, in his thirties, and fairly short, with a helmet, visor, and gun. And yes, he has the number on the green license plate of the small gray van stored on his Sony Ericsson mobile phone. The police issue an all-points bulletin.

Around four in the afternoon a message goes out to the national media that Norway's prime minister is unharmed and safe. A journalist at an online newspaper unfortunately forgets to type two crucial letters, so his message appears as "Stoltenberg is injured." The flowers for Marianne remain wrapped on the kitchen counter in the Torvbakkgata building.

Domestic Violence

9

Domestic Violence

Fredrik Reinfeldt and his political allies declared their love for the Nordic welfare system when the conservative bloc won the parliamentary elections in Sweden in October 2006, but according to the Swedish economist and politician Ali Esbati, no one has done more to destroy that system than this conservative government. That's also why Esbati has been invited to Utøya on July 22—to warn the campers about the so-called "conservative brothers." For the past five years Sweden has seen a rise in unemployment, a widening social and economic gap, and a deteriorating work environment. Esbati doesn't want to see the same brutalization happen in Norway. The Norwegian right—with the Conservative Party, Progress Party, Confederation of Norwegian Enterprise, and the conservative think tank Civita at the forefront—has emulated Reinfeldt's policies and pressed the government to dismantle the welfare state. The Labor Party must endure. And who better suited to keeping the party on the right course than the youngsters on Utøya?

It's half past three. Around fifty youngsters have shown up for the political workshop in the little hall to hear the high-prolife social commentator talk about his experiences from the neighboring country. Esbati is originally Swedish, of Iranian descent. He settled in Norway in 2008, when he became an editor of *Klassekampen*, and he decided to stay when he met his current girlfriend. People from immigrant backgrounds in Norway are generally invited to debates about Muslims and integration. Esbati has often discussed the growing Islamophobia in Europe, but he is best known for his radical analysis of economic policy issues in the form of reports from the think tank Manifest Center for Social Analysis, where he works as a researcher. Esbati was the leader of the AUF's sister organization in Sweden, Young Left, during the early 2000s, and the thirty-five-year-old has often been mentioned as a future leader of the Left Party in Sweden. He hasn't decided whether he will stand as a candidate. His girlfriend is pregnant.

Esbati's girlfriend, Marte Michelet, spoke at Utøya two days earlier on the polarized discussion climate in Norway. In the main hall the thirty-six-year-old brought up her in-laws as an example of what it's like to come to a new country. She expressed concern that hatred of Muslims has become acceptable. She believes that since the fall of the Berlin Wall, Islamophobia has become the dominant form of European racism. "[Muslims] can't integrate. They lack manners. They will only exploit our welfare system. They are potential terrorists." Such statements abound in online debates, often even though the topic isn't even about immigration. She could choose whether she wanted to come to Utøya on Wednesday or Friday. She chose Wednesday.

She and Esbati are among the biggest hate objects of the Islamophobic bloc in Norway. She represents everything that far-right extremists hate: she's a feminist, she's radical, she's a "traitor" as she grew up partly in Africa and partly in Oslo, and she's not afraid to engage with those who slander the Norwegian immigrant population. In short she's a "cultural Marxist." Some weeks earlier she published a newspaper commentary in which she criticized the toxic rhetoric among the so-called "people"—that is, academics and politicians. The opening line in the commentary was, "Hi, my name is Marte Michelet, and I'm going to give birth to the welfare state's demise."

The point of departure for Michelet's speech on Wednesday was the Brochmann Committee, which had come to the conclusion that immigrants were a demographic time bomb. "Even though my baby's father has less faith in God than most people, she will be counted as part of the Muslim population; she will become part of the 'demographic time bomb'—you know, the lazy, screwed up, indoctrinated masses who are here only to steal our tax money and propagate jihad. She will be counted as part of the dreaded 'minority quota' in kindergarten, in school, in sports—you know, the ones who spoil everything for the poor 'ethnic Norwegian' children. On top of everything else, I have to tolerate some damn billionaire writing off my unborn child as a net loss. I must tolerate a government-appointed committee people deeming my partner and in-laws as 'liabilities' in their hypothetical financial projections and warning that such as those growing in my womb may be the doom of the Norwegian welfare state. I don't want to write commentaries; I want to smash things." Esbati and Michelet have long warned of the consequences of the emerging Islamophobia in Norway and Europe. Tore Sinding Bekkedal was so impressed with Marte Michelet's speech that he went up to her afterward and thanked her.

Johanne Butenschøn Lindheim sits leaning against the wall in the main hall and listens to a political refugee talk about the situation in

Western Sahara, the disputed area that the Moroccans and Sahrawis have been fighting and quarreling over for three decades. Johanne sits next to people from Georgia and Uganda. Accounts of the difficult living conditions in refugee camps in Tindouf make her forget her own gloomy mood. A girlfriend from Oslo came to Utøya on the express errand of hearing Gro, and when she left after dinner, Johanne felt so sad, cold, and tired that she wanted to go home. She bought cookies in the kiosk and went into the tent to try to hold back her tears. She thought about how nice it would be to sit with her family in the cabin on Hvaler now or to enjoy the summer on a bike in the city. Johanne has many friends and acquaintances on Utøya and even more potential friends and acquaintances, but it's easy to feel sad when you don't have your best friend by your side. And she's scheduled to arrive now, at four o'clock, directly from the United States. Johanne presumes that she's been delayed.

Morten Djupdal takes the boat over to the mainland around four in the afternoon. The excuse was that he needed to buy bread and spreads for the Oppland campsite, and it is the perfect cover story for a hot shower at his uncle and aunt's in Hønefoss. Unfortunately it turned out that his relatives didn't come home until 6:00 p.m. They'd made appointments that had to be kept. A bit of time in a heated car should be a welcome distraction. Besides, Morten had less of a guilty conscience when it turned out that the white lie, against his best intentions, turned out to be unavoidable reality. What he is most concerned about on board the MS *Thorbjørn* is whether the red campaign car will start. On Tuesday the battery was dead. On Wednesday he rented a car to go buy a battery charger in Hønefoss. Morten managed to charge the battery up so that it was possible to start the car, but he still has doubts about the Volkswagen Sharan's condition. The bright red car of 1998 vintage has 320,000 kilometers on the odometer. The AUF replaced the water pump and painted it, as well as stuck on decals of a rose, the AUF logo, and "Vote Labor," so the Sharan now looks like it was worth the 35,000 Norwegian kroner that the AUF in Oppland County paid for it. There's still a problem with the fuel injection, whereby the wrong amount of air is injected so that the car doesn't start easily each time. Therefore Morten has asked the work crew on the mainland not to start the car.

Someone has moved the car. From Tuesday to Thursday he managed to keep the ignition key in his pocket despite repeated requests that he deliver it back. The night before, after a reminder from the camp administration, he finally relented and sent the key over with the MS *Thorbjørn*. Now someone not only moved the red campaign car, but that person also moved it into a mud pit. "Damn it." Morten is normally a calm guy, but now he's pissed. His mood gets even worse when he learns that the key isn't in the tent but that Ingrid Endrerud has unwittingly taken it to Sundvollen, where she's meeting her boyfriend. Morten and his two passengers from the island have barely one hour in which to shop for groceries before they have to take the five o'clock boat back to Utøya. The exact words Morten Djupdal used in the telephone conversation with Ingrid are not really clear, but when he hung up, he thought, "Oh, I may have been a little too harsh."

If you're wondering why the Oppland County AUF secretary and the others around him are concerned only with prosaic and practical matters such as keys, bread, and spreads after more than half an hour has gone by since the bomb explosion in Oslo, there's a logical explanation. No one has informed them yet.

Member of Parliament Stine Renate Håheim is holding the third political workshop for the afternoon. It will be held on the stage where Datarock played its concert the previous night. The Valdres girl has been on Utøya many times as an AUF party member. Although the workshop is being held today, she came to the island on Thursday morning to hear Foreign Minister Støre talk about the Middle East. Besides, she loves that "Utøya feeling." "Coming here is like coming home," the twenty-seven-year-old says. It was here that she learned that the party leadership isn't always right. It's here that she's reminded of how important it is to be idealistic. In parliament paper is shuffled around from one office to another. The procedures have to be rigorous, and things take time. In a busy workday marked by practical matters, sometimes it's necessary to look away from the paperwork and try to remember youthful idealism. The AUF believes that it's possible to save the world, just so long as one has enough political will.

Hence Stine Renate has left political propositions and her black work clothes behind in the parliamentary apartment on Parkveien in Oslo. She has been playing volleyball and cheering on the soccer players; she has played the card game Bohnanza at the campground; she has attended the Datarock concert and eaten hamburger and French fries at the night cafe. Try to imagine a member of parliament from France, the Netherlands, or Denmark who voluntarily stays overnight on a mosquito-infested island in a bunk bed in a small, sparsely furnished room in a dormitory. Also imagine her going to the toilet early in the morning, putting on some clothing and walking through a mud pit in light canvas shoes to a communal outhouse, covering her head—perhaps with a black garbage bag—to protect herself from the rain. Norway is in most cases not that different from other countries, but our politicians' preference for the "good communal life" and willingness to mingle with the masses is atypical in the global context. The rooms below the cafeteria building where Stine Renate and others are staying this summer are called the Ski Wing. One can be misled into thinking that the name is related to the typical Norwegian winter activity, but the fact of the matter is that the Ski Municipality AUF has contributed substantial sums to Utøya over the years, including money for the construction of the wing, which was completed in spring 2010.

Stine Renate talks about violence against women and children. In the Justice Ministry's violence index for 2008, 1,357 calls for help due to domestic violence were registered in the course of one week. The vast majority were reports of abuse against those who were physically the weakest in a household. Cases of rape frequently make the headlines in the dailies, *Dagbladet* and *VG*. Such headlines are followed by a public outcry and debate, and answers and accountability are sought from the elected officials. Domestic violence, which occurs within the confines of the home, is more widespread but receives only a fraction of the media attention. Stine Renate tells the circa forty youths at the workshop that the time has come for them to get more engaged with this issue. A new action plan on domestic violence is currently being prepared, and the AUF should contribute input. Proposals shouldn't be overly complicated and should be written in plain language. They can be basic and practical so that they can be readily implemented in municipalities and counties around the country. There's a separate hotline to call if children are subjected to sexual abuse. Is the hotline number, 116111, noticeable in the schools in your area? The ombudsman for children has asked children how they can tell that a message on a sheet of paper is important. The answer is that it's important if the sheet is laminated. Stine Renate asks the youngsters to check whether the hotline number is hanging in the classroom at their schools—and whether the sheet is laminated.

The workshop participants in front of the outdoor stage grinned and wrinkled their eyebrows worriedly at each other, and they asked questions. Stine Renate felt that the meeting was productive and that their enthusiasm was genuine. Hence she picked up her mobile phone to reject the call from her brother, although she did briefly wondered about the fact that he was calling during working hours, something that he rarely did. She did the same when a friend called. And then another friend called. After that, the mobile phone kept demanding her attention to the point that Stine Renate became convinced that something terrible had happened to her parents. Why else would her brother and her friends be calling? Before she had time to really start worrying, someone from the central committee came over to the outdoor stage and signaled with his hand at his throat that it was time to conclude the session.

Not all the youngsters are attending the political workshops when messages from concerned friends and family start to arrive. Arshad M. Ali has been a prominent politician in Stavanger for years. Now the twenty-three-year-old is the campaign secretary of the AUF in the capital, in addition to working on a master's degree in Nordic Viking and medieval culture at the University of Oslo. Last night he had a dispute with a friend. He went to bed before the Datarock concert but couldn't sleep because of the concert and the dispute. After Gro's speech Arshad and his friend found a room in Ski Wing where they could try to resolve their differences. In the midst of their conversation someone comes in to say that a bomb has exploded in the government quarter. Arshad thinks about the consequences if it turns out that a Muslim is responsible. He wonders how Norway will be after that, what it will be like to be a Muslim in Norway—or just a person from a minority background. He thinks Norway as a society will become more inhospitable, where notions of "us" and "them," which have so far been discussed only in the public arena, will become more pronounced in practice. He thinks that what he and other minority citizens have done to engage with society will have been in vain. Arshad calls his parents in Stavanger, but they don't answer the phone. Then he realizes that it's Friday. They're at Friday prayers.

Jorid Nordmelan stood outside the schoolhouse talking on the mobile phone with her boyfriend, Lasse Juliussen, in Bruvoll in North Odal municipality. They talked about the weather forecast and the size of suitcases. Next week they're going to the IUSY Festival (near Salzburg in Austria), which is going to be a mix of work and pleasure. IUSY is the acronym for the International Union of Socialist Youth. Every other year the AUF's sister organizations gather at the festival along with several thousand participants and some big-name draws, and according to Jorid, it is tremendous fun to participate in it. At least that was the case in 2009 in Hungary. Then she had sleeping accommodations indoors. This year they have to sleep outside in a three-man tent. The couple hatched a plan for preventing another person from sleeping in the tent with them—not because of the issue of space but because the person will be a poor third wheel in the tent. Lasse said that rain is forecast for the week, which annoyed Jorid no end. Packing rubber boots into the suitcase will be at the expense of at least one pair of high-heel shoes.

Jorid complains when Lasse interrupts her with an "Oh." She hears from his tone of voice that it's not a comment on her footwear dilemma. "What is it?" Jorid asks. "Oh," Lasse says again. She concedes that it may be a geeky, irrelevant comment on the sweaty, pedaling men in tights in the Tour de France on TV, but she repeats the question. "Shush," comes the response. Now Jorid feels she has been needlessly kept in suspense and ignored. "What is it? Tell me." Her boyfriend tells her that there has been an explosion in Oslo.

Lasse is an editorial assistant at the VG daily, so it's natural for him to go to the vg.no website. There's nothing there about an explosion. Nor is there anything on the websites of the other dailies, dagbladet.no and aftenposten.no. Jorid asks him to call back when he knows more, and then she starts running around in a panic, asking people to check their phones, first in the schoolhouse, then in the Oslo and North Trøndelag campsites. No one knows anything. The Internet is down, but Jorid's best friend gets through on the phone from Oslo. She says she heard the blast from Holmlia. It's quite a distance from the city center to Holmlia. "There's speculation that it's a gas explosion, but it's a bomb," her friend says, adding, "I don't dare go out on the streets now." Her fear has to be understood in the context of her religious background. For Jorid and her friend it's almost a given that Muslim terrorists are responsible for the blast. Jorid thinks that Norway is going to become a terrible country to live in.

In tenth grade Jorid attended Hersleb School in Oslo. Ninety-three percent of the students came from minority backgrounds. She was the single ethnic Norwegian girl in her class. The transition from homogeneous and *hijab*-free small-town Namsos to Oslo was notable, but her cultural enlightenment was remarkable. She made new friends, experienced cultural diversity, and became fond of Islam. Since then she has taken it personally whenever someone expresses a simplified view of Muslims. She has no doubt that most Norwegians are not able to tell the difference between an ordinary Muslim and a terrorist who blows himself up. Jorid thinks that Norway is an impoverished country when it comes to the inclusiveness of others. Now Norwegians have the perfect excuse to be even more racist. The Labor Party won't be able to rally in the short time left before the election. The Progress Party is going to win in September. She has thought about it before, and she thinks about it again: if Norway becomes a country run by the Progress Party, won't it be better to emigrate to Canada?

Tore Sinding Bekkedal compresses the video file of Gro Harlem Brundtland's speech to the party members in the cafeteria building before uploading it to YouTube. To the others in the room next to the kiosk he comments that the Mother of the Nation is still looking good, and then they joke about how the self-confessed technophobe has revealed that she actually has a Facebook account under a false name just to keep in touch with her grandchildren. The Gro video is almost uploaded when a twitter message pops up about the explosion in Oslo. The online newspapers provide little information. The dagbladet.no website is not accessible. Neither is vg.no or nrk.no. The Wi-Fi connection on the island, going through an ADSL router, is useless when too many people connect simultaneously. But Tore's worn-out Nokia phone has one luxury item that many envy him for: FM radio. Hence he takes on the task of informing others about the news from Oslo to try to stem the tide of wild rumors. Some talk about another bomb in the parliament building, while others say that the jihadist who is under an expulsion order, Mullah Krekar, has been observed in the government quarter. Tore leaves the media room through the little hall and down the stone steps to the campsite and then goes up the hill toward the information house, where he knows that FM reception is optimal.

Eskil Pedersen met with the leadership in the white information house to sum up Gro's visit. She hadn't been as intimidating as rumor had it, and the youngsters were visibly fascinated by the history lesson from the postwar period told by one who had actually lived through it. Eskil's normal work day on Utøya starts around seven in the morning. He sleeps in a guest room linked to the lavatory block because he's a little afraid of the dark and because it's close to all the essential facilities such as the showers. By the time the youngsters get up around ten or eleven to listen to the day's lecture, the leader has already spent several hours scrutiniz-ing media pictures and preparing for the day. It's only when the speakers leave at three in the afternoon that he can relax and put his feet up. But then a phone call comes in from Oslo to Utøya's camp administrator, who exclaims, "What!" in front of an exclusive assembly of youths with question marks on their faces.

Like the online newspapers, radio channel P1 had nothing new to report at first. A gas explosion was the most realistic theory, while a bomb was a secondary, unlikely, and perhaps undesirable explanation. They were saying there were shattered windows from the Gunerius building to the Parliament, but it's a bit difficult to sit on an island on Lake Tyri and envision what such a cityscape would look like. Eskil knew it was big when TV2 called and canceled the evening's program on the talk show *Sommertid*, where he was supposed to meet Gro again. Supposedly no one is injured at party headquarters, but soon afterward, he sees images from the government quarter. The question of whether it was a gas explo-sion or a bomb seems by then a minor issue. Human lives must have been lost.

The news spreads at an uneven pace and with varying degrees of accu-racy. Hildegunn Fallang is relaxing in the red party tent in the Oppland campsite when a youngster mentions something about a bomb. "Bomb? I've written about that issue," Hildegunn says. She has a summer job as a journalist for the newspaper *Oppland Arbeiderblad*. At 2:00 a.m. on a Saturday night a ruffian threw a smoke bomb into Saft, a club in Gjøvik. The club was evacuated, one person was admitted to the hospital, and three others were sent to the emergency ward. Hildegunn covered the incident in the Tuesday edition of the newspaper. "Have you written about the bomb in Oslo?" "Bomb in Oslo?" Confusion reigns until they hear a voice over the intercom telling everyone to meet in the main hall at half past four. There's no reason given. Many think the meeting will be about the flooding of the campsite or that they will be chewed out because they've been going into the cafeteria with their shoes on. It's pretty muddy out there today. It has rained incessantly since the morn-ing hours. The cloud cover hangs low over the island on Lake Tyri.

10

You People Are in Serious Trouble Now

Beyond Utøya, the world continues on its winding path, and it has a goal and a direction. Oslo University Hospital is put on red alert. The hospital expects more than fifty patients—some killed, many injured. The first patient arrives at the emergency room at Ullevål Hospital at 3:50 p.m. In the next twenty minutes an additional seven patients arrive. The chief physician was about to go on vacation. Now they have to prioritize who should be operated on immediately and who should wait. On Youngstorget Square injured people sit with fleece blankets around them. *VG* set up temporary editorial offices at the Bristol Hotel. Journalists have to buy chargers and computer equipment to keep the newspaper running. *Dagsavisen* moves its offices to chief editor Arne Strand's home in Pilestredet Park. The police have succeeded in closing off the government quarter, but they remain on high alert. Police personnel on duty in Oslo are told to stop everyone in a police or security guard uniform who doesn't comply when challenged. They have been given permission to use "all means possible." Oslo Central Station, Oslo City shopping mall, and Byporten are evacuated, with many people not knowing the reason why. The capital's residents don't know what has hit the city, and no one dares to reassure them that the danger is over.

Hanne Gro Lille-Mæhlum and other ministry staff members are at the emergency ward. One of them says he was in S-Block when the bomb went off, a piece of information that gives the poor receptionist a bad conscience. What if it was she who let in someone who shouldn't have been? Another says that it would have taken a large amount of explosives to cause an explosion of this magnitude. The terrorist attack must have been carefully planned. Hanne Gro is relieved that she didn't sign in someone who could have brought in large amounts of explosives. A nurse comes with juice and biscuits.

Why today of all days? It's the vacation period, it's after three, and there are few ministry employees at work. "There's no ministers' meeting today, right?" Hanne Gro asks. She's fairly confident of the answer but is a bit embarrassed that the statement is followed by a question mark. She feels like a summer intern. "What about Stoltenberg? Is he on vacation?" No, she's told. He's going to Utøya this weekend. "Utøya? What's actually happening there?" she asks a little awkwardly. She's interested enough in social news that she should have known the reason why the prime minister was going to Utøya. "Oh yes, of course," Hanne Gro says in a vain attempt to save some dignity when someone mentions the AUF summer camp. "Right; it's this weekend."

The doctor asks if it's okay that she take off her blood-stained uniform so he can check whether she has glass shards on her body. "Do you have to? I'm pretty sure I don't have any," the reception guard says. She has had many strange hands touching her in the past few hours. "It's amazing that all's well with my eyes," says Hanne Gro, who's glad she chose to put on contact lenses that morning. "There's a reason why the eyes are located in an indented area," the doctor says while checking whether the pupils are symmetrical. Hanne Gro gets stitches on her eyebrows and arm. She puts on her uniform and is given blue shoe-cover socks. The blood-stained pantyhose is thrown into the trash. Hanne Gro is ready to go home to her apartment in Majorstua with three stitches over her eyes and three on her arm. She goes to the exit to wait for her boyfriend to pick her up in a taxi. A large TV screen shows images from the government quarter.

In the suburb of Nordstrand a young man sits with a mild expression on his face. Friendly eyes peer out from behind round glasses, and jaunty curls encircle his head. The thirty-six-year-old, originally from Ålesund, has a job that suits his quiet demeanor at the Radarveien Day Care Center in Lambertseter, where he takes care of the mentally handicapped. He sits in front of the PC in his apartment. When the bomb exploded in the city, Peder Are Nøstvold Jensen thought it sounded like a thunderclap. Now he has learned that it's most likely a bomb. With that information it's not difficult for the thought processes to take their natural course. Only organized Muslims have the resolve to commit a terrorist act against the Norwegian government. When he blogs, some consider his opinions rather extreme. He's no extremist, at least not in his own eyes. He is passionate. Nevertheless, he hasn't told his friends, work colleagues, or family that he is the persona behind the influential blog name "Fjordman"—otherwise known as Peder Jensen, a native of the municipality of Sunmøre in western Norway who was raised in a resourceful socialist family. According to his parents, there's no one who is more peaceful or nonviolent than he.

It's been almost ten years since he attained ideological enlightenment. Arabic studies at the University of Bergen led him to the American University in Cairo and a thesis in which he wrote about blogging and censorship in Iran. Peder Jensen was in Egypt when the two planes hit the World Trade Center. He has claimed that Egyptians danced in the streets with excitement. Osama bin Laden became a heroic figure in the Arab world. But no one has written the unvarnished truth about Islam and Muslims in Norwegian newspapers. Peder Jensen tried to warn us but felt that he was being censored, just like the voices of dissent in Iran.

Only a few years earlier Peder Jensen would have had to actively seek out local groups, associations, or milieus to find the like-minded. On the Internet he can garner support for his viewpoint without leaving the house. It's a new phase in political activism. Radicalization campaigns no longer take place in cafes or illicit places of assembly. Instead they spring forth in darkened rooms with online computers and are spread to the whole world with one mouse click. Hate groups provide lone wolves with a sense of belonging to a community. With this in mind Fjordman established his own blog in 2005, and eventually he gained the status of a prophet in the international anti-Islam and anti-immigration Internet environment. Here he has been able to accuse politicians, academics, and journalists of betraying his country by allowing the immigration of Muslims. Islam is taking over Europe while the traitors do nothing.

When Fjordman finds out about the explosion in the government quarter, he posts on the Gates of Vienna website that the Norwegian government is "suicidal" and "cowardly." Fjordman writes that Jens Stoltenberg is a "pathetic sucker for Islam." He quotes indirectly from his own book, *Defeating Eurabia*, in which the relationship between Muslims in Norway and the multicultural elite is stated as follows: "Yes, we should be angry with them, but we should first and foremost be angry with those who fed us false information, flooded our countries with enemies, and forced us to live with them. They constitute enemy number one. We should never forget that." Muslims are bad, but those who like Muslims are even worse.

Most people in Norway don't take the time to visit the Gates of Vienna website, but they don't need to do that. The public debate has for years primed Norwegians for a scenario in which al Qaeda–inspired Muslims would attack our democratic institutions. Oslo is in shock and in a smoldering mood. A supermarket employee was told by a customer, "We know where you live." General Secretary Mehtab Afsar of the Islamic Council of Norway receives a text message in Tanzania, where he was under the auspices of Norwegian Church Aid, telling him to move to a new country. Many Oslo citizens encounter the fury of the population in the first minutes after the explosion. Religion becomes a secondary issue; having a dark complexion is what matters. A man of Somali origin is told in no uncertain terms, "You people are in serious trouble now. I hate you fucking niggers." Harassment, curse words, spitting. The form of communication varies, but the message is clear. A man of Pakistani origin is greeted with Nazi salutes on his way through Sofienberg Park.

Khan Laal is a director of the Islamic Cultural Center in Oslo. The mosque shook when the bomb exploded in the government quarter. Soon after, the mosque receives an email: "If Muslims are responsible, you'll have to find another place to stay." The fifty-four-year-old thinks it a strange statement. He's also scared. He too has encountered a form of terrorism today. A friend of Khan's, wearing a white robe, was told by a man to get the hell out of the subway car. Khan tried to soothe the angry man, but another man got up from his seat in a threatening manner.

Muslim terrorists. The Statoil company contacts Norwegian authorities to secure its oil installations and facilities. Nobody wants the Norwegian kroner after the terrorist attack, so its value plunges in the stock market. Norway's central bank tightens its security. Journalists for the major newspapers and television stations call around to experts on al-Qaeda and the wars in Iraq, Afghanistan, and Libya. Researcher Anders Romer Heim at the Institute of Defense Studies feels pressured by NRK TV to conclude that al-Qaeda is behind the attack. Most of the commentaries consist of indignant opinions about the Islamist threat in Norway. One group, Helpers of the Global Jihad, assumes responsibility and says that this is just one of many attacks against Norway. Most Norwegians are convinced that Islamic terrorists are behind the attack against Norway, even though Islamists have been responsible for only 0.3 percent of all attacks in Europe since 2006. In Norway studies have mainly been done on integration challenges, female genital mutilation, and forced marriages in Muslim communities, while minimal research has been done on xenophobia, racism, and Islamophobia among the majority population. Hence we easily see the connection between Islam and terrorism but not the relationship between national chauvinism and organized violence.

Nor is there a historical reason to associate terrorism with Muslims alone. The purity-cultivating, nationalist, and revolutionary Jewish Zealots are considered to be civilization's first terrorists. In the 1800s the word "terrorist" was associated with Russian anarchists and nihilists. The world's first letter bomb exploded in Stockholm on August 19, 1904, and was called "the Russian Affair" because it was first assumed that it was related to a wave of terror in the east. Several more assassination attempts using letter bombs followed in subsequent years. Although the letter bombs clearly pointed to the Jews as perpetrators, suspicions turned to the working class. Someone who called himself the "Social-Democrats' Court" claimed that the upper classes had been guilty of deceiving, plundering, and oppressing poor workers and their families. "We believe in the wonderful impact that a bomb may have now and then," he declared. It turned out that the perpetrator was a solid pillar of society—an engineer, inventor, and philosopher named Martin Ekenberg who had made the bombs himself and fabricated the letters to newspaper editors to deflect attention away from his real motive: a personal vendetta against specific members of the Swedish business community who, according to Ekenberg, had contributed toward turning his entrepreneurial venture into a fiasco.

In the 1980s the Palestinians started using suicide bombing as a political weapon. At the same time acts of terror were perpetrated by the ETA in Spain, the IRA in Ireland, the RAF in Germany, and the Red Brigades in Italy. In the 1990s the Aum Shinrikyo sect attacked the subway in Tokyo, Japan, while the Americans were exposed to terror through the Unabomber and the Oklahoma attacks. Islamist-funded terrorism was nothing new when the planes crashed into the World Trade Center and the Pentagon on September 11, 2001, but in the following decade, caught in the slipstream of the "war on terror," terrorism became synonymous with Muslims and al-Qaeda.

Right-wing extremism has disappeared somewhat from the radar, but it has been a greater threat to Europeans than violent Islamism. The neofascist group Nuclei Armati Rivoluzionaria killed eighty-five people and injured two hundred in a bomb attack in the Italian city of Bologna in 1980. In the same year a German neo-Nazi, Gundolf Köhler, attacked a festival in Munich and killed thirteen people. Another neo-Nazi, David Copeland, perpetrated three bomb attacks on civilians in London in 1999, one of which was on Hitler's birthday. In 2003 German authorities managed to stop a neo-Nazi group from carrying out several bomb attacks at the last minute. Nevertheless, both ordinary people and the authorities and security services have, since 2001, been mostly occupied with the threat from Islamist terrorists. The Swedish journalist and author Lisa Bjurwald has pointed out that it's as if we are unable to conceive of two threats at the same time.

Hence the murder of Somali-Norwegian Mahmed Jamal Shirwac on August 23, 2008, was considered the work of a madman. The twenty-six-year-old man from Oppdal who killed Mahmed, a forty-six-year-old father of four, by firing thirteen shots into his car in Trondheim was indeed diagnosed as psychotic, but before carrying out the racially motivated killing, he was active on the stormfront.org website, which fights for "white power all over the world." On the floor of his apartment police found a note with plans for the summer that included killing Muslims and burning down mosques. Because the man, who had a wife and three children, was diagnosed as "psychotic," his activities on the far-right website were never investigated thoroughly. The thirty-two-year-old man from Skøyen who had just detonated a bomb in the government quarter in Oslo had participated in five different discussion groups on stormfront.org.

Prejudice blinds not only so-called ordinary people; even sober, well-educated columnists for liberal publications can get carried away. In *Dagsavisen*'s temporary office in Pilestredet, an editor sits and polishes his statements about the worst attack on Norway since April 9, 1940: "It's too early to tell for sure who is behind the attack. But the extent and degree of planning required to implement something like that clearly points in the direction of an international terror network."

The editor's sentence does start with a caveat. At the same time it suggests a certain direction that should be followed and comes to grips with what has happened and where the culprits are to be found: "It's natural to ask why we have been attacked by people who want to hurt us so badly that they try to kill ordinary citizens and our political leaders. It may be connected to our troops in Afghanistan and Libya or with the cartoon controversy. Cappelen Damm, which recently published a book with the controversial cartoons, is just a few meters from ground zero. We must now take the time to find out the truth. One thing is certain: terror will not determine Norwegian policy." The words are written under deadline pressure in the midst of a chaotic situation at a time when the state broadcasting channel's waiting room is full of terror experts who will try to explain to listeners and television viewers about the causes of such hate: colonialism, poverty, hatred of the West, the Iranian Revolution, the Afghan war against the Soviet Union, the first Iraq war, the World Trade Center, Iraq and Afghanistan, Libya, Muhammad cartoons, the murder of Dutch filmmaker Theo van Gogh. The newspaper columnist writes that terror will not determine Norwegian policy. We must not let fear rule over us.

Nevertheless, that's what happens. Not in the aftermath of big events, like the attacks in London, Madrid, and Mumbai, but in daily life. Fear of Muslims chronically characterizes public debate in Europe, so much so that hate can flare up when we least expect it to. It's symptomatic that the guard duty inspector and police operations leader first reported that the uniformed man who left the white van outside the High Rise was "darker in complexion than a Norwegian." At the same time he is described as "light skinned." Physical characteristics collide so long as one doesn't think that it's either a Norwegian or a Pakistani but a man from the Middle East. We see what we want to see.

The terrorist is a blond Norwegian from Skøyen, armed and dangerous. But by the time the police in the capital are notified to stop a suspicious person in a police or security guard uniform, he is already beyond the city limits. The thirty-two-year-old did not drive from Hammersborg Square to the interchange and highway; he chose smaller streets to avoid the traffic out of the city via Bygdøylokket—Henrik Ibsensgate toward Solliplass into Bygdøy Allé, and from there into Drammensveien to Skøyen. He did not drive past his mother's apartment in Hoffsveien as it would have been too risky. Instead he turned the Fiat left a hundred meters before the street, by Harbitz Allé. From there he drove on several backroads to the ring road, which took him out to the highway to Drammen. In Sandvika he took the turnoff to Hønefoss. From there on he is able to feel fairly secure. The entire police emergency response team is focusing on the government quarter in Oslo. On radio station P4 he listens to the journalists' ongoing and conflicting reports. He is curious to know whether the High Rise has collapsed and the number of people killed. In 2083 he has described how important the element of surprise is. Create a diversion in the east, then strike in the west. Attack the enemy where he least expects it by creating false expectations. Everyone thinks there will be new attacks in Oslo.

In the back of the little gray van he has a customized rifle, a shotgun, and ammunition. They are his private weapons with cryptic, significant names such as "5.56 Ruger M14." He bought the Ruger from Winge Weapons in Moss on November 18, 2010. He paid 9,000 Norwegian kroner for it. The weapon is semi-automatic and legal. But he has customized it in order to give it a more military look and feel. It was a well-dressed, urbane man who entered the premises of Winge Weapons the previous fall. He did not talk about moose hunting as customers usually do. He bought the Glock pistol in late winter from the Intersport shop on Bogstadveien in Oslo. A month later he bought a silencer, but it didn't fit. He purchased a laser sight, bayonet, and light from the United States via eBay. Each cartridge clip contains thirty bullets. He has four cartridge clips, which he procured through the arms dealer Capsicum Solutions in Skien. There he also purchased an easyloader, which helps to prevent sore fingers when the weapon is reloaded. He engraved "Mjöllnir" in runic characters on the pistol's grip; Mjöllnir is Thor's hammer, which, according to Norse mythology, always strikes its target and always comes back. The rifle's barrel is engraved with "Gungnir," Odin's spear, which has the same amazing capabilities. The thirty-two-year-old Christian has a predilection for pagan words infused with talismanic powers.

He has cut the tips off the bullets with a pair of pliers so that they would inflict maximum damage. American air marshals on board aircraft use similar bullets as they don't go through a body and hit other passengers or puncture the fuselage. The bullets break up into smaller pieces when they hit something. He has one thousand bullets in a hard black case. In the CamelBak backpack, the kind used in the Birkebeiner ski race, he has a water bottle with a tube. He plans to take a cocktail of ephedrine, caffeine, and aspirin—medications that he has purchased duty free over the Internet—twenty minutes before the mission. He has already been doing a course of steroids. He estimates that all these preparations will increase his physical and mental capacity by 100 percent. The man driving past Sollihøgda along the E16 motorway by Lake Tyri believes that the energy cocktail will transform him into an "unstoppable one-man army."

He passes small, red-painted cottages and spacious yellow villas with large green manicured gardens. Families are enjoying themselves at campsites with coffee, juice, and waffles. Kids are jumping on trampolines even though the weather is rough. Father and son are out in the old brown wooden boat, fishing for perch. Mute swans, ospreys, and marsh harriers are hunting for fish, mice, frogs, and small animals for a late lunch. In the car he's eating chocolate, drinking Red Bull, and listening to the P4 radio channel. At the Nes tunnel, just before the exit down to Utøya, the traffic is redirected. The over 1,200-meter-long tunnel was closed in March after concrete from the ceiling and walls collapsed, and all the control and security systems are being replaced. This means a further delay for the thirty-two-year-old man in a hurry. On average each day eleven thousand vehicles pass through Hol municipality, and even more on Fridays and Sundays. A speed camera at the exit to Utøya captures the gray Fiat at twenty-two minutes past four. He parks in a grove. He was here just a couple of weeks ago to do reconnaissance and to enter the location coordinates into his GPS.

The thirty-two-year-old sits in the car a while. He fears that doubts may start to creep in; hence the energy drink in the CamelBak. The high shores him up mentally before the act of martyrdom and convinces him that it's necessary. He will stifle recruitment to the "Quisling Party" from below by eliminating AUF members, who believe in a multicultural society; who fight for gay rights; and who support social justice, gender equality, and other politically correct feminist values. He believes that 60–70 percent of all cultural Marxists are women. "If you hesitate as much as a second due to the fact that your opponent is female, you will fail. You must therefore embrace and familiarize yourself with the concept of killing women, even very attractive women," he wrote in 2083. Gro Harlem Brundtland is the symbol for everything he hates about the labor movement and Norwegian society, but he's not certain she's still on the island. If not, he will find Eskil Pedersen. He believes that the Labor Party is relatively moderate politically. The AUF, however, is full of extreme Marxists. After the explosion in Oslo he expects the police to send reinforcements to protect Utøya since it could be a political target for terrorists.

Under his vest he has earphones attached to an iPod filled with what he considers inspirational music. In 2083 he has written about music that invokes rage and how, during a terrorist operation, he will be listening to the soundtrack from the *Lord of the Rings: Two Towers* trailer to drown out the screams. The soundtrack is called "Lux Aeterna"—the eternal light. The music starts with quiet, innocent notes that rise to a hypnotic, repetitive crescendo, where the leitmotif is repeated with choir and orchestra, becoming darker, more aggressive, and insistent. Maybe he'll play the same track over and over again at full blast to maintain his trance state. He's going to pump himself up with steroids, ephedrine, and epic music. Clint Mansell, who is English, composed the original "Lux Aeterna" for an American movie in 2000 called *Requiem for a Dream*, in which the protagonist suffers from amphetamine psychosis and hallucinates that the refrigerator is a menacing living monster.

Disco Is Canceled

The AUF members are gathered in the cafeteria building. People sit and stand close to each other, stretching from the main hall through the little hall and out into the long corridor. Body heat from hundreds of young people causes the air to turn sluggish and humid in the building. The windows go from slightly ajar to wide open. It's with a knot in his stomach that Eskil Pedersen climbs onto the elevated stage in the main hall. No one has fully confirmed that the explosion was caused by a bomb. The leaders don't know any more than the other youngsters, who have been able to obtain information via their laptops and smartphones. Eskil shares his concerns with the others on Utøya: that those closest to them could be affected; that Norway will become a different country if it turns out there's a premeditated, political decision behind the explosion; that Norway will in any case have a tough time if civil servants, secretaries, and ministers have lost their lives in a gas explosion. The last thing Eskil saw before he went to the main hall was the web page from an online newspaper in the editing room of *Planet Utøya*. On the PC screen were large black letters: "Stoltenberg is injured."

Eskil's face is pale, his eyes are glazed, and he is clearly trembling. He says that there has been an explosion in the government quarter, that the surrounding buildings are damaged, and that no one knows whether it was a bomb or a gas explosion. He tells the youngsters what he knows while taking care not to provoke fanciful speculations. But the AUF's leader has to make an effort to put his words in the correct order. Utøya's camp administrator is more comforting with her responsible, determined voice. The forty-five-year-old is said to be authoritative but fair. She has done everything on the island, from replacing door frames to feeding the youngsters. She has defied the ice in winter and dealt with liquidity crises. She has served prime ministers waffles when they arrived and sandwiches before they left. The youngsters couldn't be in better hands. "We are in the safest place there is—on a desert island on Lake Tyri. We will grill sausages, we will get the news on the big screen, and we will eat all the goodies we have on the island." She reckons there should be one or two sausages for each person. It's her last summer on the island; she has been the administrator for over twenty years. Starting in the fall, she will be the director of the Norwegian Maritime Museum. A big farewell and thank-you party has already been planned.

When Stine Renate Håheim found out that the High Rise was most likely to have been the worst affected in the government quarter, she became worried. As a member of the Justice Committee, she has become close to the minister and the political leadership. Stine Renate sends a text message to the committee's adviser in parliament to enquire whether people she knows in the Justice Department have been harmed. She gets an answer back that they are unharmed. However, the member of parliament is still uneasy. Before the information meeting she visited the media room behind the little hall and got to see pictures from the government quarter on the Internet. It did not look like a gas explosion.

In the course of the fifteen-minute-long meeting the youngsters are told that the rest of the day's program will be canceled. There will be no self-defense course, which was supposed to start at five o'clock. There will be no stand-up show with Terje Sporsem, which was scheduled for half past eight. There will be no disco and no late-night movie. "There won't be any disco?" a youngster asks in the auditorium. The banal, naive question, full of expectation and disappointment, temporarily lightens the grave, serious mood in the room. "No, there will be no disco," Eskil replies in an overbearing manner and with a slight smile on his face. Finally the leaders say that there won't be any boats going over to the mainland for the rest of the day because there are no buses going to the capital. It's best that everyone stay on Utøya.

The youngsters are encouraged to call or send text messages home to their families. An eighteen-year-old from Levanger gets a pessimistic text message from his mother: "Be careful on Utøya. You all can easily become a target if terrorists are on the move." Likewise a twenty-year-old from Orkdal gets the message: "Has security been tightened for you all now? This is certainly an attack against the Labor Party, and you all must also be protected." Matti Brox is a young guy who doesn't worry unnecessarily. The scope and the cause of the explosion are still unknown. For the time being the Oslo boy smiles and reassures those whose eyes have gone blank. The sixteen-year-old is a little smitten with a girl from his old class in Oslo and takes the opportunity to invite her for a stroll along Lovers' Lane later in the evening. The girl says yes.

Hildegunn Fallang calls home. Her mother is sitting in front of the TV and tells her daughter what she sees on the news channel. There's a huge crater in front of the High Rise. A burned-out car lies on its roof. There's a lot of smoke. "Oh, oh, don't zoom in on those people lying there," she says to the cameraman while her daughter is listening at the other end. They agree to call each other up again in a couple of hours. Hildegunn is a local politician while working as a journalist. In the long run this combination will create too many conflicts of interest, and she will have to choose. She believes it will be difficult to abandon politics while study-ing at the Journalism College. This spring her class did a course on Tuni-sia and the Arab Spring uprising. For the entire fall she will do an intern-ship at *Dagsavisen*'s foreign news department. The explosion in Oslo affects her on many levels, both privately and professionally. The AUF office is located just a stone's throw away from the government quarter, while the newspaper's editorial office is even closer.

Jorid struggles to hold back her tears in the dining hall. She doesn't understand why she's in such distress. Perhaps it's because the messages are too unstructured and conflicting. The Petroleum and Energy Minis-try was the target, they say. If that's true, it can't be Muslim terrorists who are behind this. Environmental activists perhaps. One dead—no, two dead. A new car bomb? The only thing she wants to do is read the online newspapers and get more detailed and precise information, but the Inter-net is currently an unattainable luxury. She has called her mother, who's at the Molde Jazz Festival; she has called her father, who's in Italy; and she has called her boyfriend again. Someone asks Jorid whether she's okay, and she answers, "Yes, thanks; it's just that I was worried about Lasse for a second." It's a blatant lie to justify her lack of self-control. "I must pull myself together," she thinks. Jorid belongs to the old guard on the island, and she's employed by the party as a delegation leader. But she can't manage to pull herself together.

Before Jorid goes into the woods to see whether a change of environ-ment and a phone call to Lasse will help, she goes to see her Namsos girl-friends, who are charging their mobile phones at the far corner of the main hall. Hanne Hestø Ness and Lene Maria Bergum have just picked up their phones from the North Trøndelag campsite so that they can send messages. Outside the tent they ran into their county friends, who were gathered around the portable radio they had hung on a peg in the mid-dle of the camp. They were asked whether they wanted to stay to listen to the news, but they declined because they had to charge their devices. "My God, if it's the Muslims, then we'll lose the election to the Progressive Party," Jorid says to Hanne and Lene Maria in the main hall. The statement makes the three of them smile for a few seconds. "I'm just going for a walk but will be right back," she says, and she gives the girls a hug.

The party leaders' emotional words have affected Hanne. She cries and feels sorry for them and for herself. At the same time she thinks to herself that the grief is primarily theirs and not hers. She knows no one in Oslo, at least none who are in the vicinity of the government quarter. Hanne should be the one who comforts, not the one who's crying and needs to be comforted. She sends a text message to her parents, who are in Östersund, on the way home from a camping trip: "I'm doing fine." She sends the same message to friends, without realizing that not all of them will understand the actual context of the short, reassuring message. Hanne's mother calls back and asks how it's going. The nineteen-year-old says that they are actually having great fun, and she tells her about the Datarock concert and working at the night cafe. Her parents update Hanne on the latest news about the explosion in Oslo, and her mother corrects her daughter's gaffe. It's the government quarter, not Youngstorget Square. Hanne knows that. Still she thinks that Youngstorget Square has been hardest hit. The initial information is difficult to erase from her mind.

Johanne Butenschøn Lindheim is embarrassed. Her face is swollen and her makeup is running, but she sees that none of the others in the dining hall are in tears. Thankfully the film crew has left the island and won't be returning until tomorrow. It's whispered about that some have already been confirmed dead in the government quarter. Uncertainty is the worst thing. How extensive is the damage? What and who are affected? Johanne manages to borrow a mobile phone and goes halfway into the kitchen to call her parents at the cabin in Hvaler. She's shaky and scared while her father is calm and collected. Doesn't he understand the gravity of the situation? He says that they still don't know what it is. Johanne is convinced that it's a bomb, so she knows the follow-up question must be: "When will the next bomb go off?" Johanne puts on her no-longer-white shoes in the hallway, goes down to her tent, and lies down in her sleeping bag. She's cold, but that's not why she's trembling.

While the youngsters are calling around to family and friends, Tore Sinding Bekkedal tries to set up the projector and computer in the main hall so that those without smartphones can have access to news broadcasts. It turns out to be complicated. Internet access and mobile phone coverage on Utøya are weak to begin with. When hundreds of youngsters call and surf at the same time, the open network collapses. Hence the camp administration has decided that only a select few can have access. The twenty-three-year-old computer nerd from Oslo waits for someone to come with the password and is quite annoyed that he's not allowed to fix the connection himself.

A little before five o'clock on Friday afternoon, July 22, a national emergency message is issued by the National Criminal Investigation Service (KRIPOS):

NATIONAL ALARM—

POSSIBLE EXPLOSION BOMB(S) IN OSLO CITY CENTER

With reference to media coverage of the case. It's advised that one keep a lookout for a small gray van, possible reg. no. VH24605. As of now, the connection between the explosion and the vehicle is not known, but if it is encountered, notify the Kripos Desk or Oslo PD for further instructions. It's advised to exercise due caution when approaching the vehicle.

Further information will follow.

PLEASE CONFIRM RECEIPT OF THIS MESSAGE!

Sincerely
Kripos Desk

Ingrid Endrerud has had a baguette with ham and cheese and coffee with her boyfriend at the Sundvolden Hotel. She has told him about Datarock, Gro, and choir practice, while he has given her a present. A passing remark, that was all—just a remark filled with irony—that she wanted a CD of the staid Irish band *The Dubliners*, and he went and bought it. While Ingrid chuckled gratefully at having gotten a CD that she certainly hadn't wish for, Morten Djupdal called and asked for the keys to the campaign car. He needed it to buy bread and cold cuts for the Oppland camp. After making preparations for choir practice in the little hall, Ingrid took the MS *Thorbjørn* over to the mainland to meet her boyfriend. Either she was early or he had been delayed. Anyway she went to the registration booth and picked up the keys to the red campaign car in order to have a dry place to sit. She inadvertently took the car keys with her when she got into her boyfriend's car. On the way from Sundvollen to meet

Morten in Utstranda, her mother called and told her about the explosion in Oslo. "Okay, thanks for telling me," she thought. The range of the explosion did not sink in, not until she began to think about the AUF office, located close by in Youngstorget Square, where she had been a week ago. The couple listened silently to the radio while he drove her to meet Morten at the ferry berth. After that they drove around the area randomly to delay their parting. It occurred to Ingrid that it was Friday, the Oppland delegates would be going home on Sunday, and the travel route was via Oslo. She would have to arrange for an alternative route. She has to inform the youngsters and their parents. She has to cross over to Utøya as soon as possible.

Now Ingrid Endrerud stands on the mainland side and waits for the MS *Thorbjørn* along with other youngsters, including a twenty-two-year-old who, on the number 171 bus to Utøya, was listening to his new audiobook, *Fooled by Randomness*. The Lebanese American author, Nassim Nicholas Taleb, argues that everything is more random than we think. The youngster has just arrived at the ferry berth in a rain poncho that his brother used in the scouts twenty years ago. The participant is registered, and his bag is thoroughly checked for alcohol or drugs. The older guard always tells the same old joke: "Yes, yes, I'm just checking to see whether you have some sawn-off shotguns or rifles."

Down the hill rolls a little gray van and parks by the waterside just south of the pier. The AUF guard, Simen Brænden Mortensen, sees that the driver is a policeman. He walks over to present himself, "Simen." The policeman says his name is Martin Nilsen of the Oslo police and that he is being sent to the island to check on security and to inform the people about the incident in the government quarter. It's purely routine. Simen notes that the policeman, whom he perceives as firm and determined, calls the explosion a "terrorist attack"—information that has not been confirmed by official sources. Simen sees the gun in the holster on his thigh. He is puzzled that he came in a van and asks to see some ID. The policeman holds up the ID card hanging around his neck. Then Simen asks whether people on the island have been notified of his coming. "Yes," he replies. The guard calls up the information house on the island and says that a police officer is coming over to the island. "Fine," they answer at the other end. They will send the MS *Thorbjørn* over to the mainland now.

Jannike Arnesen sits cross-legged on the pier. The information house is to her right, while the MS *Thorbjørn* is to her left. She leans over her mobile phone so that her upper body shields it from the rain. Under her jacket she has a white T-shirt with the encouraging slogan "The Beat Goes On." But it doesn't. Not here anyway. Arnesen wants to go home to Kristiansand. The Utøya stay has so far been about reconsidering her plans. Originally she was supposed to go home today because she was starting work at the cafe in Ravnedalen Park in Kristiansand. But on Tuesday night, unfortunately, she injured her hand. It's difficult to work as a waitress with a bandaged hand. So why not just stay on Utøya for a few more days?

The accident happened in the schoolhouse. To relieve back pain Jannike slept on a mattress under a roof and shared a four-square-meter bedroom with five other girls. One of them was allergic to the cold. Hence the windows remained shut. The still, stuffy air meant that Jannike could neither breathe nor sleep properly, so she concluded that she would probably be better off on the couch in the living room. The opening of the living room window did not go as expected. Her hand went right through the glass, and she was cut. Her nightgown was spattered with large, blotchy red spots. Jannike put on warmer clothes, sneaked out of the schoolhouse, and walked the few meters over the grass to the Norwegian People's Aid tent. She was given a temporary bandage, taken over to Utstranda, and driven to the emergency ward in Hønefoss, where she got three stitches on her wrist.

After learning about the bomb explosion in Oslo, Jannike has thought only about going home. She wants to go to her sister, who is alone in Kristiansand while her parents are vacationing in Germany. In any case it's what she says to the others—that she must go home to her sister—but strictly speaking, it's a pretext. The hand works fine, the weather is miserable, and Jens Stoltenberg is definitely not coming tomorrow. Plausible reasons all of them, but the justification is just a veneer covering an abrupt, irrevocable desire to leave Utøya. People are told that the ferry won't be operating anymore that day and neither will any buses on the mainland. She accepted the situation until someone told her confidentially that Norwegian People's Aid would soon be crossing over to fetch some people with their own boat. Perhaps she could tag along with them. And then hitchhike further on?

Jannike is half-lying, half-sitting on the pier, alone and waiting for fear that she will miss the Norwegian People's Aid boat when Utøya's camp administrator comes from the information house and wonders what's going on. Jannike says she's going home and makes up the little white lie about her sister's situation in Kristiansand. She's told that she's not allowed to leave. The administration doesn't want to have too many youngsters milling around on the mainland side. And anyway it's certainly not wise to hitchhike to Drammen, as Jannike said she's planning to do. Jannike responds in an evasive and noncommittal manner, ever steadfast in her resolution—if only the Norwegian People's Aid team keeps its word. The nineteen-year-old isn't a petite, nimble blonde but measures 1.82 meters from head to toe. It's broad daylight. Jannike reasons that motorists will be more inclined to give her a ride because of the explosion in Oslo. She's not afraid to hitchhike to Drammen. Jannike browses the online newspapers and calls her sister again. "Don't stay by yourself. Go to a girlfriend's or something." She's reminded that no more boats are crossing over and that she must go up to the cafeteria building. Jannike answers back in a surly manner: "Is it a problem that I'm sitting down here? I have to make some calls." Then she sees crewman Johannes Giske, the camp administrator, and the ferry captain on the MS *Thorbjørn* heading toward the mainland.

Giske sees the policeman in a bomber uniform from the wheelhouse of the MS *Thorbjørn*. He sees that he has a quite heavy hard plastic case with him. "Equipment to defuse a bomb," he thinks. In reality it contains the hundred-liter black Pelican case with ammunition and two four-liter cans of diesel. The policeman is focused but clearly disconcerted. It's no wonder, considering what happened in Oslo. Giske is taken aback for a moment that he has iPod earphones in his ears, but he doesn't think any more about it.

Ingrid Endrerud also doesn't think it strange that a police officer is going to Utøya. She has heard that the AUF and Labor Party building on Youngstorget Square was severely damaged. But she reacts to the policeman's black garment, which is reminiscent of the kind of compression jersey that cyclists wear to make the blood pump faster. She also doesn't know what the tube over his shoulder is for—she thinks it resembles a CamelBak straw. The most troubling is the bare skin between the jersey and the pants. The jersey has ridden up, creating an embarrassing opening on the back. "Strange that a police officer doesn't dress properly," the county chairman from Oppland thinks to herself. Ingrid notes that it is 5.04 p.m. when the MS *Thorbjørn* sets off from the pier on the mainland side.

Morten Djupdal was upset because someone had moved the red campaign car. He was upset because the driver had parked it in a mud pit.

And he was angry because the car was stuck. "Everyone understands that it's impossible to park there," said Morten to the guys in the tent on the mainland side. "Come and help push." They found gravel and stones to put under the tires. Morten was hit by a stone in the leg, and the mud splashed on his shorts and AUF sweater. On top of everything else it was raining. It was then that his father called and told him what had happened in Oslo. The three youngsters—Morten and the two who came with him from the island—jumped in the car, concluded that they wouldn't manage to shop in Hønefoss, and headed toward the Joker grocery store in Sundvollen. Because there were speed cameras along the way, Morten couldn't press down on the gas pedal as much as he wanted to.

Since it was difficult to start the car, Morten kept the engine running while they shopped. "It may not look so good that an AUF car is idling, but the hell with it," he said to the other two and added that they had to hurry. The two youngsters from Oslo filled some bags with provisions while Morten wanted only two loaves of bread and a tube of cheese. While he was standing in front of the bread slicer, his father called again from Fagernes, and he was talkative. With one hand holding the phone and a cheese tube under his arm, Morten got so distracted that he dropped the sliced bread on the floor. "Oh, now we really have to hurry," thought Morten, and he hung up and bent down to pick up four slices of bread. Getting into the idling car, he realized that they were probably not going to catch the five o'clock ferry to Utøya. Edvin Søvik, who was en route from Oslo with the current issue of *Planet Utøya* and who had just posted a message on Facebook—"Left Youngstorget before the bomb; am doing fine and on the way back to Utøya"—had told him that there weren't going to be any more ferry crossings to Utøya today. The five o'clock ferry would be the last one of the day.

The story of how Morten and the two youngsters from Oslo missed the MS *Thorbjørn* by one minute and had to sit in the car on the ramp down to the ferry berth and watch it head out into Lake Tyri begins with Morten deciding that he needed a hot shower at his uncle and aunt's place in Hønefoss. But the reason for the delay is hidden among the chance events that occurred after four o'clock: if the car hadn't been moved, if Ingrid hadn't taken the car keys, if the car hadn't gotten stuck in the mud, if there had been no speed cameras on the road, if Morten hadn't dropped the bread on the floor by the bread slicer in the Joker grocery store. If only one of these events had not occurred, Morten and the two youngsters would have managed to catch the five o'clock ferry over to Utøya. For the county secretary of Oppland standing on the mainland watching the MS *Thorbjørn* heading steadily toward the pier in front of the white information house on Utøya, this single minute-too-late was but one in a series of bad luck moments he has had to endure during the last hour.

12

I'm So Glad You're on Utøya Today

Jannike Arnesen sees him take the step from the deck of the MS *Thorbjørn* onto terra firma on Utøya. Behind him come Utøya's camp administrator and the captain. Jannike smiles at the policeman as he passes her on the pier. The crew member, Giske, is staying onboard because he's been told that there will be two more officers from Oslo who need a ride over from the mainland. Ingrid Endrerud goes quickly up the hill past the information house. Outside the cafeteria building she meets a friend who has become sick, as is wont to happen after one has slept in a damp tent and stayed up late into the night. He's going back to Gjøvik. His father is on the way by car to fetch him. Ingrid says that a police officer is on Utøya. In the main hall many are still gathered after the information meeting. The youngsters sob, comfort each other, or talk about the explosion. Many can't get in touch with their parents in Oslo because the phone lines are down. Hildegunn Fallang waits for news to appear on the big screen. The girl from Hadeland gets a call from a slightly irritated Morten Djupdal. By now there are many youngsters waiting on the mainland. He asks them to send the MS *Thorbjørn* over or, alternatively, the smaller boat *Reiulf*.

Tore Sinding Bekkedal has a dark cloud hanging over his head. The plan was that he would set up a webcast via the screen on the wall behind the stage in the main hall. He is a computer geek and is best suited for the job; end of story. But some of the work crew decided that they had to set the password on the wireless network rather than Tore, who could do it the fastest. Tore doesn't think this is the right time to talk about who has the formal authority to change a configuration. It's just silly. It's stupid at a moment when there's no time for stupidity. The computer geek waits for the password from someone who isn't a computer geek and mopes by the edge of the stage with a big gray-black cloud hanging over his head.

The camp administrator spoke to the policeman en route from the mainland to Utøya. There was something about him that did not instill confidence. While the captain goes up to get her car so that they can take the policeman's equipment up behind the information house, she walks quickly up to the hired guard for the island. The policeman from Oslo has asked her to gather the guards on the island. The captain loads up the gear. As the car drives up the hill, the guard walks toward the policeman. He wants to make sure that a black trash bag is not hiding a weapon so that the youngsters won't be more alarmed than necessary. Jannike sees the camp administrator, guard, and policeman walk up the hill and over the grassy field to the information house, twenty meters to her left. In front of the old white building is a collapsed yellow rodeo ring—the island's most light-hearted entertainment next to the bouncy castle, which was never set up. Morten Djupdal picked up the packages for the rodeo in Vestfold on Tuesday with a white van from Bislett Car Rental. The mechanical bull was used for an hour yesterday, but today it's taking shelter from the rain.

Morten is still waiting for a ride from the mainland when he hears popping sounds from Utøya. Firecrackers? Morten calls up Hildegunn in the main hall again. "We heard some popping sounds from the island," he says. Hildegunn asks the others with her if they have heard anything. "Nothing," they reply. The windows are wide open. "See you soon," she says and hangs up, thinking that the Oppland delegation leader has gone off his head. Morten doesn't like the sounds but is no more worried about them than that he goes into the woods to do what one has to do every now and then.

Jannike is typing on her mobile phone when she hears two bangs. She can't see the grass field up there because of the height difference in the terrain, but she sees the policeman pulling the garbage bag off the large weapon. The camp administrator and the guard become the first victims of the fake policeman. A youngster from Oslo is standing not that far from the information house and watches the whole scene unfold. He thinks it's a joke. The fifteen-year-old calls his father and asks whether all is well in Oslo. "It's going well on Utøya," he says.

When the captain realizes what has happened, he runs up the hill to warn the young people around the cafeteria building. Jannike is still sitting unawares on the pier. She sees the policeman go to the right of the information house and up the hill to the cafeteria building, but she doesn't think anything of it. She hears seven more gunshots. Giske shouts and waves her down to the MS *Thorbjørn*. She saunters across the gravel, turns for a moment, and considers bringing her backpack before she puts it down. "What is this?" she asks, looking up toward the top of the island. "The kind of crazy guy we see on television?" "I don't know," Giske replies.

Eskil Pedersen sits on the second floor of the information house and waits for the TV broadcast of a press conference when he hears the sound of a hammer striking a nail three times. He thinks, "What was that?" Two others in the room go down to the reception area. One of them quickly comes up again and says there's shooting on Utøya. Eskil doesn't think so. That is, not until he opens the door to the porch and hears the disturbing sounds. His twenty-two-year old political adviser, who is already on board the MS *Thorbjørn*, calls to say that he must come to the boat. Immediately. Eskil runs down the stairs to the ground floor, storms out of the building in stocking feet, and pauses for a second at the two bodies on the lawn before he runs further down the steps, across the gravel, and toward the pier and the old Swedish cargo boat. About the same time the captain comes out of the woods to the left of the pier with two youngsters from northern Norway.

Eskil runs into the wheelhouse, where Jannike, Johannes, and the others are lying flat on the floor. Eight youngsters and the captain. "Lie down, lie down!" The others tell him what they have seen: a policeman shot Utøya's camp administrator and guard before he moved up to the cafeteria building. The AUF leader doesn't know what to think. Is he witnessing a large-scale, well-planned attack on the political structure of Norway? What has taken place in Oslo and now on Utøya—is it happening all over the country? Is Norway under attack? Is anyone in the military and police involved in the conspiracy? He is powerless and helpless. "We must get off the island," the youngsters say to the captain. Some of them fear that their leader, Eskil, is the primary target on Utøya. The captain starts the engine and backs out into Lake Tyri. Eskil and the others think there're two more policemen on the mainland. They first head toward the ferry berth, but midway they turn toward the island of Storøya. Jannike is convinced that these eight people on the deck of the MS *Thorbjørn*, plus the captain, are the only ones who will survive the massacre.

Most youngsters in the main hall, the kiosk, the tents, or the toilet stalls don't hear the gunshots and warnings. The slope from the information house to the cafeteria building is steep, so the sounds of the gunshots would have been muted. Morten Djupdal heard popping sounds from the mainland, six hundred meters to the east. Hildegunn in the main hall, just a stone's throw from the shooting, heard nothing. The youngsters are not aware that a broad-shouldered, armed policeman is walking with determined steps up the gravel road to the big green cafeteria building.

Matti Brox is on his way to the cafeteria building from the back, up the stone steps to the little hall, after talking with his mother. For a moment he forgot that his mother was visiting relatives in Mehamn in Finnmark, so his voice was a little shaky when he asked how she was. Matti's phone is worn out and has to be charged more or less constantly. Therefore he has to find a free electrical socket in the dining hall. Through the window he sees a dozen youngsters running past the gravel yard. Curiosity gets the better of him, and he returns to the little hall to see where the youngsters are running. At the top of the stone steps he hears four or five gunshots. They sound close.

The youngsters are scrambling into the little hall. Matti blocks the hallway with his arms. He doesn't know how many are pressing to get in, but the little hall is already full. The youngsters are impatient and their adrenaline levels are running high. The sixteen-year-old flexes his muscles, makes eye contact, and shouts with a compelling voice: "Silee-ence!" In reality he's asking them to stay calm, but in this self-conscious moment Matti sees himself in the role of the eccentric bearded headmaster in the Harry Potter movies, Albus Dumbledore. His authority lasts about one minute. Then the youngsters turn around and run in the opposite direction toward the main hall and dining hall, looking for an escape route out of the cafeteria building. Matti follows behind.

The atmosphere around the cafeteria building on Utøya is one of surreal pandemonium. Everything happens either really fast or in slow motion. There's no past and no future, only a chaotic now, detached from time and space. Utøya is the safest place on earth. This is not supposed to happen. Many people are panic stricken while others remain paralyzed. Some hear the whooshing or popping sounds and move toward them out of curiosity. Jorid Nordmelan is sure that she hears guns being fired, but she comes to the conclusion that the sounds must be coming from hunters. Others think it sounds like someone is bursting balloons, kicking a trashcan, firing a nail gun, or blowing up a smoke bomb made from baking powder and water. The youngsters hear shooting and screaming right outside the windows of the little hall, main hall, and dining hall, where they have congregated, but many can't comprehend what's going on as they don't see who or what is behind the sounds. Some say the shooter is a man in police uniform, while others say he's wearing a green reflective vest and a military hat. Some of the youngsters seem to have gone over the edge.

The cafeteria building is huge. What happens in the main hall isn't necessarily noticed in the kiosk, and what happens in the little hall is shielded from what is going on in the dining hall. The policeman's ambiguous signals create further confusion. He shoots the boys and girls while he calms the youngsters by saying he's come to protect them. A man dressed in a uniform that represents law and order and authority is committing criminal acts. The mind is not capable of comprehending conflicting signals such as these. The mind looks for causal relationships and familiar sensory patterns, whereas the adrenaline rush in the body is an instinctive reaction. Your brain tells you to stay until you get a plausible explanation; then your legs tell you to run.

Stine Renate Håheim is in the dining hall when she hears gunshots in the yard and sees youngsters running down to the woods. Her annoyance over someone playing an outlandishly tasteless prank dissolves when she hears new disturbing sounds. She stands motionless in the little hall. She has no recollection of how she got from A to B, how long it took, or who was running with her. Whether she misunderstands on the way back to the dining hall or whether the girl who comes running in from the gravel yard in front of the kiosk is babbling in incomplete sentences and hyperventilating is now moot. The only thing that Stine Renate understands of what the girl is saying is, "Bullet holes in the wall."

The sound of gunshots in the campground outside the little hall leads to wild panic in the cafeteria building. A youngster has locked the main door of the kiosk from the inside. So using the door to the campground from the little hall is not an option. That leaves only the exits from the kitchen and dining hall. People run, fall, or scramble to get out, amid shouts of "Get down!" Stine Renate stands still and watches the people squeezing through the doors. Some jump out of the windows. The twenty-seven-year-old waits her turn among the people trying slowly to get out. She considers throwing a chair through a high window but drops the idea. There will be too much broken glass to sweep up afterward.

"Are you okay?" Johanne Butenschøn Lindheim has heard the commotion outside the cafeteria building but has not taken the trouble to check it out. The question puts a halt to her sobbing, as it's followed by news about her best friend. She has just arrived on Utøya. Johanne doesn't dare stick her head out of the tent as her face is lumpy and swollen and her makeup is a mess. She looks at herself in the mirror of the iPhone and notes that she has looked better. Then her friend, who's flown in from America, comes into the tent. As the friends hug and cry in the tent, Johanne hears loud bangs and screaming outside. The nineteen-year-old thinks it must be firecrackers going off. That's not cool, not cool at all. She opens the tent zipper and turns her head toward the gravel yard in front of the cafeteria building by the waffle booth. There's a policeman standing there. He's shooting at something red on the ground. Johanne thinks it's a bag. She's seen it before, at an airport in Paris. The bag was shot at because it had been left unclaimed for a suspiciously long time. "Relax," her friend says. She took the boat over with him. The policeman is going to check that everything is okay on Utøya.

"Run for your lives!" The phrase is often heard in American movies. Now it's shouted by youths running past Johanne's tent, with desperate looks and flailing arms. The nineteen-year-old thinks that it's mass hysteria. Nerves are on edge. Yet she and her friend crawl out of the tent. Johanne first puts on shoes but then takes them off as it's impossible to move fast with them on. They run up toward the Buskerud campsite and into the woods on the west side of Utøya. Although Johanne hears gunshots and sees the panic in the youngsters' eyes, she still wonders if this is worth getting dirty for. She and her friend slide down a steep and slippery slope, clinging to blueberry bushes and ferns, until they end up looking at a fifteen-meter plunge straight down into Lake Tyri. Johanne's hands are bloodied. They hide under a tree. She hears several gunshots, rubber boots splashing in the mud on Lovers' Lane, and someone shouting, "We need a knife!"

Panic is spreading. It spreads, unreasonably slowly or reasonably fast, from youngster to youngster, in and around the cafeteria building. Many still believe they are unwitting spectators to a scene staged for their entertainment. When one is on the safest island in the safest country on earth, it's rational to think that a deadly weapon is something else. They don't see a mass murderer but a uniformed man with a paintball gun. Experience and logical deduction suggest that a man in uniform is there to help you. "I'm from the police. I'll make sure that you're safe. I just need to gather you in one place so it'll be easier for me to protect you," he says calmly. Meanwhile, turmoil is spreading. The desperate commands are firm but confusing. "Run in!" "Run out!" "Get down!" "Get up!"

Hildegunn Fallang dismissed the concerns of Morten Djupdal. Now she also hears the loud bangs as she sits barefoot on the floor of the main hall in a signal yellow raincoat. The bangs—light pops—don't sound like gunshots. Hildegunn served compulsory military service from 2009 to 2010. She was stationed on Norway's border with Russia. She has handled both the military-issue AG3 and HK416 rifles. She thinks that these pops sound like the kind of dummy ammunition used when soldiers are on exercise. The administration must have forgotten to inform them about the exercise.

Boys and girls jump over the unfortunate ones who have stumbled, blocking the exits that are not wide enough, bumping into the Norwegian Textile Workers' Union poster with the slogan, "In the nuclear age, our destiny is woven together into one pattern." They shatter the windows to climb out, cutting themselves on the glass; hide under tables, chairs, or behind the piano; and sprain their arms and legs as they tumble down the slope at the back of the building. Every one of them is running only in socks. The wet boots are left helter-skelter in the hallway.

Tore Sinding Bekkedal is in one of the toilet stalls in the cafeteria building. Outside the stalls there are wash basins and a door leading out to the long corridor in the cafeteria building. Tore hears an air gun. He thinks someone is trying to cause panic just for fun. He finishes up and prepares to march out to reprimand the prankster. He opens the stall door and sees Arshad Ali hiding behind the wall that leads out to the corridor. Tore has always known Arshad as a Stavanger guy with nerves of steel and one who never gets ruffled, exuding a relaxed equanimity to the outside world. Not now. Arshad signals with his arms, hands, and fingers, but above all with his eyes that Tore must get back inside the stall.

The thirty-two-year-old comes into the main hall through the door from the little hall. Hanne Hestø Ness notes that he steps over the threshold, but she is unable to put down her phone and moves her body away from the corner by the window and the wall. The nineteen-year-old sits paralyzed on the floor with her girlfriend, Lene Maria, on her lap, equally paralyzed. This isn't a firecracker prank. She could have gotten up and run out with everyone else, but she had calmed down after the international guest from Lebanon had told her that the sounds did not come from a gun. Besides, she was enthralled by the sight of young people, desperate and disorganized, trying to push their way out of the main hall through the three doors. The echo in the main hall also meant that it was difficult to determine the direction of the sounds of the gunshots.

The deputy of the North Trøndelag AUF sees the stony-faced man approaching. Hanne thinks that with his clenched teeth he looks like a neo-Nazi, just as he comes to within two meters of them. The bullets first hit the boy next to them, then Lene Maria, and finally Hanne. One shot strikes the little finger, one the upper arm, and one the neck. The second shot goes through the arm and out the back of the shoulder. She's flung backward and her head hits the wall. She thinks that she's going to get a concussion. Since Hanne got her first single-lens reflex camera for her confirmation, her plan has been to become a press photographer. Next year she planned on studying photography in England. She needs her hands. "This is the end," thinks the nineteen-year-old girl in the main hall on the island on Lake Tyri. Her body is motionless, not because she doesn't want to move it but because it no longer obeys her. This is the end. Her right hand has stiffened, clenched around the mobile phone. Blood stains the gray linoleum floor. There's a ringing in her ears. She closes her eyes. Try to sleep. This is the end.

Hanne doesn't go to sleep. That's how the body is put together. Different parts of the brain work together to bring forth positive thoughts. Behind alien names such as amygdala, caudata, thalamus, and hippocampus is concealed the will to live itself, the ability to make you see light when it's actually dark. The amygdala is associated with emotional responses. It's only human. The frontal lobe of the cortex dampens signals from the amygdala. It's just as human. Hanne wants to sleep, but her body doesn't. She feels pain only in the arm that isn't injured since it's pressed against the hard floor by her body. It's hard to breathe. Lene Maria lies on top of her chest. The ringing in her ears subsides. Instead she hears mobile phones and feels the linoleum floor vibrating. She reckons that many of the youngsters have iPhones. Parents can't get hold of their kids. The thought of their loss overshadows the response of the selfish gene.

On the wall in the main hall hang two campaign posters from the 1930s in budget-black IKEA frames. On one poster, depicting the parliamentary election in 1936, is a handsome young boy with a coat, flat cap, and scarf around his neck, looking hopefully into the future. On the red background the map of Norway is lit up with the slogan "Norway for young people" in bold black letters. The other poster illustrates the Nygaardsvold government's disarmament policy, launched after its winning the 1936 election and for which it was criticized after the German invasion of April 9, 1940: a muscular Gustav Vigeland–inspired arm with a clenched fist smashing a stack of weapons of war. "The Norwegian Labor Party" is printed in pale yellow. In red, against a yellow background, are the words, "Down with weapons!"

Hanne is convinced that she's the only survivor in the main hall. Because of her unnatural supine position, she can only look up at the ceiling or down at the floor. Her ear is pressed against the linoleum, which conveys the sound of heavy footsteps. She thinks it strange that a couple of minutes ago she was hysterical and so terrified that it caused physical pain in her body. Now she's no longer afraid. She's not in pain. She's not frantic but focuses on spreading her stiffened fingers around the phone so that she can free her hand. She tries to move her upper body so that her girlfriend can slide down. She succeeds with the phone. The display lights up. Her feet feel as if they are up in the air, but that's not the case. Hanne comes to the conclusion that she must be paralyzed. She has broken her neck and is paralyzed. It's not the thought of losing her life that makes her so furious—it's because of her own state, because of her best friend's death, because of the other youngsters' fate—and shouts after the man who is to blame, "You're a coward! You don't even dare to come back to finish the job!"

Tore Sinding Bekkedal feels painted into a corner. He checks the door of the toilet stall and confirms that it won't resist the bullets. The material seems to be made of corrugated cardboard. Tore wants to get out of the building, out in the open, where there're more avenues of escape. He doesn't know where the gunshots are coming from; whether they're heading in his direction or away from him; or whether they're coming from the cafeteria building's south, east, or west side. All he knows is that he must get out. Tore opens the door carefully and goes out into the long corridor. There he makes eye contact with a young boy lying shot on the floor who waves him into the staff toilet by the entrance to the dining hall. The door here is at least more solid and has a cylinder lock. Tore assumes that a small-caliber pistol won't be able to penetrate it. He hears moaning outside.

Several people are hiding in the toilet stalls in the cafeteria building. They're unsure about their hiding place. There's no escape. All it takes is a bullet through the thin door. Metallic banging sounds are coming from the hallways and rooms outside, followed by groaning and strained calls for help. Each fiber and cell in the young human bodies is working in high gear. Feelings run the gamut from fear to panic to disdain of death and back to fear. Gunshots are soon heard in other parts of the building. There could be one shooter or there could be many. All sounds are heard. Watches are ticking annoyingly loudly. The mosquito sounds like an airplane, and the rumbling in the stomach sounds like thunder. Any trivial movement is transformed into the sounds of those metal garbage cans in American movies being overturned at night by cats or drunks. In several of the toilet stalls a verse from the Gospel of Matthew is repeated: "Deliver us from evil."

Outside there's a symphony of unsynchronized ringtones. The girls and boys have selected the musical snippets of the songs that they love. Many have bought the ringtone to Chris Medina's big summer hit, "What are words / If you really do not mean them / When you say them." The more tech-savvy among them have set friends and family members to exclusive ringtones so as to more easily identify the caller. Some phones are still connected to chargers inserted in sockets, left by the girls who were put to flight. "And I know an angel was sent just for me." Other phones are in the trouser pockets of guys who lie lifeless on the floor. What they have in common is that they're ringing constantly because someone is trying to get hold of them. "Those words, They never go away / They live on, even when we're gone."

Along the waterside, at the campsite, in the schoolhouse, or in the woods, youths are texting about what has happened—privately to friends and family or publicly via Twitter and Facebook. A Gjøvik boy calls his father as he runs along Lovers' Lane. "Dad, there's someone shooting at us. A crazy person. I love you. I love mom. And I love everyone else." When he finishes the brief conversation, he hears his father scream at the other end, "Nooo!" Many have to keep the calls back home brief. They're young, they don't work, they've no fixed mobile phone subscriptions that generate recurring bills; they've a prepaid card that always needs to be topped up. And the battery, of course, is never fully charged. Others destroy their phones for fear of being exposed, even on silent, in airplane mode, or completely turned off. Phone messages from the island home to parents are stark and precise but not easy to make sense of: "Police are shooting; contact the police."

The youths storm out of the cafeteria building, running helter-skelter in all directions. Many run to the woods; most of them run to the waterside; to the north, east, west, and south; to Bolsjevika Bay; and to the Nakenodden and Stoltenberget promontories. They run alone or in groups, through scrub and thorny rose hips bushes, on prickly pine needles, over gnarled roots and slippery rocks, between hardwood forests and wild pine, not heeding that their bare t feet and legs are being scratched bloody. The terrain toward the waterside is varied. In some places the ground ends at high cliffs that rise thirty meters above the lake, while in others gently sloping paths lead down to the beach. Lovers' Lane isn't wide enough for everyone. The youngsters run for their lives, jostling and saying, "Sorry," while they pass yellow warning triangles that say, "Do not lean against the fence." They run past the dark green pine trees, past the sparse, light green birches, running further and further away.

The discussion between philosophers and brain researchers on whether it's fear that makes you run or the running that creates fear merely seems amateurish and irrelevant here and now. The youngsters run to get away from the killer, and they're afraid because they don't want to feel the bullets in their bodies. There are no obvious secure hiding places other than some inaccessible caves in the cliffs facing the lake. The youngsters hiding in high reed grass, under the lavatory block, or by the pump house are at the mercy of the killer's whim and fancy.

Stine Renate Håheim runs through the woods toward the northern side of the island. Her father, who is in the cabin with her mother in Valdres, calls to tell her how glad he is that she's on Utøya today. "Dad, someone's shooting here," she said breathlessly. "Yes, but have you heard about what happened in Oslo? A bomb has exploded in the government quarter." Under other circumstances Stine Renate would have appreciated the unintended humor, but instead she becomes frustrated. "Dad, you have to call the police. Do you understand?" He replies that it's best if she calls the emergency number. "But I'm running in the woods," the twenty-seven-year-old says helplessly. It takes a lot of practice to dial phone numbers on a touch screen while running fast over roots, branches, and rocks. "Dad, you have to call," Stine Renate says and hangs up. She fears that her father thinks his daughter has lost her mind, but she's banking on his uncertainty to make him call the emergency number. Moreover, taken literally, one could claim that she has already called the authorities since her father works as a police officer in Valdres.

Ingrid Endrerud runs from the cafeteria building down the scree at the rear of the building, through dense woods, and out to Lovers' Lane on the north side of the island, where she stops after a few meters. "I'm wearing a big yellow raincoat. It's too obvious," the eighteen-year-old thinks. On one side of the path there's shrubbery and trees and on the other side, a fence that blocks off the steep cliffs down to Lake Tyri. Ingrid is clear-headed and sharp. She realizes she has to tear off the Helly Hansen raincoat, and she does so straightaway. The bag on her back shares the same fate.

When she was in Sundvollen with her boyfriend, she bought a one-and-a-half-liter bottle of Solo soft drink for the Oppland contingent. It's Friday. Coca Cola was out of the question for political reasons. Her little backpack wasn't big enough for the soft drink bottle. The red cap stuck out of the bag. As she ran from the cafeteria building down the scree and through the woods to Lovers' Lane, the zipper on the bag got opened. So when she tore off the yellow raincoat and backpack, everything in it ended up in the bushes except for the toiletries bag, which ended up on the other side of the path. My God, what a mess, she thinks. Her stuff can't be left scattered all over the ground. As she's about to bend down to collect her stuff, she hears gunshots in the background. She imagines what it would be like to be shot in the back. That's when Ingrid understands that she mustn't stop. She retrieves the small red purse with credit cards and a lip balm from her yellow raincoat. Ingrid puts her phone into the purse and runs northward along the fence.

From the toilet stalls in the cafeteria building by the campsite calls are being made to the 112 police emergency number. "There's a cop here shooting wildly" is the first message they get at the police station in Høne-foss. A police officer is alone on duty. The risk and vulnerability analysis for Buskerud County deals with floods, landslides, and major train accidents; there's nothing about a massacre at a youth camp. Most of the youngsters get a busy signal when they call because in North Buskerud they can answer only two incoming calls to the emergency number at the same time. In a more ideal world their calls would have been transferred to other police districts. In Oslo they can receive sixty calls simultaneously. The next caller to get through says that the perpetrator is wearing a police uniform and that he's shooting with an automatic weapon. Gunshots can be heard in the background.

On the way out of the cafeteria building the tall blond man picks up an old Nokia mobile phone that was being charged in the kitchen by the dining hall. His own phone was blown to smithereens in the government quarter. The thirty-two-year-old calls and gets a busy signal. The call capacity of the Hønefoss police station has been exceeded. He goes toward the campground, which is full of yellow, brown, and blue picnic blankets where the youngsters had been playing cards before they ran off. He chooses the tents that have been zipped up. No one hides in an open tent.

Matti Brox runs through the woods and thinks about "Call of Duty." The sixteen-year-old wonders whether he can convert his gaming skills into reality. "Camping" is a term from the popular shooter video game, often used in contrast to "rushing," where a player hunts relentlessly for his target. Campers hide and prefer to ambush the target. But if they are stationary for long periods, they will likely be liquidated. Even campers have to move around. Matti has no intention of attacking anybody; he just needs to find a hiding place, using rocks, shrubs, and trees as camouflage. The Oslo boy must reluctantly concede that the video game world has no analogue in the real one. On his old TV it's impossible to spot a target at a hundred meters as the quality is too poor. Here, in the woods on Utøya, reality is in high definition. The trees are spread out and the visibility is excellent. The "camping" strategy has to be abandoned in favor of "rushing." Matti flees further on, to the north side of the island, where he meets Khamshajiny Gunaratnam. They hold hands and run toward Bolsjevika Bay.

Many of the youngsters have sought refuge in the woods behind the campground. Some are in small clusters while others are scattered, lying low in the grass because they think they're less visible that way. They are barefooted and soaking wet in their overly colorful clothes. Trembling clumps of color peek out everywhere in the scrub forest on Utøya. A group hides under some large, jungle-like leaves. They hope they'll be safe there. That is, until a phone starts vibrating and they are discovered. White, red, and blue T-shirts jump up from the grass and bushes, running toward the paths that are wet and rugged. It's been raining incessantly throughout the day.

Youths hiding along Lovers' Lane keep hearing frenzied, thumping, and sloshing footsteps coming in their direction. "He's taking the path!" someone yells. They see no one but know that it must be him. No youngster will think about whistling, humming, or singing now. The youngsters can also hear him humming a little, innocent tune punctuated by angry victory chants. The smell of gunpowder is becoming stronger. There's no sound of human breathing, just the wind in the trees, twigs cracking under heavy black boots, scattered raindrops falling on leaves, and those damned mosquitoes. The man in the police uniform goes calmly along the trail and says he's come to save them. Many haven't seen him yet and lie with their heads buried in white lilies and green, wet moss. Some choose to hope. From his vantage point in a tree a thirty-year-old guest from Uganda sees youths being shot and killed in a controlled and calm manner. A girl goes up to the killer and asks what he's doing. He turns calmly to the girl, "Your turn is coming."

Kjetil Klakegg Bergheim hides in the woods under a tree with branches growing out and down the hill, not far from Lovers' Lane. He thinks about what it would be like to die and what his last words to his father would be. While the rain pours down and ants crawl frenziedly up his legs, he draws the following conclusion: it won't take more than two seconds from the time he registers that he's dying until he actually dies. In other words he won't have time to say much before everything goes black. Or will it be black? The Florø boy thinks that energy can neither dissipate nor materialize, so consequently he'll also not dissipate. Maybe he'll be in a state in which he'll be conscious of someone mourning over him? But does he want that—to experience the sorrow that others feel for him? No, actually not. I hope everything goes black. The end. That's what the twenty-three-year-old from Sogn og Fjordane County thinks under a rain-soaked bush on Utøya.

We don't know much about how it is to die, but we do know a little about how it feels to think that one will die. The twenty-seven-year-old Fyodor Dostoevsky was sentenced to death for challenging the Russian Orthodox Church and tsarist autocracy. When he was led to the execution ground on the morning of December 22, 1849, he thought of the cold, a Victor Hugo novel, and the sun lighting up the domes of the church. In *The Idiot* he describes his mixed feelings about the moments before death. According to the Russian, the heaviest of these moments is the nagging suspicion that death isn't going to happen anyway. "What should I do if I were not to die now? What if I were to return to life again? What an eternity of days, and all mine! How I should grudge and count up every minute of them, so as to waste not a single instant!" Pretty soon the mood changes. The still-to-be world famous Russian writer is seized with the most profound indifference. He doesn't care about life or the people around him. Everything is trivial compared with that awful moment that's coming. At the last minute, as sixteen men stand with raised, loaded guns aimed at the insurrectionists with hoods over their heads, Dostoevsky and his accomplices are pardoned by the tsar. One of the condemned men loses his mind right then and there. The others don't even smile. When you think you're going to die, it's a strain when you don't.

Banalities are triggered by fear, indifference, or loss of reason but often lead to clear insights. The realization of death leads to clarification, reconciliation, and precocity. Letters from doomed men and women during World War II bear witness to this, as published in the anthology *Last Letters*: "As long as one is free, it seems like such a terrible fate. But now I know that it's not," wrote a thirty-year-old Polish housewife, Mira Cikota. "I can't explain it, but my mind is completely calm," wrote a twenty-one-year-old Danish sailor, Kim Malthe-Bruun. "Death has lost all its bitterness. I'm filled with a great peace and sense of relief," wrote a forty-eight-year-old teacher from Germany, Alfred Schmidt-Sas. "A lyrical mind may sometimes be defeated by this. But the tree feels no pain; it's all so natural and logical," wrote a forty-year-old Czech author, Julius Fucik. "I have, at this moment, a feeling that my life has served its purpose," wrote Lucien Legro, an eighteen-year-old student from France. That's how it may feel to know that your time has come. Whether you're forty-eight or sixteen years old is of little consequence. When all hope is gone, one's life work is accomplished. For these letter writers, as for many on Utøya that afternoon, it's liberating to have reconciled oneself to death. What bothers them the most is a deep sense of guilt for the suffering they'll cause the ones they leave behind.

A twenty-one-year-old with a broken heel rests against a tree, covered by earth, moss, and branches. Ants crawl all over her, biting where they fine pale skin. She sees that the decomposition process has started. Many will remain lying like that after meeting the murderer, in the woods or along the waterside—motionless, with bleeding, burning wounds under the popular, drenched AUF hooded sweater. The mind switches between agony and shame as one defecates in one's underpants. The rain fills the ears while one's thirst is chronic and banalities intrude. Some are bored or long to be pumped full of drugs in the hospital, while others are looking forward to supper.

Johanne Butenschøn Lindheim and her friend have been running from the west side of the island to the north, where they sit on a stone ledge, a couple of meters from Lake Tyri. They have plowed their way through the crowd that ran too slowly, over mud, slippery roots, and unforgiving stones, and they jumped over a curved fence, looking for hiding places by the waterside without others nearby. They took off their colorful garments, but Johanne still feels quite noticeable with light, long hair and a pink and blue sweater. Thoughts and words fly through their heads and between the friends at a breathless pace, while pine cones and leaves fall on them from the path: What's going on? Is the hideout good enough? Shall we swim, run on, or press ourselves closer to the rough and sharp rock wall? Johanne runs into an existential conundrum. Can it all be a dream? How will this be portrayed in history books? But she also thinks about her stock investments. The nineteen-year-old has worked as a trainee at an asset management firm and knows that it's wise to have a consistent investment policy. Make a decision and stick to it. They're not going to move. "There're so many damned mosquitoes," whispers Johanne. "Hell with them," is the response.

Johanne is so scared that she no longer knows whether she exists or not. She has never been more physically tough, yet she feels dead already. Her body is shaking wildly while her legs are starting to weaken because of reduced blood circulation. It may seem a trivial issue, but if the body doesn't obey when the mind directs it to, it's impossible to run away from a killer. In order to suppress the most dystopian scenarios, she thinks of the German movie *Sophie Scholl: The Final Days*. The movie depicts the period from February 18, 1943, when the twenty-one-year-old student and anti-Nazi resistance woman was arrested, until she was executed four days later. Through the bars of the prison window she could see the clouds drifting past, and she was reminded that the sky above condensed water vapor is always blue. Johanne motivates herself with the same thought, but it's not easy to imagine anything beyond the massive dark cloud that hangs over Utøya.

Her friend uses her mobile phone to call the police. In contrast to so many other young people on the island who call the emergency number at the same time, she gets through on the second attempt. She's stressed and asks for emergency aid immediately. The woman on the other end answers in a provocatively calm manner. Johanne is no less than outraged when she learns what the woman says when they end the phone conversation: "Have a good day, then." The everyday phrase of politeness has long since been emptied of meaning, but in this context it gets renewed life as an ironic comment.

A spider crawls onto Johanne's hand. She regrets it the instant she kills it. The nineteen-year-old takes it as a sign that she's going to be killed. Her anxiety decreases when a centipede craws onto her left hand. Johanne lets the jointed creature crawl around on her hand. She thinks that it moves so graciously and nobly around in its protective skin that it seems spared from any knowledge of the massacre unfolding on the island. When it leaves her hand, the anxiety returns. Johanne grips the rock wall, digs out a stone and clenches it in her right hand. She lowers her head onto her hands, resting on her knees, and wishes herself out of the world. Johanne looks up, curses herself, and vows that she won't be overwhelmed again. With veiled eyes she's not able to see clearly.

The Oslo girl sees the same man she saw shooting at something red on the ground outside the cafeteria building. Fair-faced with fair hair. Black police uniform under a black bulletproof vest. Police insignias. Weapon. He comes walking down through the trees, looking calmly and systematically from side to side. "He's here," Johanne whispers to her friend. Through the tree in the water she sees two youths running. She imagines the scenes before they happen, and the images cause her brain to come to a conclusion: I'm not afraid to die. The first shot is followed by screaming, retching, groaning, and splashing. The boy running toward her falls into the water after two shots at short intervals. Johanne hears him shouting at the boy and girl in an angry, agitated voice. He comes in their direction. He's only fifteen meters away. "He's coming to us," Johanne whispers to her friend, who crouches down. Johanne doesn't crouch as she wants to look at him. Has to look at him. She looks him in the eye. He looks her in the eye. Johanne casts her eyes down, not making a sound. Each move may be interpreted as a provocation. Why he moves on, just two meters from them, and disappears from her field of vision is hard for Johanne to understand. All she knows is that the fear of death has paralyzed every part of her body.

Stine Renate Håheim is with five boys near Bolsjevika Bay, four of them between the ages of seventeen and nineteen. The waterside is stony and impassable on both sides. She's reluctant to swim for it. It would be too easy for someone to shoot at swimmers in the lake. Stine Renate gets down on her knees in front of the boys and says, "Oh, I'd been so looking forward to the stand-up show tonight." The twenty-seven-year-old isn't saying this to be funny. Any reaction—aggravation, anger, despair— would have been a misplaced comment. Stine Renate doesn't want them to disappear inside themselves and become inaccessible. One of the boys says brusquely, "You're not thinking about that now?" "No, no, it was a joke," she says and smiles. "That wasn't particularly funny," she's told. Yet she thinks that a couple of them have a hint of a smile on their faces.

Stine Renate speaks several times with her father on the mobile phone. He tells her that the police have been informed. Unlike most parents, he didn't call the emergency number and not get through. Her father contacted the emergency operations center in the capital directly. Even though it's been twenty years since he worked in the Oslo police, he still had the number when he called from the Valdres cabin. Stine Renate smiles to herself when he tries giving her good advice. "You have to hide," he says. She chooses to interpret the obvious advice as a sign that her father is more frustrated than she. His concern reminds her that a mobile phone is a scarce commodity now on the island. The boys' parents are probably just as worried as he is. She passes the phone around, telling them to call or write text messages home.

The mobile phone is Stine Renate's lifeline to the outside world, and the physical object—having it, touching it, fiddling with it—provides a sense of security. Even the fact that the touch phone is tricky to handle in the rain provides a welcome distraction. She tries out different ways to shield the phone display and ends up by lifting her dress over her head. Her reaction is mixed when the radio news program *Dagsnytt Atten* calls up. The fact that the radio program wants her on a live broadcast is basically good news. This means that the appropriate authorities have been informed about what's happening on Utøya. At the same time the request is inappropriate and a source of irritation. Stine Renate whispers as softly as she can, as she tries to make her voice sound determined: "I'm hiding right now. People have been shot here. I can't participate in a debate now." The radio program researcher sends her a text message in case she changes her mind. The voice at the other end is so practical, so light, so trusting, and so far removed from reality that her annoyance turns into frustration. So now people out there know that something disturbing is happening on Utøya, but they obviously haven't understood the gravity of the situation.

Even if one is in the middle of a massacre, it doesn't mean that basic needs cease to exist. On the contrary, Stine Renate notices that the more basic, everyday challenges appear, the more reassured she is. Trifling matters provide a semblance of normalcy. Hence she gets up from the rock, takes a few steps toward the woods, points, and says to the others, "Do you think it's okay that I go up there to pee?" The boys have gotten used to Stine Renate saying weird things, but now she's proposing something foolhardy. Her movements could alert the shooter, and she'll be stuck in a position that could delay their possible flight. Perhaps that's another inappropriate joke? "Don't ever do that," Stine Renate is told. Oh, well. But the need for a soothing palliative persists. A round box that she got from one of the older party members should do the trick. Stine Renate is a polite lady, so she holds up the box and offers the young guys a snuff pouch. The generous offer is rejected. "That's good. You mustn't start taking snuff; it's dangerous." She doesn't manage to feel the light anesthetic intoxication of the snuff before they have to flee from Bolsjevika Bay. They head west, toward the gray pump house, along the waterside. Stine Renate is afraid that she won't be able to run anymore if she cuts herself on the rocks. Yesterday Norwegian People's Aid warned about the sharp rocks in the lake and recommended the use of bathing shoes because several people had injured themselves while swimming. She hears shooting and is pretty certain that the sound is coming from the place they just left.

Hildegunn Fallang runs out of the cafeteria building through the woods toward Lake Tyri, where she finds a hiding place under a rock between Bolsjevika Bay and the pump house on the north side. On the way she fiddles with her brand new HTC smartphone, which she doesn't feel particularly comfortable using. It's simply impossible to type on the screen, especially in the rain, and it freezes constantly. Eventually she gets in touch with her mother and explains what's going on, but the heavy, breathless sobbing and hysterical screams force her mother to say in an insistent tone, "Get a hold of yourself!" Hildegunn takes a deep breath and reiterates that the youngsters on the island are being shot at. "I love you; now I've got to run." The mother realizes that her daughter's not joking, but there's nothing she can do other than calling Hildegunn's father, who's the sheriff of the neighboring municipality, Jevnaker. As Hildegunn runs, she takes off the watch she's so fond of, a stylish Calvin Klein in polished stainless steel with a white dial and steel band. Hildegunn got it for her confirmation, with her name and date engraved, so the sentimental value over time will have at least tripled. She takes off her most precious possession and puts it in a safe place in case she needs to get into the water.

The shortest distance over to the mainland is six hundred meters. Swimming over would be more hazardous than the distance would indicate, as even small waves and weak currents can pose a challenge to skinny, chilled, and weary bodies. There are two currents between Utøya and Utvika Camping, one going north and the other going south. The water level in Lake Tyri may well rise by 20–30 centimeters in one day, especially if the inflow from the mountains is intense enough. This means that the water temperature varies when you swim from Utøya to Utstranda on the mainland. Small temperature variations can be a shock to the system, and the point to which you're swimming may shift because you're also being carried slightly northward or southward by the current. A badly chilled person also can't think clearly. This may lead to one's making the wrong decision or becoming indifferent.

Furthermore, there's the psychological stress of swimming away from a mass murderer, swimming from vulnerable friends, swimming breathlessly past a pair of sneakers floating in the water. Lake Tyri is not a small pond. Norway's fifth largest lake is 137 square kilometers and nearly 300 meters at its deepest point. The Drammen River overflows its banks when the water level of Lake Tyri rises precipitously. The killer's systematic route around the island, from the campsite via Lovers' Lane and the woods out to the Nakenodden promontory, forces more and more people out toward the waterside. The youths have horrendous images in their heads of their recent experience, and they don't know whether the perpetrator is alone. The waterside is safer, despite the fact that there's a risk they may encounter obstacles with no way of turning back. They can try to hide, they can continue to run along the waterside, or they can swim.

Hildegunn Fallang sits under a rock on the north side, clutching her purse, and wondering whether to swim or not. She ponders until it's no longer safe, when she hears gunshots first to the left, then to the right, from the path behind her. Almost as soon as the first shot is fired, Hildegunn starts running up to Lovers' Lane in the direction of the Nakenodden promontory on the south side. The small brown frogs are everywhere, but the creatures that caused anxiety yesterday are now merely trifles. She loses the little red purse on the way. In it she has credit cards; a driver's license; and a small compact camera with pictures of the foreign minister, Datarock band, Ingrid giving her speech after the Mother of the Nation, and the Calvin Klein watch she got for her confirmation six years ago.

The killer dressed like a police officer has driven the youngsters away from the center of the island through the woods and onto the cliffs, promontories, and beaches. He now walks along the waterside, round and round several times. It doesn't take him long to walk around the entire island. The number of hiding places is limited. Only the fortunate ones avoid running into him. A fifteen-year-old and a sixteen-year-old hide under the old, dilapidated skating ramp in the woods behind the cafeteria building. The killer passes by several times. Three youths hide in the so-called "rock tent" on the southwest of the island. At one point they glimpse black pant legs outside. "Come to me, you're safe with me," they hear him say to many. To dehumanize their enemies the Nazis called the Jews "rats." The Hutus called the Tutsis "cockroaches" during the genocide in Rwanda. The killer on Utøya doesn't draw parallels to pests or vermin. On the contrary, he uses trust-inducing, soothing words. "You can call home to your parents and tell them everything's fine, you're safe," a youngster hears him say soothingly before adding, "Good night."

The scenes that play out on the island are detached from a precise time and place. They take place on various parts of the island, yet they are concurrent in time. One youngster starts swimming on the east side, while another clings to the caves by the waterside on the north. Some hide in the toilet stalls in the main building, while others keep running around and around along Lovers' Lane. The killer doesn't always know where he is, and the victims often don't know either. Time passes fast and slowly at the same time. The pitter-patter of rain, waves against the rocky edge, and wind rustling in the grass are constant, while the gunshots are distant or close.

Tore Sinding Bekkedal has contact with the outside world from the toilet stall in the cafeteria building. He thinks about the paradox that the foreign guests on Utøya this summer repeatedly expressed admiration for the country's democracy, where political opponents openly disagree without fear of reprisals. His frame of mind alternates between grandiose scenarios and prosaic concerns, such as when one of the three in his stall gets a craving for cigarettes and is put in his place with a short moral sermon: "Smoking isn't good for you." The smiles and laughter are quickly replaced by guilt. Tore's text message, which he sent out to concerned friends and acquaintances, says that there are dead people outside his door.

Tore has no time for political analysis; he's more concerned about how he'll survive. He tries all the emergency numbers for the police, ambulance, and fire department. Since he can't get through to the emergency services, he calls his acquaintance at NRK broadcasting. The news photographer is in the government quarter, so Tore is given another NRK number. He whispers as softly as possible that there's shooting on Utøya. When the person on duty, a little perplexed, asks him where Utøya is, Tore gives up any semblance of politeness and shifts from a whisper to a hiss: "Damn

Swede; just ask any Norwegian where Utøya is." The NRK man excuses himself by saying that he's only a technician.

Utøya is no longer a paradise. It's no longer a shining light in the universe, other than those created by an electric current through wafer-thin wires. Mobile phone displays flash under dark tree roots. Computer software refreshes the dagbladet.no webpage automatically in the cafeteria building. The refrigerator lights up the darkened schoolhouse because someone is using its door as a shield.

Human beings are complex creatures. A boy lies bloodied by the waterside and gives a thumbs up to his comrades clinging to the rock face. A seventeen-year-old swims out onto the lake while keeping his buddy with cramps afloat. "Well, now we can finally swim." A nineteen-year-old loses his mobile phone when he jumps from a ledge into Lake Tyri and thinks he's finally got an excuse to buy an iPhone 4. An eighteen-year-old uses his one good eye to count the fingers of his left hand, which hangs by some skin, and is encouraged by the thought that he can still drive a snowmobile because the thumb and index finger are intact. For many youngsters on Utøya, even among the victims, the wounded, and the terrified, humor becomes a defense mechanism; a source of strength; a confirmation of self-control, individuality, and free will.

It's paradoxical to resort to humor in life-threatening situations. But similar paradoxes emerge throughout Utøya this Friday afternoon. The unharmed are the ones who express despair and fear, getting anxious at the sight of abrasions and cuts. They are the ones who panic at the sight of dead bodies. In general the young people who've been shot and badly wounded don't scream. They're not paralyzed with fear or overwhelmed by the chaos, and they don't lose their heads. A fourteen-year-old who has been shot four times in the stomach, shoulder, and thighs thinks it really annoying that she won't get to see the final Harry Potter movie. One reaction is no more human than another. A person's own morphine, the endorphins, reduces pain, anxiety, and stress. The body pumps out more endorphins into the brain and spinal cord of those who are wounded.

"School Massacre." The thought goes through the minds of the forty-seven who have sought refuge in the schoolhouse on the southern tip of the island. The thought association is not unreasonable, even though it's been a long time since the red-painted room was used for teaching. The classroom is supposed to be a safe place, surrounded by staid, reliable adults in a setting where relevant knowledge of the world is transmitted. There're responsible people in the schoolhouse too. The adults from Norwegian People's Aid have ushered the youngsters in, one by one. Some of the girls howl, while some of the guys try to appear tough, saying, "What's up, huh?" Eventually it gets so crowded in the main room that some of the youngsters prefer to hide in one of the four bedrooms. Others pull out the door of the kitchen fridge and use it as a shield. The youngsters do as they're told by the adults: lock the door; turn off the lights; close the thin, purple-green curtains; slide the red sofas in front of openings; take the thin foam mattresses off of the beds and lean them up against the walls to cover the windows; and push tables, chairs, and sofas up against the mattresses. Then they spread themselves out on the floor, lying or sitting against the wall or the big white fireplace. All these measures provide an illusion of safety. All it takes is a kick to the door, a blow against the window, a shot to the lock. Whoever wants to come in is going to come in. Then there'll be no escape for the forty-seven. Some of them are already thinking that this must be the worst place on the island to hide.

A seventeen-year-old imagines how he'll have to escape to Sweden with a bag, weapons, and provisions. A sixteen-year-old doesn't even think that far ahead. He wonders what to have for dinner. When one is paralyzed with the fear of death, other predicaments can seem trivial. A twenty-year-old wonders where she left her purse. A seventeen-year-old answers with just "Love you" to a text message from her unsuspecting father, who wonders what's going on. A younger brother calls his elder brother, who calls his younger brother. Both are on Utøya and both get voicemail. Other youngsters in the schoolhouse are reluctant to close their eyes because of all the surreal images in their heads. Under one of the unpainted pinewood bunk beds a twenty-seven-year-old thinks about a brave girl who went up to the gunman and begged him to stop shooting. The man in the police uniform waited until she came closer. He shot her, first in the chest, then in the head. The boy under the bed sends a text message to his girlfriend and family: "Thanks for everything. You're amazing."

Jorid Nordmelan was sitting on the couch in the living room of the schoolhouse, charging her mobile phone and talking with Lasse when the youngsters and adults from Norwegian People's Aid came rushing in. She did as she was told and pulled the foam mattress off of the bunk bed. Inadvertently the valuables she had hidden under the sleeping bag—a

PC, iPod, and purse—all fell out. After placing a chair in front of the mattress, she hid in the most obvious place: by the doorway between the bedroom and living room.

In Norway it doesn't make any sense, but if you take into consideration the fact that for a year Jorid lived in Indonesia and Vietnam, where the doorway is the safest place to be during the frequent earthquakes, the twenty-year-old is acting logically. Jorid gets intensely irritated by all the whispering and asks the others to shut up. She then feels a little guilty about the harsh tone of voice she has used on the party members, who are younger than she is. So she adds in a milder tone, "It's going to be all right."

The adults from Norwegian People's Aid don't share Jorid's perception of safety. They say the bed is safer. So she moves over to the bunk bed in the far corner, curls her legs up in front of her stomach, and rests her head on her knees. She's scared, but she's even more afraid to show that she's scared. That's because she's one of the oldest, one of those with courage in the heart and sense in the head. When the girl next to her suggests that they should hold each other's hands, it's like a gift from heaven. Those five fingers feel more secure than the doorway, and Jorid feels that she's breathing more calmly. The overwhelming momentary feeling of joy becomes greater when the girl also suggests that they hide under the bed. "Oh God, I'm so glad that you suggested that," Jorid thinks. The best hiding place is obviously under the bed, but again her maturity and pride prevented her from making the proposal. Imagine if Jorid had hidden under the bed, trembling by herself, scared to death, and then it turned out that all the fuss was caused by a game or a prank. Imagine how embarrassing that would have been. The others would have laughed at her nonstop, from Friday afternoon to Sunday morning. Now at least there are two of them who may be making fools of themselves.

Jorid squeezes under the bed by a hair's breadth. She creeps centimeter by centimeter on her stomach. Her buttocks and thighs are thoroughly scraped. She keeps creeping until she can't go any further and is stuck. And there she lies, trapped between the underside of the bed and the laminated floor. The girl who came up with the suggestion weighs a few grams more and is filled with a sudden, inane angst when she realizes she's not able to squeeze under the bed. Instead she has to lie exposed on the floor, with a sleeping bag over her. One of her arms sticks out to hold Jorid's hand under the bed.

Jorid's stomach is rumbling like never before. Had she been sitting in the lecture hall at Oslo University, she would have blushed an intense red, but now she doesn't even get embarrassed. Jorid isn't afraid of losing face anymore; she's just afraid of losing her life. It would have been meaningless if they were discovered and shot due to the sounds of her digestive tract. Seriously. And on top of everything else, she also has to pee. Her buttocks take up too much space under the bed, thus pressing the bladder against the floor, and it's so unfair and painful and incomprehensible. Jorid doesn't understand why her body behaves this way. She and her father lived in Oslo when she was in high school, and they sometimes drove home to Namsos on weekends. Her father is one of those people who likes to beat his own record. No matter how many bottles of soft drinks she had on the way, there was no question of stopping before they arrived home. Hence Jorid developed an admirable ability to hold on. It's no problem for her to hold on for ten hours. But now it's as if her body doesn't belong to her anymore.

Every muscle in the body is set in motion when the gunshots come closer. And then comes the damned silence. Crackling twigs, rustling grass, rhythmical, heavy steps. The dark shadow outside takes hold of the door handle. Next to the door hangs a laminated white sheet of paper announcing a political workshop with Member of Parliament Anette Trettebergstuen. On Thursday she talked for an hour in the schoolhouse on women's part-time work in the health sector: "What's important in the fight for the right to full-time work? What can be done locally in the municipalities?" On the other side of the door a note says, "Remove shoes here." A rusty horseshoe is nailed upside down onto a red pillar outside the building. According to folklore, it should bring good luck to the house.

The thirty-two-year-old takes a few steps back, raises his firearm, and aims at the glass window of the white door. The bullet makes a hole in the couch. Some run into the shower to hide, while one brandishes a knife, ready to counterattack. One of the people from Norwegian People's Aid picks up a lady's shoe that she intends to use as a weapon. The concept of time disintegrates; seconds seem like minutes. The lack of control is paralyzing. The youths and the adults in the schoolhouse have only two choices. If he comes in, everyone dies. If he doesn't come in, everyone survives. Two choices—and the choices are not theirs to make.

Will he bomb the schoolhouse as he bombed the government buildings? A seventeen-year-old from North Trøndelag County wonders what it would feel like to be blown up before the staggering enormity of the thought is replaced by heartwarming platitudes. She wishes the older generation could see them now. The old folks would be so proud! They're only sixteen or seventeen years old, but they hold and comfort each other with reassuring words, telling themselves that they're actually quite all right. Only sixteen or seventeen years old, and they've already acquired the wisdom of war veterans. Jorid sobs under the bed. She's sobbing out of guilt because she's safe. Because she's relieved when the gunshots fade away. Great for them, but a tragedy for others. In the schoolhouse many are crying. They're crying, hyperventilating, and peeing on themselves, out of necessity or fear. One of them gets cold sweats and faints. Another one throws up the remnants of a meal of meatballs and mashed potatoes. Nobody can grasp what has just happened. Why didn't he shoot his way in? Kick down the door? Break a window? He kills in cold blood, unscrupulously and mechanically, but he doesn't dare to open doors for fear of being overpowered by the youths. He needs a raised, loaded weapon between him and his visible victim. One of the folks from Norwegian People's Aid knows about this. He has been on terrorism exercises with the police, where he learned that perpetrators are usually reluctant to go into places where they have no control. Like the fox in the hen house, the thirty-two-year-old goes after the easiest prey. Outside the schoolhouse the youngsters can hear someone begging for life. "No! Don't shoot me!"

The youngsters haven't become cynics yet. Even youngsters who are shot, injured, or in danger have a guilty conscience because they are still alive while others have died. Because they're less injured than their friends. Because they ran past them, didn't help enough, and didn't say the right words when there was a chance. They also worry about the abrupt messages to mom and dad that are causing uncertainty and anxiety back home. The boys and girls have been, or may become, victims of a mass murderer, and yet they're still more concerned about the family back home. The feeling is real and not false modesty. At the same time other emotional forces that are just as difficult to control—panic, fear, the selfish survival instinct—are thrown into the mix. The combination is not unusual. All around the island hundreds of youths are hiding, swimming, or running for their lives with an uneasy feeling in their guts because they may survive. Fifty years ago researchers discovered "KZ syndrome," also known as "survivor guilt." It was widespread among Jews who survived the concentration camps in Germany and Poland. They suffered from depression, fatigue, recurring traumas, nightmares, feelings of guilt and shame, and melancholia, and they were often institutionalized and prescribed alcohol and pills as a cure. The syndrome didn't occur at the time of liberation in 1945 but much later, about 15–20 years after the war.

Ingrid Endrerud has sought refuge in a crevice under a cliff not far from the pump house. The hiding place is good as long as the killer doesn't come by sea. All rock crevices on the north side are shaped the same way except for the one that Ingrid is in. The crevice tapers down toward the water so that her rear and the tips of her rubber boots rest against opposite walls. Moss and pine needles drift down over her. Ingrid took the boat over to Utøya along with the man in the police uniform. She knows what he looks like. It's not unreasonable to imagine that what happened in Oslo is related to what's happening on Utøya now. The eighteen-year-old wonders what would happen if he detonated bombs here too. Would the rock crevice she was in then move and squeeze her flat? A young boy sits and shivers next to her, wearing only underpants. She lends him her beige wool jacket and long gray scarf. Ingrid hasn't seen him before, so she asks him his name, where he comes from, and whether he has been on the island before. "No," the boy says, adding, "This is the first and last time." Ingrid looks at him and smiles sadly. She wants to tell him that it doesn't usually turn out this way on the island.

"What shall we do?" Emma Martinovic asked in a text message. "Swim!" was Eskil Pedersen's forthright reply. The Kristiansand girl and the others in the group on the north side of Utøya take off their clothes. They set their sights on the island of Geitøya. A twenty-six-year-old from Arendal is going in the same direction, so he puts his wallet in his boxer shorts. Emma starts to swim in the freezing water, and the others follow suit. In a few hours, days, months, the eighteen-year-old would say the same thing that hundreds of others on Utøya would say that Friday afternoon that was just turning to dusk: "Suddenly he was just standing there." It happens now—suddenly he's just standing there, on the island, and aiming at those fleeing from him. One youngster in front of Emma is struck. She takes quicker strokes, turns over on her back for a few seconds, and watches him shoot those who never made it to the water. One is shot as he plunges into the water. Emma swims for her life, dedicating each stroke—this one is for mom, this one is for dad, this one is for little brother, and this one is for Robin, my best friend. Emma was born in the middle of the war in Sarajevo. Her father has talked about massacres. Now she finally knows what he's talking about.

Someone tells Emma that she's bleeding. She looks for the wound. Emma doesn't know when she was shot in the left arm. She hears screams, gunshots, and chilling laughter on the island. Then a boy suddenly appears behind her. He wasn't there before. The boy is very young, just a kid. "You're a really good swimmer," she says. He looks at Emma with empty eyes and says, "Dad is dead." She asks him not to look back, just look forward, and swim for dad. "You're really good!" He doesn't need any help, he says, as he's good at swimming. His father has taught him. Emma prays to God while they swim further on. The boy says, "I thought policemen were kind." Emma thought so too. She has long thought about becoming a police officer. She dips her head under water so that he doesn't see her crying. A beautiful, innocent view of the world is shattered. The dream of becoming a firefighter or a police officer, such as young boys like to envision as their calling, is no more. Helping people in need. Fighting evil.

The youngsters are forced out into Lake Tyri, whether they're injured or have aquaphobia, whether they're on the east side, closest to the mainland, or on the west side, facing what seems to be a sea of nothing. Some are swimming with gunshot wounds or dislocated knees, while others console themselves with "To Youth" by Nordahl Grieg to block out the sound of gunshots: "Love and enrich with dreams / all that was great! / Go toward the unknown / wring answers out of it." One girl is on her back, with eyes closed and doing double strokes because she can't actually swim, and she goes off course. A seventeen-year-old from Longyearbyen swims on his back and alternately calls the police, ambulance, and firefighters. On his chest a sixteen-year-old carries a kid who's been shot in the thigh and swims further on, and when he meets a girl suffering from cramps, he takes her in tow to Utstranda on the mainland. Studies show that when people think they're completely depleted of energy, they've actually just used up a third of it. The feats of the sixteen-year-old support that theory.

Khamshajiny Gunaratnam swims from Bolsjevika Bay behind Matti Brox. They have been warned not to do so. Several who've tried have come back because the lake is freezing cold. Before they set off, Matti borrowed a mobile phone that he used to call the police. He hung up instantly when he saw the number to an institution because it occurred to him that it might be a trap. The killer could have placed telephone guards around or even answered himself. Maybe he can trace them. Matti asked "Kamzy," as he calls her, whether they're selfish if they swim off and leave their party colleagues behind on the island. The night before, they'd discussed just that: selfishness, solidarity, community.

"Central committee member seen with sixteen-year-old on Lovers' Lane," was what they could read in *Planet Utøya* earlier in the day, but Matti and Kamzy don't take notice of gossip like that. Last night they repeated the tour and ended up on a rock by the pump house. Matti wondered: if you sacrificed yourself for others, were you doing something altruistic, or did you do it for selfish reasons so you could feel better? The philosophical discussion went back and forth without coming to any conclusion. This afternoon the circumstances demanded a clear answer. "No," Kamzy said.

Kamzy takes off her shirt while Matti does the same with his T-shirt and jacket. He has hidden his valuables—iPod, wallet, keys, and mobile phone—in the soft shell jacket in a bush but has kept his Ray Ban glasses in his jeans. After a few strokes in the water, Kamzy removes her pants. She's not that good a swimmer and is afraid of going into the water. The waves are not as bad as on the ocean on a windy day, but they are taxing. Matti has gone swimming 2–3 times every day since he came to Utøya on Tuesday instead of using the crowded, worn-out lavatory block. He doesn't think that the temperature is excessively low in Lake Tyri. Moreover, he is well trained, thanks to his interest in sports such as soccer, kickboxing, jogging, cycling, skiing, and swimming. He knows he'll manage to cross over to the mainland unless the rumor is true that the police-uniform-clad man has allies who're circling the island by boat. Unlike on Utøya, there are no means of escape on the lake. It's not possible to swim away from a motorboat.

After a hundred meters Matti tells Kamzy to stay focused on reaching Utstranda on the mainland. "Kamzy, don't look back now. You should look straight at the mainland and visualize that as your goal." She says okay. Matti tells her that because he sees the killer on the island aiming at a youngster in a red T-shirt. First, he fires a couple of shots from a distance; then he gets closer and fires three shots to the head. A few minutes ago Matti and Kamzy, as well as twenty-five other youngsters, were hiding there. "If I get shot," Matti says, "or if I show any signs of panic, you must swim further on and fend for yourself and leave me behind." Kamzy doesn't respond. The sixteen-year-old repeats what he has said. "Yeah, whatever; shut up and swim," Kamzy says. When they've come a good distance from the island, Matti turns to Kamzy, puts on an encouraging face, and says "Smile a little, then." The twenty-three-year-old smiles back.

"Someone's shooting; get the hell out," was the message Morten Djupdal and the other youngsters got by the ferry berth on the mainland. The police-uniform-clad man said that two colleagues were coming from Oslo, which meant that they would soon be arriving at the ferry berth. The youngsters saw the MS *Thorbjørn* coming toward them at an unusually high speed and then, midway on the lake, turning right and heading northward. Eskil was reportedly unharmed on board. "We can't just leave," Morten said, but the others insisted on doing so. They piled into a couple of cars and drove up the hill toward county road 155. Morten stopped by a bus stop and looked over to Utøya. The sounds of gunshots were louder and more frequent, and he saw around 40–50 people swimming away from the island. Morten sent a text message to someone he knew was on board the MS *Thorbjørn*, urging the ferry to turn around and pick up the youngsters who were at risk of drowning, but he got no answer. Tearfully he called his father and asked him for advice. "Are there any boats there?" his father asked. Eureka.

The twenty-year-old doesn't answer the question. He and the two youngsters who were with him in the car to Sundvollen drive down to the ferry berth and into a side road where the boats are located. The first vessel they find for their purpose is a yellow paddle boat of the kind that is so popular on tropical beaches. It's not particularly fast and not easy to steer, but Morten is determined to use it as a life raft. The problem is that it's too heavy. They can't budge it at all. Next to it is an unlocked ten-foot motorboat that is full of water. Morten starts to bail the water out but realizes that it's going to take all night to empty it. The consequence of bending down to bail out the water would be felt in the strain on his back in the course of the autumn.

Morten is in the boat alone, wearing only shorts and an AUF T-shirt, and he is barefoot as his slippers are stuck in the mud at the bottom of the boat. He is alone because what he's going to do is dangerous and also because that way he can pick up more people. Morten takes down the engine too early and it gets stuck in the bottom, so he grabs the oars and rows out. "Is there anyone who's struggling?" he yells out on Lake Tyri. The answers are many, ambiguous, and scattered. Some swim away because they think Morten is a killer. All the youngsters don't know all the other youngsters. Behind the youngsters swimming toward him he sees the police-uniform-clad man standing on the Nakenodden promontory and aiming a gun at a youth. And another one goes down. Morten stops for a moment and reasons: the man is obviously aiming to take as many lives as possible. I'm trying to save people, so he will certainly kill me. The twenty-year-old turns his head to the east, south, and north but sees no other boats on the lake. He's the only one who's trying to rescue the youngsters. Morten turns and rows back to the mainland with a boy and a girl in tow.

"We're going to die," Morten says and runs to the campaign car. The youngsters whom he rescued also jump in. He is so afraid that the battery will die on him that he reverses recklessly fast up the narrow slope. He drives at full throttle, causing the clutch to give off a burning smell, and he goes up the slope toward the main road. When he approaches the detour around the Nes tunnel, he runs into Friday traffic going into Oslo. The cars ahead are barely budging. Morten is so scared that he ignores all traffic regulations. He turns the car to the side, blows the horn, and presses his way forward in the direction of the Sandvika police station.

Morten Djupdal hasn't had time to think about the who, what, or why of the events of the day before driving the car to the police station. Nor has he, until now, thought about the explosion in Oslo as a terrorist act. No one knows the motivation of the desperado on Utøya or whether he's alone or part of a larger group, but Morten concludes that the killer must be a man who hates immigrants. He estimates that around a third of the camp participants come from minority backgrounds. Racial diversity in the Labor Party is greater than in other parties. It's not only that the AUF is the largest political youth organization, but also that the party has a deliberate policy of recruiting people from all ethnic backgrounds and sexual orientations. Morten's passengers are a bit worried about his driving speed, especially since he's driving barefoot and speaking incessantly on the phone, so they ask him to calm down. "It would be incredibly tragicomic if we were to die in a car crash now," Morten says and elicits smiles from the two youths who've just swum away from a killer on Utøya.

Around six o'clock the youngsters who are still hiding on the island notice that the shooting has stopped for a few minutes. However, it's not quiet. They can hear an ambulance helicopter above and ambulances on the mainland. In the helicopter are four anesthesiologists who departed from Lørenskog district twenty minutes earlier. They need clearance from the police and have to go toward Sollihøgda district. The youngsters hear and see an ambulance helicopter, but they no longer hear the bullets whizzing toward cliffs, pine trees, and human bodies. The youngsters are hoping that salvation has come. "The world has forgotten us," a nineteen-year-old thinks on a rock ledge at Bolsjevika Bay. Where are the police? Why don't they save us? Johanne Butenschøn Lindheim hears a helicopter circling over Utøya, and she sees blue emergency lights on the mainland and small boats on the lake. Her friend receives disturbing messages on her mobile phone that they can't be saved because the killer has allies who're shooting on the mainland. They really want to escape, but they're getting messages indicating that they can trust neither the police nor the rescue personnel. They have to wait.

The killer has his own plan. According to the plan, the police should have stormed the island by now. The sound of sirens will be clearer when he takes off his earphones. He has called several times without making contact. A youngster's mobile phone is used to call the police emergency phone again. This time he gets through to the operations center. He says that he's a commando in the Norwegian anti-Communist resistance movement, is currently on Utøya, and wishes to surrender. The operator asks what phone number he's calling from. He doesn't know. "Yes. It's not my phone; it's another ...," the thirty-two-year-old says before the call is cut off. "Another? What's your name? Hello ... hello. ..."

The mobile phone network has been brought to its knees. The police can't call back as the phone number doesn't appear on the display. They must wait for him to call back. He throws away the mobile phone. He has killed enough people for the 2083 compendium to get the attention it deserves. He could sit down and wait. But he doesn't. He goes further on, into the woods. He screams, "You'll die today, Marxists!" in order to frighten the youngsters and herd them into the lake. He lures them out with reassuring words: "I'm from Police Security! I'll protect you! Don't be afraid." When he is at his most calculating, he says the things that young people want to hear. They've called the police several times—sooner or later help should arrive. It could be right now or it could be later.

One of those who really wants to believe him is Stine Renate Håheim. The member of parliament is hiding under a rock ledge with younger party members. There are many such groups along the waterside, and there's one not too far away from them, about thirty meters west, at the pump house. Brightly colored clothes are discarded and thrown far away.

The younger ones sob while the older ones comfort them or hold their hands over their mouths to stop them from screaming. Regardless of age, they're soaking wet and cold. There are sounds of sobbing, waves crashing on the rocks, and the fear of soft footsteps on the rugged forest terrain. Stine Renate stands barefoot on slippery rocks in a thin red and white checkered dress, wet and thoroughly frozen, and doesn't feel the bleeding from wounds she got while she was running along the waterside from Bolsjevika Bay.

Up until now she has kept despair at bay with the help of trivialities and practical challenges. But even little things threaten to paralyze her into inaction. On Bolsjevika Bay she'd lent her mobile phone to others. When responses from mothers, fathers, or friends came in, she had to deal with them. "Are you my son? I must speak with him," one text message said. Stine Renate turned and looked at the boy. She didn't dare to get up to deliver the message to him. Moreover, the phone battery was low. She had to answer but couldn't respond rashly and thoughtlessly. She couldn't write that he was safe. That everything was okay. She couldn't write that he'd come safely home as that was a promise she didn't know she could keep. The sequence of letters was not arbitrary. Words come with obligations. Sentences mean something. "He's here. We're doing the best we can," Stine Renate replied to a mother who wanted to talk to her son.

A man comes down from Lovers' Lane toward the pump house. Glad tidings spread from youth to youth on the north side of the island: "The police are here, we're safe." Stine Renate throws herself around the neck of a friend, sobbing with relief. A couple of happy youngsters spring up from their hiding places. The Valdres girl raises her head and looks toward the pump house. Up to now she'd thought that the perpetrator was a crazy loner who stood in the cafeteria building shooting around wildly and that he would keep shooting until he ran out of ammunition. She thought that the shooter believed that a Muslim terrorist organization was behind the explosion in Oslo and that he had come here to Utøya to take revenge on the foremost defender of multicultural Norway—the AUF. Now she sees that he has been carrying out his plan. Wearing a uniform, controlled and systematic, he was going to take six hundred lives. There's no escape on the island anymore because sooner or later he'll get every last one. The politician from Oppland County and the boys turn around and run back to Bolsjevika Bay. Stine Renate loses her mobile phone among the rocks on Lake Tyri.

13

Rubber Boots Left Behind

Visitors from Norway and abroad return to Utvika Camping year after year. The population of the little summer community is varied and is far from the homogeneous common perception. People such as roofers, teachers, bank managers, and doctors come to this campsite. Utvika Camping is managed by Torill and Brede Johbraaten and their daughter Anita, and it is a place that's suitable for families with children. Loud laughter and music is frowned upon after eleven in the evening. The regulars feel that Utvika Camping has everything: swimming and fishing, swings, a playhouse, two trampolines, and a sandy beach for the children. The campers are very neighborly; there's fresh bread for sale every day, a licensed cafe, shrimp evenings, and often a red sunset over the hills to the west of Lake Tyri.

Today has been a day of nature trails, ball playing, air-gun shooting, and other activities for the campers to get to know each other better. Hence many are enjoying a glass of wine or a beer together and talking about the explosion in Oslo before they fire up the grill. In the part of the camp called Hylla guests have an unobstructed view of Utøya. They have seen the ferry, the MS *Thorbjørn*, turn abruptly northward midway through the lake, and they have thought no more about it. They have been taken aback by yellowish- and reddish-brown fumes by the schoolhouse and the information house on Utøya. They thought it strange that there were fireworks on the island, considering what has happened in Oslo. They have seen that some youngsters have been running a swimming race over to the mainland again, as a couple of them have been doing each year, to show off. They have seen the smaller Utøya boat, the *Reiulf*, and thought that it was serving as an escort to those in the swimming race. All these observations could be logically explained. On the other hand, cries for help can hardly be misinterpreted.

When there's a roar from the soccer field or messages are broadcast on speakers on Utøya, they can hear it at Utvika Camping. Music and noise late into the night have diminished in recent years, but the noise problem has been a recurring topic of discussion between Utøya's administrator and the island's neighbors. In the summer of 2002 VG wrote an article about an Irish family who was chased away from Utøya. The family, who had borrowed a boat from the camp, wanted to go ashore on the island to soak up the sun on a rock face. The case was embarrassing for the AUF and the Labor Party. A party that was supposed to keep the beaches of Norway open to all and sundry had denied harmless, friendly tourists access to its property. This wasn't the first time this had happened either, as the campsite owner told the journalist. Utøya's administrator maintained that the party had full rights to safeguard the Labor movement's private paradise. The argument was that closed events require admission. Boat tourists could come and visit when there wasn't something special happening on the island, but in reality there were events on Utøya almost continuously all summer.

The cards have now been reshuffled. Now other temporary and paradoxical rules of the game prevail. The cornerstones of the Norwegian welfare state are the police, the military, the fire departments, and the health care system. Soldiers, nurses, police officers, and firefighters come to our aid in times of need, protect us from internal and external threats, salve our wounds, and put out fires. We trust the state and its servants. The threshold for calling the emergency phone number is low. On the other hand, neighbors, colleagues, or random passersby at the tram stop are looked on with suspicion. But green, black, and white uniforms, with yellow stripes or badges, put us at ease. But the reality is quite different. When your boat is about to sink, your Toyota has run off the road, or you have been struck down on a street downtown, the people who come to your aid are ordinary men and women. It's the man in the street or the woman on the sidewalk who saves your life—those who happen to be present there and then, before the professionals arrive at the scene. And so it was to be at Lake Tyri on a Friday afternoon, July 22.

While the local police are waiting impatiently for the Emergency Response Unit from Oslo, the campers and local residents get into their boats and head toward Utøya. The boatmen have no rule books, hierarchical structures, or strict instructions; they have not undergone countless exercises; nor have they bulletproof vests, visors, or weapons with scopes. The people on the mainland set the operation in motion via autopilot. Some start the engine or set in the oars to row; many pick up life jackets, blankets, towels, and sweaters from the caravans. It's not possible to just stand and watch young people drown.

Four boats head out at roughly the same time from the campsite: a yellow boat; a white, open console boat with superstructure; a white dinghy; and a red rental boat from Utvika. The boats spread out between the north and west sides and the east and south sides. The boatmen find out from the first youngsters they pick up that there's shooting on Utøya, but the information is confusing and inconsistent. Most of those who are pulled up into the boats are not very talkative. They cling to the deck, dig their nails into the plastic, or mumble "Bloody hell" repeatedly until they are set down on the campsite pier. One youngster is so angry that he tries to lift up a huge stone weighing hundreds of kilos from the pier. Some swim away from the boats out of fear, while others ask suspiciously about the boatman's name, occupation, and motivation. Conflicts are inevitable. For some girls and boys it's unacceptable to get closer to the island to pick up more people, while the boatman feels obliged to fill up the vessel. At other times it's the youngsters who insist on going all the way back to the island to pick up friends while the boatman is reluctant to get too close. Misunderstandings are just as unavoidable: the boatmen who first head toward the island to get a wider turning radius before swinging the bow around are met with howls of protest from the youths who are convinced that they have been abandoned. Such a U-turn is made only once by the boatman.

Considering the number of youngsters who swim out from Utøya and the condition some of them are in, it's a miracle that only one of them drowns. This can be explained by the fact that the boatmen, campers on shore, and the youngsters keep calm during the most critical phases. The boatmen don't yell at each other; they signal with their hands. Youngsters who don't have life jackets or other buoyant objects to cling to are taken up first. Generally the boats are not filled with too many people at a time; if a boat gets too heavy, it slows down or risks taking in water. Some youngsters with leadership experience take responsibility and direct boatmen to the ones most in need. Some are more than stoical—in any case seemingly so. The first thing a boy says to one of the boatmen who pulls him up is, "Oh, I left my rubber boots behind." When one of the boats runs out of gas, it gets a refill from a camper who has the presence of mind to mix oil with gasoline before he hands the can over.

A dozen civilian boats pick up hundreds of young people while bullets whizz around them. Out on the water they not only risk their lives, but they also have to make difficult choices. Sometimes they head toward the mainland while youngsters scream for help behind them. The gratitude of the youngsters will be eternal, but the cabin residents and campers on the mainland are also witnesses to a sight that will be hard to forget: young girls and boys who are struck by expanding bullets and have gunshot wounds the size of saucers, who have all their teeth shot out, and who hyperventilate and scream in despair because they have seen their brothers and sisters killed.

Matti Brox and Khamshajiny Gunaratnam suspect that the boats they have seen set out from Utvika Camping belong to accomplices of the assailant. The thought is, paradoxically enough, rational. What happens, happens. They are less certain when an approaching boatman throws out life jackets to them before heading on to Utøya. Matti tries to signal to the next boat that they should pick up people who are further away from the mainland, but the boat has already stopped beside them. Matti and Kamzy have been swimming for thirty minutes and have covered about half the distance between Utøya and the mainland. The rescue boat is bobbing beside them.

Kamzy doesn't feel safe. She thinks they are still within range of the killer's machine gun. She climbs up the ladder at the rear of the boat and sits on the deck. Matti follows close after and takes a seat. The boat operator turns the bow around and returns to the pier at Utvika Camping.

Ingrid Endrerud is still standing in the rock crevice at the north side of the island. A gang of youths was just swimming away from the pump house and stopped a moment in front of her. "No, don't stop here," she thought, a desperate look in her eyes. The hiding place is perfect for one or two persons but not for twenty. When they swam on, she took off her T-shirt, pants, and rubber boots. She kept her woolen socks on because she has learned that wool stays warm even if it gets wet. But probably not if you're swimming, which she intends to do now. She has kept a cool head for a period that now feels like an eternity. After two strokes she realizes that it is the most stupid thing she has ever done.

She's convinced that the killer is on the cliff above her. She takes quick, short strokes and is absolutely sure that he is raising his rifle and aiming at her. Ingrid swims for her life, not because there actually is a person on top of the cliff aiming at her but because she *knows* that he is and that at any moment she'll be shot in her legs, back, and head. The eighteen-year-old is so convinced of this that she doesn't swim the shortest route to the boat but swims around the back, to stay under cover. Ingrid is dragged over the boat's gunwale and can see with her own eyes that there's no man on the cliff at the north side of Utøya. A dripping wet and ice-cold

Ingrid, with wet socks, is given a towel before the boat moves further on. The boat has a Manchester United soccer club logo. "My brother isn't going to like that," she thinks. Ingrid's brother is a Liverpool fan.

Stine Renate doesn't have much physical stamina, but she's a good swimmer. Nevertheless, she has been reluctant to start swimming in the lake from the north side due to the cold and the distance. After seeing the gunman at the pump house, she's no longer in doubt. They must get as far away as possible from Utøya. As she and the boys are about to swim out from Bolsjevika Bay on the north side, she sees two boats on the lake. "Can we trust them?" asks one of the youngsters. "No," Stine Renate replies, but she believes that they no longer have a choice. When they swim out, with her in front, they see that one boat is heading west toward youngsters who are further away from the mainland. Stine Renate thinks that it makes sense. She becomes more worried when she sees that the other boat is also moving away. On board she sees the foreign guest from Lebanon with whom she played volleyball. "We can't leave without Stine," he says to the boatman in English.

The twenty-seven-year-old swims with all the strength her arms can muster until her hands grip the gunwale. The boat, bobbing a hundred meters from shore, is high above the water surface and without a ladder. Stine Renate hangs on to the boat, without the strength to lift herself up. She's told that she has to try to raise herself up, and she manages to lift one leg up. It's not working. She hangs on until the boys reach the boat and push her up from behind. Stine Renate rolls over onto the boat in her wet summer dress and with bruised feet. She has to crawl forward to make room for the others. Foremost on the boat there's already a boy wearing only boxer shorts, with chattering teeth, shaking and howling wildly. She tries futilely to make contact with him. She cozies up to the boy to try to warm him. She's not aware that her body temperature is as cold as his.

The first two youngsters from Utøya to arrive at Utvika Camping are led up to the Johbraaten family's private house. The shocked boys get towels and are offered coffee or tea, food, and a hot shower, but they don't have much of an appetite. Torill calls the emergency number and requests ambulances to the campsite. She's told that it's not possible. Torill is too busy taking care of the youngsters to be bothered by the rejection. She will have to manage by herself. The youngsters say they want to get as far away as possible, away from the man dressed in a police uniform "with blond hair," and she has to try to convince them that they are safe now. After that there are so many boys and girls arriving at the white house that the youngsters have to be diverted to the camp's cafeteria. When the towel cabinet is empty and some of the towels have been used a second time around, sheets, blankets, pillows, shirts, and sweaters are taken from private houses, cabins, and caravans. In the cafeteria there's more than enough food and beverages, but the youngsters are more concerned about borrowing phones to find out how their friends have fared. The TV sets in the cafeteria and in the camp owners' house are turned off. Not everyone can bear to watch any more distressing news.

While Torill takes care of the youngsters in the house and Anita organizes help in the cafeteria, Brede drives the youngsters off to Sundvollen in his Subaru. He meets ambulances on the road and asks them to go to the campsite, where a steady stream of youngsters is arriving. They answer that their orders are to stay exactly where they are until the area has been secured. Brede thinks it strange that civilians are still allowed to drive around in the area. He makes several trips back and forth between Utvika and Sundvollen. Neighbors and campers also make trips back and forth. Private cars are stopped along the road to be packed full of young people. Several of the youngsters refuse to get into the cars. And when the kids who are in the car see a uniform, they try to hide.

Ambulances and police cars don't go to Utvika Camping, where over two hundred young people are rescued and brought to shore; they head toward the ferry berth for the MS *Thorbjørn*. Two police officers arrive at the pier a little before 6:00 p.m., armed with machine guns, but they were told to secure the suspect's vehicle, requisition boats, and wait for the Emergency Response Unit from Oslo. Three ambulances are withdrawn because there were reports of gunshots fired at the pier. The killer's assault rifle has high-velocity rounds that have a range of 3,600 meters. The distance between Utøya and Utstranda is six hundred meters. Residents, cabin owners, and campers who have flocked to offer aid are in danger.

Matti Brox and Khamshajiny Gunaratnam see neither the police nor the ambulances when they come to shore, only campers who come to them with fleece blankets. A woman asks Matti whether he is all right. "There's a massacre going on over there," Matti answers. His instinct is to keep running, up toward Krokskogen, to live as a partisan. Instead he is escorted to a house where he is offered a shower and food. Matti doesn't want to take a shower. "No thanks; I just want to get away from here."

Then a man says that an assembly point has been established at the Esso gas station in Sundvollen. Can he take them there? "Yes," he replies in a manner that sounds unnervingly stoic to Matti. He just has to fetch his driver's license first.

Matti, Kamzy, and four other youngsters are driven to the gas station in a car. A group of youngsters has already gathered there. A girl from Buskerud is crying because she doesn't know where her sister is. They borrow phones and are given promotional garments from Esso. Kamzy wants to be alone for a while and takes the garments and a cup of coffee with her into the staff cloakroom. Just when she has finished changing, a man comes abruptly through the door, making her tip the cup of coffee over the Esso garments, and she has to change again. Suddenly someone sticks a phone in Kamzy's face and says that Culture Minister Anniken Huitfeldt, who earlier in the day landed in Molde to attend the jazz festival, wants to talk to her. Huitfeldt wonders what has happened and gets a question in return: "Why have the police taken so long?"

Kamzy and the youngsters sit on bar stools by the high, round tables in the middle of the gas station, next to the rows of candy, potato chips, and DVDs, in front of the counter with bacon sausages, hamburgers, and buns. A woman, whom they assume is a police officer, comes in and starts asking them questions: "What did you see? How many were shooting? How did you escape from the island?" But something isn't right. The questions are not the ones a police officer would normally ask. Kamzy gets a queasy feeling: "I'm sorry, but are you a police officer?" "No," she replies, "I'm a journalist." The youngsters are furious. They realize that the journalist has come in under false pretenses. All the other people from the press are standing and waiting outside. One of the youngsters yells, "Get out!" Matti has picked up some words from his polyglot friends, and now they are put to good use. The sentence in Serbian contains the word "mother," but there's no chance that it would be misinterpreted as a declaration of love: "Jebem ti mater!"

Johanne Butenschøn Lindheim had expected a huge battalion of ambulance personnel, police officers, and journalists. Instead she's greeted by campers with towels on the stone pier. The boatman had said he could not take any more people in the boat, but Johanne insisted that they make room for her and her friend. A girl was crying and screaming during the whole trip over, while another kept asking for her boyfriend. A boy held Johanne around the shoulder and said, "I don't know who you

166 RUBBER BOOTS LEFT BEHIND

are, but listen to me. This is best for the dead. We have to get out of here. They would have wanted it that way, you understand?" His voice was firm and determined and effective. She pressed her friend's hand and became noticeably calmer.

On the stone pier at Utvika Camping Johanne is told that they are moving straight on to a hotel. The people from Oslo get into a Volvo xc90 and ask where they are being transported. "To Sundvollen," replies the driver. Johanne learns that her good friend, the AUF leader for Oslo, is dead. The youngsters embrace each other in the back seat. Johanne thinks people must be in shock. They don't know what they have seen. It needn't be true. It can't be true.

Stine Renate Håheim is the last to disembark from the boat onto the pier at Utvika Camping. The mood on board was ambiguous. Relief was mixed with the fear that the people on the boat were some of the very few survivors. When Stine Renate raised herself onto the boat, she saw the cuts and wounds on her feet. She had been bleeding and staining the deck. She felt sorry, apologized, and offered to wash the boat. Then she said, "Thank you for the trip." Even as the words came out of her mouth, she realized that the excessive courtesy appeared suspicious. Stine Renate went into campaign mode. She smiled and wanted to be nice to everybody. She saw a man coming down the pier from the camp with a fuel tank and smiled at him. She saw men and women come with blankets and sweaters and smiled at them. Here people actually did show up to help, she thought, and she smiled. Stine Renate gets a black fleece jacket and smiles. No one smiles back.

Stine Renate is told to go up to the camp cafeteria. She walks past the Johbraaten family's white house, the red barn, more red cabins, and a playground with a trampoline, and she thinks that it's unduly far to her destination. She walks on gravel and stones and for the first time feels the pain of her wounds. In the cafeteria she discovers that there are more youngsters who have survived than she first thought. She hugs the people there. "We need to create a system," she says to a party member from Troms. Someone has to take responsibility and make a list of those who have survived. Stine Renate shifts from campaign mode to administrative mode. "Find a pen and some paper." The party member finds a pen and paper in the lobby. "First, write down your name; then write down my name." The party member does as he is told. "Now we can go around and ask people their names." Stine Renate doesn't get very far. Someone from the camp comes over to the lobby and wonders what they are doing. "We're creating a system," she says. That's great, they're told, but someone else has already thought of that.

Stine Renate has no concrete plans to leave the camp. She has no desire to sit in a car at all. These motorists, as she calls them, have all sorts of strange motives for the things they do. She would have remained at Utvika indefinitely if she hadn't met a young girl from northern Norway. She's afraid. She can't find her brother. She fears that her brother has been shot on Utøya. "Then I think it's wisest that you go to the Sundvolden Hotel," Stine Renate says. The young girl has been told that they have set up a registration system at the hotel that is now an assembly point, but she doesn't dare to get into a stranger's car. Stine Renate thinks a bit and concludes that she needs to be accompanied. "Would it help if I sit in the car with you?" The girl nods.

The driver, who stops his car on the square in front of the cafeteria, looks trustworthy. But if there's anything the young people on Utøya have learned this day, it's that first impressions can be misleading. "Has anyone seen him before?" Stine Renate shouts down to the campers. "Do you know who he is?" They are told that he lives in the area. The driver has to remove a child seat to accommodate as many passengers as possible. That little detail—that he has children—allows Stine Renate to let her guard down, but no more so than that she deliberately sits directly behind the driver so that she can hit him over the head with something sharp if it turns out that he is driving in the wrong direction. That scenario isn't really plausible as she has no hard object with which to hit him, but the paranoid attitude nevertheless says a lot about what has been lost on Utøya—at least for now.

Full Secret Service Bonanza

14

"Hello, I'm actually awake here!" The doctors don't hear him, and they carry on digging out the heart and lungs, holding them in the palms of their hands, and weighing them, as if they are butchers, not surgeons. He needs more anesthetics and fewer concerns, but no one can make himself understood by making only gurgling sounds. This is really disgusting, thinks the young man who switches channels on the TV at home when blood appears on the screen.

Eivind Thoresen was the third one into the ER. The paramedics were convinced that he wouldn't survive. Nevertheless, they tried to save him. The siren wasn't functioning, so the driver blew the car horn from Møllergata to Ullevål Hospital, cursing all the way. Eivind was attended by doctors who concluded that he probably had internal bleeding. Therefore the twenty-five-year-old had to be operated on immediately, and they had to give him a type of anesthetic that could produce hallucinations. "Don't be afraid," the doctor said. Eivind wasn't afraid, just thirsty—a thirst that comes from having walked on foot in the desert. He wants a Coke. But the doctors couldn't give him one before the surgery. Water then? No, not that either. Eivind was irritated. What is the point of stopping internal bleeding if one dies of thirst anyway? A nurse dipped a sponge into lukewarm water and moistened the law student's lips before the anesthetic started working and the thirst disappeared.

Eivind lies on the operating table under the bright lamp and sees eight snapshots going around in a circle. First he becomes dizzy and just wants to close his eyes. Then he recognizes the contours of his own childhood. There's the boy playing soccer in the garden, in the street, and on the pitch. Still images are replaced by four-second video clips, also from his childhood and soccer playing. The images feel reassuring and comforting and serve to remind him of his safe childhood. So he gets confused and upset when the images turn into a sharp, dazzling light. Eivind is awake, conscious, and pensive. There's nothing that is feigned about him or the situation. Yet his mind brings up associations to Hollywood. The light he sees is what he has seen in countless American movies, a light

168

that always comes at the end of the story, toward the end of one's life, when the soothing, lilting, fluid music stops abruptly. Then the clear, bright light is replaced by total darkness. Eivind knows it's coming. There. Now. There are no more stills from childhood or the seductive, beautiful sunlight. Twenty-five-year-old Eivind Thoresen from the Oslo suburb of Nordstrand, once a promising soccer player, now a budding lawyer, looks into an empty void.

We've lost him. Damn it. The sound is far away. The surroundings are dark, but Eivind can still hear. Blood circulation ceases, but death is not the result. Nurses get the defibrillator. While current from a machine is pumped into Eivind's chest, he thinks of how little he has gotten out of life. He should have traveled farther and more frequently. He should have spent more time with friends, family, and his partner and said all the warm, comforting words that were thought of or not thought of. I love you. I miss you. You're amazing. But it was not to be. The funeral has started. The organist plays in a minor key, the priest speaks movingly, and family members in the front row are crying. So many people have come to the church. Eivind was popular. Eivind was a likeable boy. Eivind would have become something big. He sees his elder brother and girlfriend each put red roses on the coffin. Anne-Tine cries and breaks down. This isn't a dream. It feels intense and more real than the reality of yesterday. Doctors said that the anesthetic would give him hallucinations, that he shouldn't be afraid, and that everything would be all right. Eivind wasn't worried about that. He just wanted something to drink.

When the bomb went off just before half past three in Oslo, the explosion was the worst thing that had happened to little Norway for a long time. The government quarter looked like a war zone; eight people were killed, and dozens were injured. Add to that the sneaking suspicion that the explosion was not an accident but a terrorist act where the perpetrator or perpetrators were still at large. Every Norwegian who wasn't directly affected sat glued to the continuous stream of TV broadcasts on NRK and TV2, either at home or at the summer cabin. Even Norwegians abroad gathered spontaneously at places where they could follow the news minute by minute. Then a rumor started spreading that something had happened on Utøya. The Labor Party secretariat was holding a meeting at a private address on Heimdalsgata when the first unsettling messages from the AUF came in. Party secretary Raymond Johansen got hold of Eskil Pedersen, who confirmed the news and verified that he was safe. The party secretary got into his own private Volvo with Pål Martin Sand and drove toward Hønefoss. In the car they talked about the fact that perhaps it was the Labor Party the terrorist was trying to attack.

Up to now it has been about saving lives, while the motivation for the attack has been a subordinate issue. Yet the driving forces behind such an attack are important for an understanding of what has struck the government quarter and Utøya. A terrorist act directed against the government quarter can be interpreted as an attack on Norway and the Norwegian government, regardless of whether it's Kjell Magne Bondevik (the former Norwegian prime minister) or Jens Stoltenberg who is prime minister. From al-Qaeda's perspective it's irrelevant whether the government is red or blue politically. It wants to take revenge on what it perceives as a prolonged neo-imperialistic crusade carried out by the West against the East, by Christians against Muslims, by the rich against the poor, and where our involvement in the war in Libya fits into its established worldview. The attack on the government quarter would, reasonably enough, be considered an attack against Norway.

If the Labor movement is the target, there are concrete political motives behind the attack. The victims in the government quarter don't necessarily share the prime minister's political views. They are bureaucrats, secretaries, or security guards who will keep their jobs regardless of the political hue of the government, or they just happen to be passersby. The people on Utøya were killed for their political convictions, which are not shared by everyone in Norway. Even between the AUF and the Labor Party there are sometimes differences in opinion regarding the environment, the EU, or a multicultural society. The AUF party members were killed because they believed in something that was the opposite of that of the thirty-two-year-old from Skøyen. The attack on Utøya must be interpreted as an attack against specific political values.

Of those directly affected by the attack very few care about ideology on that Friday afternoon. State secretary Roger Ingebrigtsen in the Defense Ministry, a long-time AUF member, receives news of the massacre while he is on board a flight from Tromsø to Oslo. He knows that his fourteen-year-old stepdaughter is on the island, where he has spent many a summer. The cabin crew recognizes the state secretary. He says he has family on Utøya. The Norwegian Air stewardess gives him a hug. The captain lets him into the cockpit so he can charge his mobile phone. Originally Ingebrigtsen was going to Oslo because Defense Minister Grete Faremo had called him in to work, but now his attention has shifted from the government quarter to Utøya.

Oda Faremo Lindholm rocks back and forth on the couch. The brain has stalled. There's no room for more news. TV footage from the government quarter blends in with her own fresh, unprocessed impressions. If Joddski hadn't been delayed, if there had been fewer digressions on the tape, if she hadn't stopped writing to eat ice cream at the sendoff for the culture editor, she would probably have gone out the door to Grubbegata and past Einar Gerhardsen Square toward Ullevålsveien just about the time the bomb went off. After the explosion Oda was instructed on the phone by her mother to go to her boyfriend's in Majorstua district. Go by way of the Norwegian Theater, not the parliament building. Stay away from Karl Johansgate. Go alongside Palace Park and not through it. Oda went past all the people streaming toward the city center and wondered to herself whether they were being foolish. She broke down when she realized that she, her boyfriend, her father, and her mother were all safe. People stopped on the street to inquire whether she was injured.

Concerned friends have called, texted, or otherwise communicated via the social media. They know where Oda works and who her mother is. One friend said that she was sure that a crazy right-wing white man was behind the explosion in the government quarter, while others posted on Facebook, warning against prejudging Norwegian Muslims. Her mother mentioned nothing about the fact that she thought the bomb was related to Norway's troop deployment in Afghanistan or Libya, as the news media were speculating. Terrorism is often discussed around their dinner table. With an uncle who is a human rights philosopher with Islam as a specialty, Oda knows that terrorists like to target populated areas in order to kill as many people as possible. The explosion in the government quarter doesn't fit that profile. It seems as if the goal is to attract attention rather than to kill as many people as possible.

Furthermore, Oda has private reasons for not needing to vent dogmatic ideas about which Muslim terrorist organization is responsible, as so many others have done in the hours after the explosion. Muslims have not called up Oda in the middle of the night to tell her they're going to kill her father and kidnap her mother before they take over Norway; ethnic Norwegians have done so. Oda has never felt threatened by al-Qaeda. She feels threatened by angry and crazy individuals.

Oda noted a change in her mother after the murder of the Swedish foreign minister, Anna Lindh. Before September 2003 she had not taken death threats seriously, even when they came frequently. Politicians are just not killed, not in Norway. The day the Swedish minister died on the operating table after being stabbed while shopping at the NK mall in Stockholm was the first time the fifteen-year-old had seen her mother cry. She was crying not because she knew Anna Lindh particularly well but because she realized that the assassination most likely would involve stricter security measures around her, her family, and other politicians and that it was only a matter of time before something similar happened in Norway.

Oda calls it "full secret service bonanza." The security detail met Oda and her boyfriend in front of the house on Oslo's west side after her mother called, extremely stressed, and asked it to go there at once. The police wanted to get all those who were particularly "vulnerable" out of the city center. A few years ago Grete Faremo wouldn't have accepted such a comprehensive security detail around her and her family, especially not in private. When Oda interviewed her mother for the monthly *Natt & Dag* in 2010, the reporter asked the minister whether she felt that she could walk around Oslo safely. The answer was, "Absolutely. It's safe. It may still be risky when it comes to city traffic. That sort of thing. The fact that we have had some violent situations, assaults on trams and buses, in Norway doesn't make me change my assertion that it's safe to travel via public transport, but you should nevertheless always keep your eyes and ears open."

The age of innocence is over. Further shaken by the news from Utøya, Oda can't bear to rock back and forth on the couch anymore, and she tells the others that she's going for a walk. She's not allowed to do that unless everyone in the house joins in. So Oda, her boyfriend, and her father and mother all take a walk around the neighborhood on the west side, with bodyguards trailing behind. The security car drives behind them at three kilometers an hour.

What shall I do with my uniform? Will I ever use it again? Is my workplace likely gone? Hanne Gro Lille-Mæhlum is back home in her apartment in Majorstua and has changed from the guard uniform and blue socks she got at the emergency ward into jeans and a sweater. They're moving into a new apartment in a week's time, so the living room is full of cardboard boxes, suitcases, and stuff to be discarded. The thirty-three-year-old doesn't want to have anything behind or next to her. She feels a strong urge to get away from the mess, having been clamped under a glass window in a bombed-out government building. She wants to get out into the open, to Frogner Park. But the police have advised everyone to stay indoors.

Hanne Gro has no mobile phone. She left it in the lobby of S-Block. She logs into Facebook to search for signs of life and information from colleagues. Some respond immediately, and she sits on the couch and chats. She hears nothing from others. She also updates her own status: "Was at work when it happened—am all right under the circumstances. Have no mobile." Her partner is in the kitchen following the news. He says something about Utøya. Hanne Gro tells him that she can't bear to hear about other news now. The guard from S-Block is convinced that the car bomb must have been in the car parked next to the Aurora statue on Einar Gerhardsen Square, just a few meters from the glass enclosure in which she sat.

It's not uncommon to feel elated and immortal after one has survived a life-threatening situation. Hanne Gro has felt listless all summer. Now she feels an intense elation. She has survived, and she feels that she has come through a great trial. "Now it's my turn to get lucky," thinks Hanne Gro.

Although the people of Oslo have been advised to stay indoors and certainly away from the city center and the apartment they rent is a stone's throw away from the prime minister's residence, the Foreign Ministry, and the Royal Palace, Hanne Gro suggests they go to the supermarket to buy groceries. For them tacos are always associated with cozy dinners on Friday and amusing television entertainment. Hence they put the ingredients for pita pizza into the shopping cart. "Sauce with basil or garlic?" asks Anders. Hanne Gro doesn't care. She limps absent-mindedly and sullenly around in the local grocery store and feels uncomfortable getting too close to the shelves. She feels bruised and dizzy. The cut over her eye looks just like a nasty black eye. So when she later meets a neighbor, she feels a strong desire to explain that she hasn't been in a fight. She has only been on the job in the government quarter.

15

A Blue Hymn

When the Oslo police receive information about the shooting on Utøya at half past five, they believe the message is genuine. A second attack is likely. The police have examined the car bomb outside the government building and have discovered the identity of the person who rented the car. They already know that he has right-wing sentiments and that he has registered three weapons legally. On the third floor of the staff room at the police station in Oslo there's a policeman who is also a parent. His daughter is on Utøya. A few minutes before half past five she called and said that Utøya was under attack by a gunman. Several people had already been killed. The men in the Emergency Response Unit get into their cars in the government quarter and drive toward Utøya. Along the way they have trouble contacting the North Buskerud police, but they speak with the policeman's daughter twice and obtain information about the unfolding situation. In Oslo the communications system is modern and has a high bandwidth. In North Buskerud they have to use the emergency network the old way—with slow analog lines and a fax. Oslo and North Buskerud both use their own frequency range. Furthermore, the telecommunications network is overloaded. At two minutes past six the Emergency Response Unit finally makes contact. There's a red French-made Zodiac II 550 dinghy waiting for them. The Buskerud police bought it in 1998. The dinghy is well used. The 16.1-foot (barely five-meter) dinghy has, in theory, a payload of 1,010 kilos. Ten grown men carrying heavy equipment will try to fit into it.

They don't board the dinghy from the mainland across from Utøya, where the sound is six hundred meters wide, but from Storøya island, 3.6 kilometers further north. The police use several minutes to board the ten men. It's risky. If the dinghy sinks, ten men will end up in the water with heavy equipment. One of the police officers is the boat operator. Behind them just as many eager policemen wonder excitedly whether it's really going to work. Police cars stand fifty meters behind them, with blue emergency lights flashing. While they load the dinghy, more policemen arrive. They have no boat to get into. This is the only one. The policemen load the dinghy on land. This means that they have no idea of the weight it can handle. When it's taken into the water, it sinks up to the gunwale.

After fifteen meters the boat operator notices that the engine is starting to misfire. Colleagues on shore go across the pontoon bridge to Storøya. They walk past a dozen leisure boats that could have taken them out onto the lake. One of them tries hot-wiring the engines but to no avail. After a hundred meters the red dinghy's stern is lying dangerously low in the water. The crewmen start unzipping their jackets. Each person is wearing a bulletproof vest, helmet, and an MP5 machine gun—a total of twenty-five kilos of equipment per person. They will sink to the bottom if the Zodiac is not able to stay afloat. After a couple of hundred meters the red boat is barely visible—just black-clad men moving on the water next to a mounted blue light.

The boat takes in water. Colleagues on the bridge go back and forth. The Emergency Response Unit drives past yet another marina full of spacious fast boats. Just a little later the boat starts to slow down. The engine splutters a bit before dying. They have been on the water for five minutes. The boat operator becomes angry and frustrated. Young people are being shot at on Utøya, and here they are, goofing around on the lake. Fortunately there's a boat nearby. Fortunately but not coincidentally. A camper was helping the injured to shore at the ferry berth when he was told that the police needed assistance on Storøya. Five minutes later he comes to the crowded dinghy in a seventeen-foot Askeladden boat with a seventy-five-horsepower engine. The Emergency Response Unit is relieved that it now has a faster boat. The camper and boat operator stay behind on the red dinghy. Now the rescue team moves ahead faster, but the policemen have spent nine minutes to cover just four hundred meters. Utøya is still three kilometers away.

Soon the Askeladden boat meets a new, open-console boat owned by a couple residing on the mainland. The Emergency Response Unit splits up; four men go over to the open-console boat, two with shields and two without. "Go," says one of the men from the Emergency Response Unit. The men ask the boat owners whether they know the island well, if they know where the perpetrator is, and where the best spot to land is. The experienced, local boatmen head toward the pier area on the east side.

A combination of bad luck, poor decision making, and a complex situation has stretched the time needed in getting to their destination. After the explosion in Oslo the Armed Forces Special Command, on its own initiative, was prepared to respond, but its anti-terror troops were never called out. The police helicopter was parked at the Oslo airport because there wasn't enough funding to keep it on standby all year round. The military has helicopters at the Rygge airport, but they were never requisitioned. The local police had been ready for a while but were waiting for the Emergency Response Unit from Oslo. The ambulance drivers needed clearance from the police. Then there was the decision to use Storøya island as the base. And the useless red dinghy. The seconds tick by. Every minute counts. The massacre has been going on for over an hour now.

At 6:26 p.m. the operator on duty at the police emergency telephone line receives a different kind of call from Utøya. A man says that he is the commander of the Knights Templar, a Norwegian resistance movement against the Islamization of Europe and Norway. He has accomplished his mission and wants to surrender to the Emergency Response Unit. He has to repeat his name and location several times. "Okay," he says, "just find out what you're going to do, and then call me on this phone here, right?" "Which phone number?" wonders the operator. "Great, bye," says the thirty-two-year-old from Oslo.

A large group of youngsters is hiding at the southern tip of the island. They think they are safe there. Helicopters, ambulances, boats. Flashing blue emergency lights on the mainland. These can only mean that help is on the way. Suddenly—it seems that way to the youngsters—suddenly he's standing there. A figure in uniform. Blond and tall. With weapons. "I'm from the police." One of them is speaking with his father on the phone and says with relief that help has arrived. The thirty-two-year-old raises his arm and points the gun. Some run to the right, some to the left. Some jump into the water, wade, and swim away northward, away from the southern tip. The police-uniform-clad man shoots at them but misses. They hide behind some trees in the water and can't see the gunman but hear the gunshots.

A camera captures the killer on the beachfront. NRK TV hired a helicopter to document the attack at the government quarter, but it was redirected to Utøya. With the wind and rain it's a challenge to keep the camera still. The cameraman realizes that something is wrong. A small island with six hundred people should be teeming with life, even under harsh weather conditions. Not so now. Utøya is completely quiet. The campground seems to have been evacuated. Had we frozen and zoomed into the images, we would have seen yellow, blue, and red clothes strewn along the waterside. A rubber boot here, a raincoat there. A ball from the games played earlier in the day is left lying on the soccer field. Hovering over the island, the NRK cameraman captures disturbing images of people who lie lifeless in the water and others swimming for their lives or running away from the southern tip. He is unable to distinguish the assailant from the victims. When a sixteen-year-old from northern Norway hears the helicopter, she runs out from her hiding place in her pink raincoat.

The shot that strikes a youngster in the shoulder while he is playing dead amid the corpses in the water is the killer's last. Around two hundred shots were fired at 569 youths who were on Utøya during the last one and a half hours. Including victims from the government quarter, the mass murderer has killed over seventy people. Hundreds are injured. Norway has experienced its third largest loss of life since the war, after the Scandinavian Star ferry accident on April 7, 1990, and the Alexander Kielland drilling rig accident on March 27, 1980. The attacks on the government quarter and Utøya were no coincidence. They were conscious, ideologically driven attacks. They are the worst mass murder committed by one person in recent times. And they took place in Norway in a sleepy quarter in a peaceful little capital and on the safest island on earth.

The heavily armed officers split into two groups. One group runs along the waterside toward the left on a road leading to the schoolhouse. The officers hear gunshots and shout, "Armed police," to get the assailant's attention. It's difficult to get a complete view of the situation. They run along the waterside onto the tractor path and make their way through dense thicket. Then in the woods, not far from the schoolhouse, where forty-seven people have barricaded themselves, he stands in front of them. With hands raised above his head. He walks slowly toward them. The men in the Emergency Response Unit think about shooting him then and there, as they suspect that the cord going into his vest is part of a bomb. One officer aims his weapon at the killer's head and has his finger on the trigger.

He follows orders and lies down on the ground. The Glock pistol is in the holster on his thigh. The cartridge clip is not empty. The rifle with several shots in the cartridge clip is fifteen meters behind him. Around them are youngsters within firing range. He says that this is a coup d'état and that he is the "other cell." The first one blew up the government quarter, and the third one will create havoc when their plans are executed. He wanted to strike against the Labor Party, which has Islamized Norway. He complains that his fingers are sore. While one of the men from the Emergency Response Unit guards him, the others provide first aid to the injured youngsters. Another group is looking for other assailants. At least 186 empty bullet casings lie spread around Utøya.

The policemen smash the window in the door and break into the schoolhouse. The men point their laser sights at the youngsters, who are certain that their time has come. Anxiety and paralysis are replaced by tears of joy when it turns out that these police officers are for real. Many are in shock. A girl asks the others if they shouldn't soon be going back to their tents. Continue where they left off. Play cards, eat waffles, talk, get laughter cramps, and look forward to Jens Stoltenberg's arrival tomorrow. The fire alarm is triggered. It's triggered when the heat rises by over six degrees in one minute. Jorid Nordmelan is still hiding under the bed in one of the bedrooms. She has been there for what seems like almost a day. Now the girl from Namsos is sure that the end is nigh. She doesn't see her life pass before her eyes, as movie clichés would have it, but many thoughts, both rational and embarrassing, whirl through her head.

The registration process. Oh my God! We must find out who is alive and who is injured or dead. "It's going to take all night, and I won't even be paid overtime," thinks Jorid. The prospect of having to stay on the island while everyone else is allowed to go home seems really unfair to her. Don't they understand that she's scared and wants to go home to Lasse? "If I'm not getting time off, I'll go anyway," thinks Jorid. Lasse. Phone. I want my phone. It's in the living room being charged. Jorid gets so upset about not having a mobile phone that she begins to cry. "What is it?" asks the girl hidden under the sleeping bag next to her on the floor. "The phone," sobs Jorid. "Here, take mine." Jorid has heard many horror stories about the iPhone's erratic AutoCorrect function, but no one had prepared her for this folly. *Kanj* (can) is the word in the North Trøndelag County dialect, so why does the iPhone insist that it should be *lang* (long). She deletes it and texts again. Deletes and texts again, to no avail. "It'll just have to be the way it is," thinks Jorid. Lasse will understand that it actually should read, "Can you tell dad."

"Oh my God!" Jorid says it often, and now Lasse has texted it. Only that. She has spent so much time writing the text message, and all she gets in return is an "Oh my God!" Granted, she was glad that he did not send a long, final farewell message, but still . . . you never know. Jorid contemplates sending back a detailed description of how her funeral ought to be. They have never talked about it. What if they don't realize that I don't want to have a Christian burial? In any case the songs must be in place; they are the most important. First, it'll either be Pink Floyd's "Wish You Were Here" or "Shine On You Crazy Diamond." Erik Bye and Henning Sommerro's "A Blue Hymn" should also be included; it's so beautiful: "I sing myself a blue, blue hymn / when day tips its hat to say goodbye / and rows with slow strokes to the beach / where we end up when day turns to night." Jorid considers Michael Wiehe's "The Person I Could Be" but dismisses the idea as being too conceited. The thought of her family and friends being startled when the organist plays something countervailing and surprising, like "Wake Me Up before You Go Go" or "Highway To Hell," and then breaking out in nostalgic laughter puts Jorid in a better mood.

A policeman kicks in the door of the bedroom. "Come out with your hands above your head." Jorid crawls out hesitantly from under the bed (one of the last to do so), her body bruised red under her green singlet and black pants. She has to pee, and her stomach is rumbling. The purple iPod that Jorid saw from her hiding place but never got hold of because the earphones got tangled up around the bedpost when she pulled out the mattress rocks back and forth when she stands up and leans unsteadily against the pine bunk bed. The purple and black bag that she borrowed from Lasse is still on the chair. Jorid closes her eyes and thinks that she will soon be witness to a massacre.

The police find and gather the youngsters at the campground, pump house, cafeteria, skating ramp, woods, cliffs, and the waterside. They have to walk in line in the approaching twilight, with eyes turned downward and hands visible over their heads, among the blueberry bushes, empty bullet casings, and white bags, past the policemen and ambulance personnel who are running helter-skelter. Tore Sinding Bekkedal has spent an hour and a half in the toilet stall in the cafeteria building. The killer could have chosen to stop outside the door at any time. Tore was evacuated through the little hall and main hall and saw things he shouldn't have seen. He fetched AUF sweaters that they used to bind the wounds of his party colleagues. He sneaked out an SLR camera, which he intended to use to document the story, inside the pocket of an AUF sweater from the *Planet Utøya* office. That's how a photographer thinks. As he took out the camera in the corridor, where youngsters sat in rows against the walls, he was put in his place by the girl who had hidden in the toilet stall with him: "Don't you dare take a picture now." But it's only when Tore goes down the path to the information house that he really becomes afraid. The hill is steep, muddy, and slippery. If someone stumbles, it may cause confusion. There's a rumor going around that there are bombs on Utøya. The youngsters respond to this piece of news with empty, resigned looks.

Hanne Hestø Ness has been lying for three hours in the main hall without being able to move. The nineteen-year-old hasn't been afraid or in pain, but she heard helicopters and sirens and thought, "Finally! . . ." But then nothing more happened. The disappointment, then and there, was more difficult for her to bear than the three shots in her body. The endless waiting. It has never been so quiet on Utøya, nor will it ever be again. The heavy footsteps. The gurgling sounds. Water dripping. It may have been blood dripping. One hour, two hours. Until she suddenly heard a scuffle in the corridor outside—a youngster running and an authoritative male voice saying, "Police," and telling him to be quiet.

Hanne's vocal cords were not functioning at the time, so she tried to thump her right foot on the linoleum floor to make a sound. A youngster detected movements in the corner and told the police that there were signs of life in the main hall. The rescue team looked through the door but decided it wasn't possible to save her life. They wanted to prioritize others who were less seriously injured. Since nobody came, Hanne thumped with her right foot again. The youngster became more insistent, and a young police officer walked over to her. She could then say what her name was, what had happened, and that she was struggling to breathe. "Be careful," she said when they were about to lift Lene Maria's body. They were not careful. Hanne would have yelled and pushed them away if she could.

Then someone came over who could prioritize her. It was a youngster with first-aid skills who had been hiding in the kitchen during the massacre. The police had told her there was no hope for Hanne, but the youngster said that she knew better. As fate would have it, it turned out that Hanne's guardian angel was the same age as she and had taken the paramedic course at the same high school.

It was Hanne's new friend who prevented the police from lifting her up by her arms and legs. That thoughtless act would have been fatal for those with gunshot wounds in the neck. Instead she was put on a fleece blanket, which isn't ideal either. Hanne did not have to go from the caf-

eteria building down to the pier with her hands raised over her head like
so many other youngsters. She was carried on a blanket, held aloft by four
strong arms. Hanne had never imagined that raindrops could give her
such a feeling of joy. Rain on her face, rain on her blue pants and sweater,
and rain on her fair hair, which was now stained a dark red.

The trip from Utøya to Utstranda is arduous. Hanne is placed in a small
white boat, with her head bent forward and her legs sticking out over the
gunwale. "Like a banana," she thinks. Hanne stares non-stop at the boatman. The sight of him gives her peace of mind and lowers her adrenaline
level. Despite her condition, she thinks it sensible to remove her watch
and jewelry in case she should fall asleep. She has a habit of removing her
watch and jewelry before she lies down. She has inherited the gold watch
from her grandmother and has worn it every day for two years. As her
left hand is now useless, she can't take off the gold ring on her right hand
that her grandfather gave her grandmother many years ago. She clutches
the watch and a cheap ring from her left hand to her chest.

As they approach the mainland, the boat hits a wave that throws
Hanne's head back and forth. The hard blow causes her pain for the first
time since she was shot in the main hall. The rescue team has to hurry.
Her blood pressure has fallen alarmingly. She's placed on a stretcher and
transported by ambulance to a helicopter that heads toward Ullevål University Hospital in Oslo. "This is cool," thinks Hanne before passing out.
Thus she doesn't discover until later that her grandmother's gold watch
has gone missing.

Jorid and the others from the schoolhouse are taken along the road
north toward the pier. Outside the information house she sees a man in
a T-shirt tapping his feet vigorously. She thinks he is a party member
because he seems so excited. But when she gets a glimpse of the pale face,
she realizes that it is him. Her stomach churns. The arrested assailant turns
his head and looks at her. He has the most evil eyes she has ever seen. The
thirty-two-year-old from Oslo, his hands cuffed behind his back, smiles
at Jorid. Anders Behring Breivik tends to do that when he's nervous.

16

It's Not Over

The spaces between the ambulances and police cars outside the Sund-volden Hotel are filled with half-naked, wet youngsters wrapped in blankets. The youngsters embrace each other, search for their boyfriends or girlfriends, and tell their dramatic stories amid cries that their best friends have been killed. One group of people is conspicuous by its absence: it is the group of youths who're no longer alive or who've been sent to the hospital for emergency treatment. Parents who come in cars from Oslo or elsewhere in the country have no idea what condition their children are in.

Johanne Butenschøn Lindheim has been offered food and drink but is so physically ill that she can't bear the thought of solid food. She sits in the rain on a wet chair in socks, with a duvet around her and a bottle of mineral water in her hand, staring fixedly at the blue emergency lights. She spoke with a priest a couple of times but got the impression that he didn't think she was worth spending time on. As if she hadn't been through enough already. As if she hadn't as big a need for some reassuring words as those who swam from Utøya. As if it's not enough having seen him liquidate a boy and a girl. As if it's commonplace to look a killer in the eye. Johanne has feelings of guilt as she sits in the rain outside the hotel. In her hand she has a stone that she plucked from the cliff wall by Bolsjevika Bay on Utøya.

Ministers come to Sundvollen to comfort the survivors. The state secretaries arrive to look for their children. A meeting with psychologists and crisis managers is being held. The police conduct brief interrogations. The young people are offered food, drink, clothing, and lodging. A group of youngsters flocks around the TV to watch the news. Some prefer the cartoon movie showing on the television in another room. Johanne has come in from the rain and settled down in front of the TV to watch the news while she waits to be picked up by her parents, who have driven from the cabin on Hvaler. Channels NRK and TV2 talk mostly about the explosion in Oslo. The images are confusing. Haven't they figured out what has happened here? When news commentators first talk about the shooting on Utøya, they state a ridiculously low death toll—

ten killed. Johanne shakes her head. She and the other youngsters know that the actual figure is far, far higher.

At 10:30 p.m., Jens Stoltenberg holds a televised press conference in the government representation complex in Oslo, in front of two Norwegian flags. "Today Norway has been hit by two shocking, violent, and cowardly attacks. We don't know who has attacked us. There's much that remains uncertain. But we do know that many have died and many are injured," says a visibly shaken prime minister, and he adds, "I have a message for those who attacked us. And for those who are behind them. It's a message from the whole of Norway. You will not destroy us. You will not destroy our democracy or our commitment to bringing about a better world. We are a small nation, but we are a proud nation. No one is going to bomb us into silence. No one is going to shoot us into silence. No one is ever going to frighten us away from being Norway." At the same press conference Justice Minister Knut Storberget confirms that the perpetrator is Norwegian and that youths on Utøya have been killed, wounded, and are missing, but no death toll is given.

Tore Sinding Bekkedal tries to make himself useful. He gets hotel staff to open up rooms for youngsters so that they can make calls in private. He shows parents where they can find their children. He goes to the Esso gas station to buy mobile phone chargers. Once outside he is overwhelmed by reporters from the tabloid press. Tore attempts to answer the questions precisely, but one journalist's gum chewing is distracting. So is a photographer's animated "long-time-no-see" background chat. Besides the photographer is using a Nikon camera, which is a sacrilege.

The atmosphere at the Sundvolden Hotel is both chaotic and organized. There are lists for registration, but many don't bother to stand in line to register. Tore embraces someone whom he believes is a friend and then has to embarrassingly apologize to the man's identical twin brother. The KappAhl clothing store in Hønefoss sends a truckload of clothing to the hotel, but no one comes with shoes. A nicotine-craving youngster borrows footwear from Tore to trudge down to the gas station. Tore doesn't see his boots again. However, he has a welcome reunion with his parents, who have come to fetch him. His father has just moved back to Norway from the United States. He landed on July 19. Tore didn't manage to see him before he went to Utøya. So it's this evening at Sundvollen that father and son finally see each other for the first time in ten years. They embrace each other and are lost for words.

Stine Renate Håheim wanders around barefoot in her summer dress, happy to have found so many survivors. She hugs them and says, "Oh, you're alive," but doesn't dare to ask about the ones who aren't there. Her best friend is still missing. She's offered food but just wants coffee. She asks a Red Cross worker whether she can get an alcohol swab to clean the wounds on the soles of her feet. She was thinking of doing it herself, but he is insistent. "You need stitches," he says. He says that she has to go to the emergency ward. Stine Renate thinks the suggestion so absurd that she's disproportionately argumentative. "People have been shot, and you say I must go to the hospital because I have some abrasions on my leg? Ridiculous. Don't you have any tape?" she asks. As if the twenty-seven-year-old hasn't gone far enough, she then decides to put him on the spot: "Can you force me to go?" "No," replies the man from the Red Cross. "Exactly."

In American movies customers ask to speak with a manager when they want to complain about service. Stine Renate does the same. She asks to see a health worker who has a sense of proportion. The Valdres girl has a rich arsenal of psychological weapons to use, and she can effortlessly shift from campaign to administrative mode and bring up rhetorical arguments that she learned at a defiant age. After another man from the Red Cross has told her that she should go to the emergency ward, she fires a salvo that she believes is an unassailable argument: "What's the worst that can happen? What's the absolute worst that can happen?" She's told that the wounds may heal incorrectly. There may be inflammation. The feet may eventually have to be cut open and operated on. Stine Renate leans back, raises her hands in the air, and says, "Fine," before she's led away to the ambulance that'll take her to the emergency ward in Oslo.

On the deck of the MS *Thorbjørn* Eskil Pedersen was afraid that Norway was under attack and that some people in the police and military were involved. The perpetrator was in uniform and said that there'd be more people coming from Oslo. Some on board feared that the AUF leader was the main target on Utøya. Hence the captain didn't go directly over to the mainland but up north to a safer place called the Bråtan farm, where the youngsters stopped two private cars that took them to the Hønefoss police station. Eskil stood by the window and saw some men dressed in black suits that were bulletproof from head to toe and carrying powerful weapons. They were sent there to protect the police station. Can one feel safe in a police station when it has to be guarded by commandos?

The AUF leader isn't allowed to go to the Sundvolden Hotel until after midnight because the police aren't sure that it's safe enough. Eskil trusts the guards nearest to him, even though he runs up from the cellar when he meets a uniformed man in the toilet. Still it doesn't mean that the locale is safe. He has just survived a massacre that wasn't detected by the police and security services. There may be several perpetrators on the island or allies elsewhere in Norway. The hotel has a thousand hallways and rooms. There's a dark forest right behind the hotel. People come and go. So when he receives a text message that says, "Call the hospital—it's not over. God bless the King," the final residue of his sense of security evaporates.

Eskil knows that there are racists in Norway and that there are quite a few of them. There are also many who hate the Labor Party and the AUF. It's often the same people who hate Palestinians, Arabs, Muslims, immigrants, and people with dark skin, where everything is blended together into a stale, brown stew. When he writes in the press about why we must increase taxes to finance the welfare state, the comments from readers comprise mostly Muslim hate and personal attacks. Before, the twenty-seven-year-old just shook his head and went on with his life—to a central committee meeting, the fitness studio, or a Lady Gaga concert. We can't continue this way. Extremist views must be opposed immediately, determinedly, and emphatically. For the AUF leader, "Now it's personal."

In addition to the assembly point at the Sundvolden Hotel another place has been created to receive survivors at the Thon Hotel in Sandvika. Morten Djupdal has been to the police station and given his statement about Utøya. There he was offered food, drink, and dry clothes. The twenty-year-old asked for a cup of coffee, which he didn't touch, and was eventually persuaded to take off his wet beige shorts. In return he got a protective suit with a hood, which he tied around his waist. Now with this attire he traipses around the Sandvika shopping mall, shoeless and with muddied legs. The AUF T-shirt is quite dirty. His wallet is in his hand. The affluent shoppers from Sandvika have seen homeless persons before, but they don't usually meet them on a Friday evening at the mall.

Morten goes into the Lefdal electronics store and asks for a mobile phone charger. "You have to excuse my attire, but I just came straight from Utøya," says Morten in a quiet, subdued voice. "A normal phone charger and a car battery charger." He goes to the checkout counter and pays. Then he goes into a clothing store. "Hi. I need a cheap pair of pants, waist 36 and length 32." The lady behind the counter looks at him oddly but finds a pair on offer for 100 Norwegian kroner. "That's nice. I also need socks," he says, pointing to his dirty feet. From her facial expression he judges that it's time to apologize and tell her about the gunman on Utøya. Morten takes the pants and socks and goes into the changing room. He asks for a bag for the white protective suit.

Morten leaves the clothing store and sees a shoe store. He sees some white shoes on offer at the entrance to the store. He brings them over to the counter, pays 100 Norwegian kroner, dumps them on the floor, and sticks his feet with the new socks in. "There, I have what I need," thinks the twenty-year-old. On the way out he goes past Burger King. It's been many hours since dinner on Utøya. It's important to eat so as not to get distracted or dizzy or even pass out. Morten orders a cheeseburger. While he waits, he calls his father and asks him to send money. The chargers, beige pants, white shoes, black socks, and cheeseburger don't cost much, but his bank account is almost empty. Morten no longer looks like a homeless person, but someone seeing the jumble of colors of his clothes would probably think that there was vast room for improvement on the fashion front.

Back at the Thon Hotel Morten sets himself up in a corner. He plugs in the phone to charge and starts up the PC. On an Excel sheet the county secretary enters the names of everyone from Oppland County on Utøya and puts a check mark next to those he knows are alive. Then he calls around and fills in the blanks as he gets new information. In the end there are two names without check marks. In the meantime he checks online newspapers, Facebook, and other sites. While browsing, he comes across a manifesto supposedly written by the man who killed his friends on Utøya. Morten clicks "download" but doesn't take the time to read it. A youngster comes over to Morten and says that they're going to Sundvollen. He can catch a ride if he wants. Morten doesn't think they are allowed to go, but he packs his stuff in a backpack and leaves with them.

Hanne Hestø Ness is imprisoned in a cage in the basement. She hears gunshots and shouts that the people have to get away. Meanwhile the nineteen-year-old is confused. Hanne knows that she's lying in a bed. If you're in a hospital, no one's going to do you any harm, right? So why have they placed her in a cage? In the basement? Who's shooting? And why don't people understand the seriousness of the situation? Nurses and doctors must flee and get out of the building. There's no doubt in

Hanne's mind that she has shouted "Get out!" from a cage in the hospital basement. That's the way she sees it, and her experience is no less real than those of the nurses and doctors, who believe that the grids are curtains and that the gunshots are the sound of a heavy hospital door slamming repeatedly. They also believe that she's on a respirator at Ullevaal Hospital and can't actually speak. It doesn't really matter. Hanne is shouting anyway.

Stine Renate Håheim's parents were on the way from their cabin to Sundvollen. They were in the village of Nes i Ådal when Stine Renate called from a borrowed phone and told them that she has had to go to the emergency ward. She thought it would be difficult for them to drive into the capital. Besides, she said, she needed to be with her friends from Utøya. "It's better if you come to Oslo on Monday." It was a deliberate decision, the consequence of which was that the twenty-seven-year-old has ended up alone in the emergency ward in Oslo. She's been stitched up and bandaged but has nowhere to go. Her mobile phone is in Lake Tyri. Her money and keys are in her bag in the room below the cafeteria building on Utøya. So is the Mac. She has no shoes, just a red and white checkered dress. A nurse comes over and asks her whether she needs to talk to someone from the sv. Stine Renate has been through a lot lately, so she's only mildly startled that people from the Socialist Left Party (sv being the acronym of the party) are in the emergency ward and want to get in touch with her. "Is the sv here? I am a member of the Labor Party, but if the sv is here, I can always talk to them." The misunderstanding is then cleared up. The nurse didn't mean the Socialist Left Party but the social crisis service, which has the same acronym, sv. "Oh, no, I can't bear to talk to them. I just want to go home." The member of parliament could well have a chat with political colleagues about a future coalition. But she doesn't have the energy to talk to psychologists.

Stine Renate just wants to change clothes and curl up on a warm couch, drink tea, and talk with good friends. She borrows a phone but doesn't know her friends' numbers by heart. She can get the numbers from directory information. Stine Renate thinks she needs to get several numbers at a time because people are not necessarily up so late at night. But how will she note down the numbers? And on what? It doesn't occur to her that she could ask the operator to put her through. It doesn't occur to her that the Oslo emergency ward has both pen and paper. Stine Renate is on the verge of a breakdown. With her last ounce of energy she takes a hairpin out of her hair and stares at her medical journal. The mind is able to imagine the most implausible fantasies, but no one in human history has ever envisaged that an elected Norwegian member of parliament in a wet summer dress would be standing alone with bandaged feet in the Oslo emergency ward on a Friday night in July, engraving the phone numbers of her friends into a medical journal with a hairpin just a couple of hours after she has survived a massacre at the AUF summer camp on the island of Utøya.

Epilogue

The Trial of Anders Behring Breivik and Interviews with Survivors

The trial of Anders Behring Breivik started on April 16, 2012, in Courtroom 250 at the Oslo Courthouse, nine months after the bomb blast in the government quarter and the massacre on Utøya. The question of guilt was not in dispute. What was in dispute in the course of the ten weeks of the trial, after two teams of psychiatrists had arrived at contradictory conclusions, was whether Behring Breivik was sane or not at the time of the crimes. The first team, comprising forensic psychiatrists Torgeir Husby and Synne Sørheim, alleged that the mass murderer was psychotic and ergo should be declared legally insane. After a heated debate that lasted two months, two new psychiatrists, Terje Tørrissen and Agnar Aspaas, were appointed. They presented their findings Tuesday, April 10, six days before the trial started. The press release reads: "The experts' main conclusion is that the accused, Anders Behring Breivik, is not considered psychotic at the time of the acts on July 22, 2011. This means that he is considered legally sane at the time of the perpetration of the crime." What are we to believe?

It turned out to be ten grueling weeks. Every slight, trivial phrase that was uttered in the witness stand was cause for delving into the depths that humanity had sunk. That wasn't the way AUF party members wanted to portray Utøya. They would rather recall swimming, political workshops, karaoke, speed dating, the sun, and strolls along Lovers' Lane during the summers of 2008, 2009, 2010, and, yes, even July 2011—at least from Tuesday until Friday at 5:15 p.m. But it was no idyll that we got to see and hear about. Far from it. We got to see and hear about the horrifying images and stories of what happened during the almost half hour when the gunman walked freely around Utøya on Friday, July 22. Words such as "nightmare," "hell," and "tragedy" are clichés. The way they are used is usually disproportionate to the events or things they describe. "My back feels like hell," was heard murmured from the courtroom bench where the press corps sat.

The work crew on the mainland and the MS *Thorbjørn* ferry captain portrayed the young people's first encounter with the fake policeman. The ferry captain's testimony began factually: "It was a rainy day...." The captain was also the partner of Utøya's camp administrator, who was one of the killer's first victims on the island. Add to that the fact that his daughter was participating in the AUF summer camp on the island when the shooting started. The captain gave his testimony in a low-key, concise, and rigorous manner without unleashing the emotions that one could sense lay just below the surface. Still, with each brief sentence the abyss opened a little wider, as much because of what he didn't say and didn't know as what he said and knew. Like when he explained that he didn't remember whether he saw his partner being killed: "I think I saw it." Emotional suppression says something about the kind of mental powers that are set in motion when the sight is too overwhelming. The captain had pondered for over nine months and was still not certain whether he saw his partner being executed. In addition, he explained, he had spent the days since July 22 thinking about whether there was anything he could have done differently. Under every pro and contra argument guilt lies concealed—the ghost that haunts everyone who survived Utøya—and it can be as paralyzing as a traumatic sight.

The boat captain left Utøya early, along with Eskil Pedersen and other youngsters. For him escape was the only logical choice. The MS *Thorbjørn* would be used to transport police and rescue personnel from Utstranda to Utøya when help eventually arrived. Still this rational decision must have been exceedingly difficult to make—to leave his partner, who had been shot and had probably been killed, and the eighteen-year-old daughter who, though he didn't know it at the time, had taken refuge in a "secure" hideout. It was really heartbreaking when the captain testified that on the way north on Lake Tyri, he got a call from his other daughter, who was eleven years old and with his grandmother just a few kilometers away. The plan was that she should stay on Utøya from Friday to Saturday, so she was calling to ask whether he would soon be coming to fetch her. "No," the father replied. "Change of plans. It's really bad weather."

Prosaic statements such as these, indicating what was and what could have been, made a bigger impression than seeing blood spatters on the wall in the little hall or hearing about the number of bullet casings (fifty) that were found in the cafeteria building. "Each one represents a dead person," a police sergeant said as he showed a map of Utøya during the forensic report. Numbers and blood convey only to a limited extent what the tragedy on Utøya was about. We don't understand numbers and blood because we lack reference points. Thus the captain gives us a deeper, more realistic perspective, as when he said that his younger daughter still often cried herself to sleep at night. Wounds were inflicted on July 22, but for the survivors and the aggrieved families, new, unexpected wounds emerge daily and will do so for the foreseeable future.

Presentations of autopsy reports are as alienating as they sound. Coroners, dentists, geneticists, and radiologists used a whole week after July 22 to reconstruct heads in 3D and look for metal fragments that were not apparent to the naked eye. They found, among other things, that twenty-five people were definitely shot in the head and neck and thirty-one were struck in the head, neck, body, and limbs. One died from injuries due to a fall, while one drowned. Three seemed to have died from drowning, but they were not found at the waterside. The lungs looked like those of people who had drowned because they had been hyperventilating after being shot. A total of sixty-nine deaths; the average age was eighteen—the youngest had been fourteen, while the oldest had been fifty-two.

The wobbly gray plastic mannequin on wheels that was used in court to illustrate bullet wounds was devoid of all human attributes. Furthermore, the reports were presented at a grueling pace, allotting between five and ten minutes to each deceased, for whom phrases with key words appeared on the big screen: "A gunshot wound on the left side of the back of the head. . . . Direction from below going upward, slightly forward and to the right. . . . Exit wound on the right side of the scalp; a projectile piece lies loose in the hair."

The language was clinical and mechanical, not unlike that used by the killer in the courtroom to distance himself from his crime. But while the coroner and police used scientific language in order to shield the aggrieved families and keep a professional distance, the killer used technical language both as a form of obfuscation and to show off military jargon. The technical reports stood in contrast to the emotions evoked among the aggrieved families. Soft gasps filled the gaps in the litany between the statistics and the logistics. The mannequin didn't have a name or attributes, and it lacked character and individuality. It is precisely the dread that their child, partner, father, or mother would be seen as just a number among the dead that made the families insist their counsels say a few words about each one and put a picture of the deceased up on the video screen.

The coroners could tell us that Utøya had hired a guard, Trond Berntsen, who was shot five times from behind in front of the information house, but the picture on the screen of him with his two children showed us the extent of the loss. The counsel for the aggrieved read out a message from his ten-year-old son, who was on Utøya that day: "You were the best dad in the world." The girlfriend of Rolf Christopher Johansen Perreau, who was "kind, generous, and joyful," was present in the courtroom. Lejla Selaci, who was found on the south side of the cafeteria building by gravel road e6, was a "pleasant girl" and "much loved" and spread laughter and joy every day. "We shall meet again, Lejla."

The counsel for the aggrieved, who struggled to hold back tears when he read the message from the Lejla's family, probably felt uncomfortable and unprofessional, but it was liberating to see someone give free rein to emotions in the solemn, square area where the prosecutors, counsels for the aggrieved, defense lawyers, and experts were assembled. The words of farewell from the aggrieved families gave the mannequin a face and features and helped to put the autopsy reports into context. The counsel for the family of Utøya's camp administrator didn't read out a special message. Instead he referred to what Jens Stoltenberg had previously said about her. That her partner and their two daughters were not able to formulate anything new to say after the report perhaps says more than a thousand words could say under the circumstances.

We heard two short phrases often during the ten weeks: "Head injury resulting in instantaneous unconsciousness" and "They had no shoes on." It was at the cafeteria building that they ate meatballs for dinner, had a vegetarian spring roll at the cafe, or bought a packet of biscuits at the kiosk. It was here that karaoke, disco, and speed dating were arranged. It was here that Marte Michelet had spoken about the growing Islamophobia in Norway on Wednesday. The *Planet Utøya* camp newsletter was put together here, in the room next to the kiosk. It was here that the electronic rock band Datarock had signed autographs and hung out with the youngsters after the concert Thursday night. It was here that Gro had talked about her long life in politics on Friday morning, and it was here that a visibly moved AUF leader had informed the others of the explosion in Oslo later in the day. And it was here, in the cafeteria building on Utøya—the safest building on "the safest place on earth"—that thirteen people were killed on July 22.

Thirteen deaths are thirteen too many, but the number is still low considering how many people were in the building when the shooting started. The information meeting about the explosion in Oslo was mandatory. Everyone was there to seek refuge from the rain and to recharge mobile phones. Hence the witnesses who survived the massacre at the cafeteria building heard a long-drawn-out cacophony of unsynchronized ringtones in the ensuing hours. The killer didn't say anything about all the mobile phones being charged. He didn't remember much from the cafeteria building except for someone pretending to be dead in the little hall, his head resting on the piano (which he thought was in the main hall), and that he had to reload. He also remembers that he was surprised because the youngsters didn't run away but remained standing, sitting, or lying in clusters. "It looked very strange. I shot them all."

The images from the cafeteria building displayed in the courtroom suggested that many youngsters were paralyzed. The press and the aggrieved families got to see the little hall and the main hall as they looked after the youngsters had been carried out, with red dots indicating their locations. They lay close together and partially on top of each other in the far corner against the wall. The meager consolation for the aggrieved families was the coroner's oft repeated phrase, "Head injury resulting in instantaneous unconsciousness." One would have thought that the shooting in the little hall would have scared away the boys and girls from the main hall, which is separated by a thin wall, but surviving witnesses said that it was impossible to discern where the shots were coming from. Nothing is mentioned of what the young people did before they were killed—whether they were paralyzed or trying to escape or hide—but some details emerged that gave an inkling of how terrified they must have been. One youngster was shot through the right wrist, probably because he had lifted his arm to shield his face.

The police superintendent testified on where the dead were found and what clothes they were wearing. The information on clothes tells a lot about what went on before, during, and after the killings. Most of the youngsters were wearing clothes one often uses to relax in or changes into after having been soaked: leisure wear, jogging pants, or jeans. Many were wearing gray hoodies with the AUF logo, which were especially popular among rookies. And, as the police superintendent often repeated, they were not wearing shoes. They were allowed to wear shoes inside the cafeteria building during lunch, but during the information meeting the ban came into effect again. Consequently one of the starkest images from the courtroom was a picture of the entrance to the cafeteria building carpeted with rubber boots, sneakers, and sandals. Hundreds of boys and girls ran out of the building in stockinged feet.

The defendant didn't pay much attention to the words from the aggrieved families conveyed via their counsels: She was "engaged and positive." He wasn't "afraid to stand out." Her favorite quote was "Before you judge me, try hard to love me." She was "very much a daddy's girl." He had a "big heart." She was "like the sun to us." He was "a splash of color." He was interested in "local politics and women." The prosecutor and the judge were brought to tears. It is the most reasonable reaction to the autopsy reports and the words from the aggrieved families. The defendant followed with interest when the coroner was describing the entrance and exit wounds on the mannequin, but he was fairly quick to look down in his lap when photo portraits of the dead came up on the video screen.

"The red dot represents the body," the police superintendent said in Courtroom 250. In the end there were ten dots in the picture of Lovers' Lane. The dots were placed close together, partly on top of each other, and some against the fence. One of the dots was Tore Eikeland, the twenty-one-year-old leader of AUF Hordaland. He was described as "caring" by his family. Words such as "kind," "joyful," and "creative" were often used in the descriptions of the dead from Utøya, but there were also characteristics that separated them from the average youth: "strong sense of justice," "wants to create a better world," "socially engaged," "was never afraid to stand up for the weak." These values formed the basis for their political engagement. They may sound like empty phrases, but they were the ones that got them killed in the first place. Eikeland's counsel quoted from an article he had written: "It may be appropriate to ask how much of the short time one has on earth one will use to fear what's alien and rage against our fellow men. And how much one will use to make life better for others and to help to ensure that everyone's welfare is taken care of. Let us live for each other!"

Instead they died for each other. The defendant argued in court that they lay down and waited for him. It was more likely that they tried to hide and kept together as a group. Twenty-five bullet casings were found among the victims and up to ten meters away from them. It was likely that the first shot was fired from a distance, followed by what the defendant called "follow-up shots" to the head. For the aggrieved families it was no trivial matter to know the order in which the shots were fired and from what distance. Clear answers leave less room for conjecture, and hopefully it would be a relief for them knowing that the first shot was fatal. Their loved ones hadn't suffer after all. The coroner's conclusion was sometimes discouraging: "The sequence of shots cannot be determined."

The victims had not only parents, but also elder brothers and younger sisters. Sibling grief is just as consuming but often different and usually not channeled through the established support system. Brothers and sisters identify more strongly with their siblings' fate. The NRK spoke with some siblings who said they had images in their heads in which they were running on Utøya, pursued by the killer. Even though they had never been there. Even though they were not AUF members. The killer didn't strike just the sixty-nine with his weapons. A message from a sister that was read by the counsel for the aggrieved during the trial revealed that the shots fired on Lovers' Lane had trajectories that extended farther than anticipated, with equally far-reaching consequences. The sister has Down's syndrome, and she responded to the news of July 22 with, "But he promised that he would look after me forever."

The defendant made many miscalculations. One of them was his idea of using Lake Tyri as a weapon of mass destruction. In his mind he thought it would be impossible to swim the six hundred meters from Utøya to Utvika (the shortest route), especially under a stressful situation. Not that it's easy, but he didn't take into account that people are strong willed when their lives are at stake. Several youngsters also swam from the opposite side of the island, facing a seemingly endless unknown. The five who were killed on the slope below Lovers' Lane on the west side may have considered swimming away, but they clung instead to the thirteen-meter-high steep cliff. He shot them. The youngest had turned fourteen five days earlier. She had just finished the eighth grade. She had dreamed of becoming a fashion designer. "Rest in peace, our beautiful angel."

Four of the five killed on the slope were transported to the mainland by boat around half past nine. Three of the eight killed by Stoltenberget/ Bolsjevika were also transported by boat from Utøya to Storøya the same evening. It is evidence of another miscalculation the defendant made. He waited for the Emergency Response Unit. Meanwhile, he had to cope with the boatmen. He fired at the boats because "they tried to pick up political activists from the AUF's indoctrination camp," as he put it in court. While police were on the way from Hønefoss and Oslo to Storøya and had the little red police boat, local residents and campers went out with their private boats. They not only saved many young people from the water and helped with evacuation efforts after the killer had been arrested, but they also witnessed the consequences of the massacre at very close range. Oddvar Hansen, a resident of Utstranda, testified in Courtroom 250. He was just one of many boatmen who had horror stories to tell about what they saw that afternoon: "They looked like dolls."

A fifteen-year-old girl who was shot by the slope below Lovers' Lane had big plans for her life. She wanted to become a lawyer. She died next to a girl who had turned fourteen five days earlier. She was going to be a fashion designer. A sixteen-year-old killed in the same area wanted to work with disadvantaged kids. A boy who died at the Stoltenberget promontory was going to work with children and youths. An eighteen-year-old girl from Bergen wanted to become a doctor, and her dream was to work for Doctors without Borders. A girl from Namsos was going to be a veterinarian. She died in the main hall. A fifteen-year-old was going to be a video game designer. She died by the pump house.

There wasn't a single case in court in which it emerged that the dead youths wanted to devote their lives to legislating cultural Marxism into the fabric of society. They were going to be teachers, musicians, photographers, and cooks. That is not to say that none of them would have ended up as politicians. Tore Eikeland from Bergen and Håvard Vederhus from Oslo were both expected to have promising political careers. As the counsel for the aggrieved read out the families' words of farewell to the dead after each autopsy report, a multitude of personalities emerged. The AUF offered a socially inclusive community within several communities, on a par with school bands, horse riding, guitar playing, dancing, and soccer training.

The killer and terrorist chose Utøya because he wanted to stem recruitment to the Labor Party and because the island was the most "attractive political target" that summer. In his mind the AUF summer camp was a "legitimate target," and he was proud of his precision, both in the choice of targets and the gun and rifle. But he missed utterly. He couldn't see into the future, and he didn't see the whole person. He didn't see the veterinarian or lawyer or chef or nurse; he saw a new prime minister. He confused six hundred individuals with the party's leadership. It may be that they would take (or would have taken) values such as liberty, equality, and fraternity into their professional lives as teachers or computer game designers. But if these values are reason enough to be murdered, then most Norwegians would be legitimate targets.

Family photographs on the screen and the obituaries make a deep impression. It was as if we were present at sixty-nine short funerals. The defendant was the only one who didn't shed a tear in Courtroom 250. The words of farewell reaffirmed why these people had been considered a threat to the defendant's reactionary ideology of purity: "She had a strong sense of justice." "He stood up for the weak." "She believed that everyone should be valued equally." At the same time they remind us that those killed were ordinary young people with very ordinary interests: horses, school bands, fashion, music, boys, Facebook, girls, books. Ismail Haji Ahmed didn't want to be prime minister of Norway; he was going to be a model and dreamed of starting a dance school. He was killed by the pump house.

"Plans had already been made for the future" was often heard in the courthouse. These must have been the most painful words to write. Plans about study choices and dream careers, bolstered by the belief that one could pick and choose. The visions would gradually have been adjusted and adapted to reality. But the youngsters also had more short-term, realistic plans. They were attending the self-defense course on Friday afternoon; they were going to see *Kick Ass* on movie night; they were going to hear Jens Stoltenberg speak on Saturday; and on Sunday they were going to pack up their tents and go home to Namsos, Romsås, or Bergen. And then they were supposed to go on summer vacation to Greece with the family, prepare for the first year of high school, take the moped driver's license exam, or travel to Bulgaria with the school band, as an eighteen-year-old from Nordland was planning on doing. As we know, nothing came of these plans. As to why these uncomplicated, innocent plans were cut short, the answer may be long and intricate, but sometimes it is the simplest answer that sounds truest, as the boatman Oddvar Hansen said in the witness stand: "What happened makes no sense."

There were not only sixty-nine aborted futures. Many of the youths who survived the massacre testified about what they saw on Utøya on July 22. Janne Hovland said she had planned to become an elementary school teacher but doubted that her dream would be realized unless her energy levels picked up considerably. The days went by slowly. Lars Henrik Rytter Øberg appeared in his high school graduation uniform. Plans to study law had to be revised because his grades were not good enough.

He was barely making it through the day. The prosecutor asked Moham-mad Abdul Rahman about school. "It's not good." She wondered whether he could elaborate. "I think I'll pass," the Hamar boy said. Five hundred youths had envisioned how life would turn out. It wasn't like they thought. They have to improvise and take one day at a time.

Generally the defendant appeared strategically smart and socially intel-ligent in the courtroom. He toned down the message in his manifesto, showed respect to the judge, and refused to be provoked by the prosecu-tors' at times condescending tones. When he yawned in the course of the sixty-nine autopsy reports, he covered his mouth with his hand.

But when the first witness from Utøya took the stand and the defen-dant was informed that he had the right to comment on every testimony, he snapped. First, he wanted to challenge party secretary Tonje Brenna on the AUF's ideological program. Just the sound of his voice appeared to be out of place after she had testified to seeing people who had been shot fall down the slope along Lovers' Lane. After boatman Oddvar Han-sen's testimony, he spoke up to clarify that he wasn't trying to shoot at the boats; he was only firing warning shots. Muhammed Abdulrahman said the killer kicked a girl outside the cafeteria building. The defendant then spoke up and said he never touched anyone on Utøya.

He executed sixty-nine people with the utmost brutality, but the most important thing for him was that he wasn't shouting for joy, shooting at civilian boats, or kicking a girl lying on the ground. He had been wronged. It was as if his moral integrity rested entirely on whether he had behaved "honorably" or not during the massacre. At one point he was really out of kilter. He was no longer strategically smart and socially intelligent. Parents and siblings had just heard the autopsy reports of those killed around the pump house, and counsels for the aggrieved had read out the beautiful obituaries of the deceased. "Her dreams are buried in the ground." Lawyers and judges cried. Families wept. Then he thought it wise to say something.

After the lunch break he was allowed to speak. The aggrieved families went out as he spoke. "There was one place on Utøya I was attacked. It was at the pump house. Someone threw an object at me, hitting me in the face. I just thought I'd mention it." Poor mass murderer.

His insensitivity in court, coupled with the hurt and self-righteous tone of his comments, was, understandably, provoking to the families. Another heavy rock was thus added to the families' burden. Throwing shoes solves nothing. But the applause in the courtroom after a sibling got up, threw a shoe, and shouted, "You killed my brother. Go to hell!" shows that he'd finally expressed a longing for emotional release that had gradually built up over time and especially during the review of the sixty-nine autopsy reports. Finally. "He said and did what many wanted to," as one family member put it. The passionate reaction was understandable, but the shoe overshadowed the last autopsy reports that were presented in court that day, except for a very strong witness testimony by Munir Osman Humed Jaber.

The survivors' stories change in line with new knowledge and insights. They were present at the cliff on the west side or the campground and saw their friends being executed, and yet (or probably because of what they saw) their memories are full of holes. There is so much that has been lost or distorted. The space-time continuum has shifted somewhat. It may have been here, or it may have been there. "I don't remember."

An eighteen-year-old told the court how he had to jump over three bodies on Lovers' Lane. The prosecutor could affirm that there were ten bodies there. He saw only three. And he remembers the flowers. The prosecutor also told him where he had clung to the rock wall for three hours, but when he was asked to show it on the photograph, he pointed consistently to a different location further north, as if he was hesitant to alter his memory. A twenty-year-old girl testified to what she saw at the southern tip as she swam from there to the mainland. The police statement is full of gory details. On the witness stand they had to be tempered. No one was shot at the southern tip the first time the killer was there. But she remembers it clearly. Perhaps she projected the images into her mind then and there; perhaps she confused others' experiences with her own. A twenty-one-year-old girl swam toward the mainland and recalls that a boy was shot dead behind her. He had brown curly hair. But according to the prosecutor, no one died there.

Their narratives are theirs alone. They saw what they saw, and all their narratives were included in the statements they made to the police in the weeks after July 22. The most intense memories, often unpleasant, form the foundation of the stories from Utøya. When this is shaken, the whole edifice starts to crumble a little. If the foundation is not true, how do I know whether all the other things are true? Their attendance at the court proceedings, with all their doubts, uncertainties, and nervousness, came at a much greater cost than the rest of us can fathom. A girl who took the witness stand was asked whether she was currently working. No; she has no energy left. "I struggle just to get into the shower." Yet she told her story in front of the mass murderer, the judges, the press, and all Norway.

The Utøya survivors cope with their traumas in different ways, but all strive to find structure and meaning in something incomprehensible and to fill the gaps in their own memories. They will be doing that for the foreseeable future. As a seventeen-year-old girl put it, "It's not as if what happened will go away. It'll never go away."

When the AUF members want to highlight something positive from July 22, they often mention dinner. It is served at one o'clock on Utøya. Outside it was cold and wet, but inside the cafeteria building the atmosphere was good at the serving counter. The servers would say, "Remember, you are amazing," as they doled out the food. The originator of the phrase is the Pollyannaish Ina Libak from Akershus.

Ina was washing dishes when she heard gunshots outside the building. She ran to the little hall, where she hid behind a piano. The twenty-one-year-old was shot in the hands, chest, and jaw. Yet she managed to run out of the cafeteria building. She stopped at the gravel yard between the outhouse and the waffle stand to try to stem the bleeding. As she explained in court, "With four to five gunshot wounds and arms that don't function, it goes without saying that you don't have enough hands." She collapsed and thought, "This is what it's like to die." She was about to give up when a boy picked her up and carried her into the woods on the north side and down a steep cliff at the decrepit skateboard ramp twenty meters away from the pump house. There she lay for a while that felt like an eternity, surrounded by good friends who used T-shirts and rocks to put pressure on her wounds. Even when the gunman shot more youngsters at the pump house and then went off on the path just two meters away from them, they didn't leave her. One whispered, "They're dying, they're dying; we've to save them," while another retorted, "Now we've got to lie damn still."

Ina laughed when she testified about the incident in court. She thought it hilarious. "It seems your outlook on life is more positive than the norm," said the prosecutor. The people in the court could easily confirm the truth of that opinion. We saw a woman who had decided that the defendant would not be allowed to make her lose focus on the bright side of life, even though she had to admit that feelings of insecurity had become part of her daily life. The laughter that regularly broke out in the courtroom during her testimony was liberating, in much the same way as the earlier tears had been. The court learned a little more about what happened on Utøya on July 22 but also learned something important about life's indomitable will, compassion in practice, and the contagiousness of optimism.

When the twenty-one-year-old was being evacuated from Utøya and she had to walk the last stretch to the boat because the people carrying her stumbled over the body bags, she met a friend from the kitchen crew. Their meeting was cordial, but Ina asked her friend to look away from her face lest it be too traumatic for her. Her friend then smiled and said, "Ina, you're very beautiful."

What made such an indelible impression on people during Ina's testimony was the disconnect between what she was saying and the way she was saying it. She showed her scars unabashedly to the court and joked that the scar on her face was hard to spot because she had spent so much time in front of the makeup mirror. The smile on her face as she talked about how beautiful the raindrops falling from the leaves were when they were hiding in the bushes contrasted with the quandary she faced about whether it was okay to spit blood on others. The situation was so "special" (the prosecutor's characterization) that she concluded that, yes, it had to be okay. After that she said there were so many AUF members at Ullevaal Hospital that they could start a small local chapter there, and she noted how good it was for gender equality that the head of the trauma team was a woman. The only drawback was that the woman was prone to cursing, something that Ina herself would never do.

The survivors of Utøya have struggled with many questions since July 22, and some of them start with "if." "If I had known how dangerous it was, I would have done something," twenty-year-old Hussein Kazemi said in court. He had come to Norway from Afghanistan in 2009 and had an interpreter with him in the courtroom in case there was something he didn't understand. It wasn't necessary. Hussein spoke in fluent Norwegian about how he had joined the AUF just before the summer camp. He barely knew what the youth organization stood for. A friend had told him about the camp, and Hussein had then persuaded two other friends who were not particularly indoctrinated with cultural Marxist ideology to come along.

Hussein had hidden behind the piano in the little hall with some girls but had run out of the cafeteria building when the man in a police uniform had come in from the campground. The girls were killed while Hussein was shot in the thigh. He didn't talk much about the injuries in court but talked instead about how guilty he felt that he didn't help the girls, that he had invited the two friends to come with him, and that he had later called out to the killer on the southern tip of the island. "If I had hidden myself better, he would not have come down to where I was and shot the people there."

"I don't think that's something you should worry about," said defense lawyer Geir Lippestad. That's easy to say, and in theory the issue at hand is even simpler: just one man is guilty, and he will serve a long sentence. But too many survivors wake up in a cold sweat even after nine or ten months have passed, still bearing a heavy burden on their young shoulders. A twenty-year-old from Buskerud testified about how he dragged a friend down to the floor of the little hall to prevent both from getting shot. Only he survived. He was shot in the head, but when he talked about his problems, it was guilt that troubled him most. He said the first thing he did when he woke up from the anesthetic at the hospital was to apologize for not managing to save his friend.

A twenty-year-old girl from Vestfold was shot in the thigh and developed an inflammation of the hip while swimming to the mainland. She too struggled most with her conscience. She was the head of a county delegation that lost its three youngest members. An eighteen-year-old choked up when he talked about his friend, who wasn't able to swim anymore and turned back to Utøya and subsequently drowned. "I felt a lot of guilt after I swam away from my buddy." Guilt because they persuaded people to join the camp and these people never came back. Guilt because they feel they failed in their duties as leaders. Guilt because they dissuaded some from swimming or told them to lie down on the floor of the cafeteria building or run to the left of Lovers' Lane. And guilt because they survived.

For those of us who covered the trial it was tempting to focus on the life force of youth, the smiles in the courtroom, and assurances that things would improve and that school curriculums have been completed in the stipulated time. "We won, you lost," as one youngster said to the killer. Optimism and hope for the future. But the dull, introverted glances spoke their own language, and not infrequently they were followed by short, vague answers about what life had been like since July 22. "It goes up and down." Behind "down" often lie anxiety, insomnia, social abstinence,

depression, fear, loss of energy, emptiness, grief, and concentration problems. Hussein didn't speak for all of the survivors, but he probably spoke
on behalf of too many:

> PROSECUTOR: "How has it been afterward?"
> HUSSEIN: "It has been hell."
> PROSECUTOR: "What has been difficult?"
> HUSSEIN: "Everything."

He wouldn't say anything more.

They are young. They should use terms such as "damn," "hurts like shit,"
and "fucking asshole," and they should say "I," "me," and "my." They did
not, in general, in Courtroom 250. Some of this may be attributed to the
fact that this is basically a resourceful bunch with a sophisticated use of
language and mature reflection, but it is not enough to explain the witnesses' systematic attempts to play down the incredible drama of their
stories.

We met many survivors of the Utøya massacre with serious gunshot
wounds. The youths talked quietly and soberly about what they remember, where they ran, what they thought, and who they met along the way.
Often they forgot to say when and where they were shot and how they
reacted to being shot. The prosecutor had to come up with friendly
reminders and ask a witness to summarize the extent of the injuries at
the end. Twenty-year-old Eirin Kjær got up from her chair in the courtroom in a fine yellow summer dress, pointed to her stomach, and said,
"It looks a bit weird now, but they say it should be fine." She was shot
four times and has undergone eleven operations. Eirin assured the court
that she was otherwise in surprisingly fine form. She was able to do whatever she was doing before, except for martial arts, in which she was not
particularly interested anyway. The counsel for the aggrieved had to draw
out of her the fact that all was not quite like it had been before. She has
an anxiety attack when Bus 20 stops where Bus 26 usually stops. She can't
handle any deviation from the norm anymore.

Not even eighteen-year-old Viljar Hanssen made a big deal of the five
bullet wounds inflicted on him on July 22. He joked when questioned
about his head injuries. That he could no longer see through his right
eye was "practical" because then he didn't have to look at "him" (Anders
Behring Breivik was sitting to the right of the witness stand). And although
parts of his brain were gone, Viljar assured us that he still had the most

important things: "sense and intelligence." He also possessed an impeccable sense of humor: "I was in a coma for four or five days, but I don't remember much of it."

The young people's sober, truncated explanations, where the experience of being shot can be characterized as "weird" (Viljar), were well suited to the court's wish to focus on the undeniable facts, but from a cynical perspective they don't serve the youngsters' cause. They are entitled to criminal injuries compensation, so they would be better served by using the strongest adjectives in their vocabulary and by churning out gruesome, traumatizing images and detailed accounts of the countless sleepless nights they have had over the past ten months. They should not be playing them down and holding back. Which they did. Eighteen-year-old Espen Myklebust was shot in the back and swam out farther and farther away on the west side on Lake Tyri. He was in the water a long time before he was picked up by a police boat. They brought him right back to Utøya, where he was put ashore without knowing whether the killer had been arrested or not. He must have been terrified, in despair, and furious. But he said nothing about it in the courtroom. He talked about the trip to the hospital.

The youngsters did not say "mass murderer" or "killer" or his name. They said "the accused," "the perpetrator," or simply "he." Some did not say "stomach" but "right flank." Or "superficial" gunshot wounds. Or "incident." Seventeen-year-old youths shouldn't be using this kind of terminology. It may be a symptom of another observation from the courtroom: often, almost imperceptibly, they slipped from using "I" to "one" and "you," although they were still talking only about themselves. Some examples from the witness stand: "One becomes totally apathetic." "Then you could feel the pain." "When you get shot, you only hear the pain." A psychologist might explain this as a need to distance oneself from what happened, to speak as rationally, objectively, and unsentimentally as possible, but it is also a reminder that what unfolded on Utøya spans the individual and the collective. The young people's experiences are unique and common at the same time. They were attacked individually and as a "we."

Often one had to read between the lines to understand what was being said or interpret words in the context of a witness's body language. The youngsters plied the art of interpretation at an advanced level. Eighteen-year-old Cathrine Trønnes Lie was shot in the back and the arm on July 22 and lost her younger sister on Utøya. The prosecutor asked her in conclusion how she was doing at present. "I feel good enough," she replied. The "enough," her facial expression, her tone of voice, and the ensuing silence made it clear that "I feel good enough" was a euphemism for "I feel totally like crap."

Some of them had begun to put July 22 behind them, but the trial brought memories to the surface again. Such was the case for all the people who were on Utøya. It was especially so for those called to testify. They all tackled the challenge in their own way. Some chose to remain anonymous, some couldn't bear to attend, and others made themselves available to journalists and photographers after their testimonies. Some requested that the killer leave the courtroom, while for others it was essential that he be present as they had a message to deliver.

After twenty-year-old Hussein Kazemi had testified for one hour, he made a final appeal, with eyes fixed to the right, where the killer sat: "Utøya was my first encounter with AUF members, but I can promise you that it'll not be my last. Those who were killed on Utøya had hopes and dreams. I'll continue to go to Utøya to continue to fulfill their hopes and dreams." Others closed their testimonies with more rousing exhortations: "We won, you lost! Norwegian youth can swim!" Several of the girls appeared in summer dresses. Fifteen-year-old Ylva Helene Schwenke had nothing against showing off her scars. On the contrary, the intention was that "he" see them. "I'm not afraid to show them. I look at it as a victory. We've paid a price for democracy, and we won. I may not be proud of them, but I wear them with dignity," she said.

An eighteen-year-old girl appeared to be quite fragile. She was on Utøya not because she was particularly concerned about the EU, power plants, or the Middle East but because a friend had convinced her to go a few weeks earlier. She testified with brevity, informed by the gravity of the moment. In closing, counsel asked about her future plans. She had been planning to work with children and youth, but because of gunshot wounds in her back she could no longer work with young children. So now she was thinking about working as a psychiatrist or a prison guard instead. Did the defendant get the implication? It seemed that way. He smiled his nervous smile.

No one made anything of Tarjei Jensen Bech's clothing during his testimony in the courtroom, but in an interview afterward the twenty-year-old from Finnmark in northern Norway explained that he had put on the indigenous Sámi costume to send a message to the mass murderer, who thought that white Norwegians were Norway's indigenous people. His testimony also revealed that when he and several of the seriously injured were taken from Utøya by boat, they began to sing a Queen song. But they found it inappropriate and sang "We Are the World" instead. He said that was more suitable and looked at the defendant. The song wasn't a random choice. The Utøya choir was supposed to perform it on the outdoor stage on Saturday, and only "My Rainbow Race" was more ideal as a cultural Marxist protest song.

Prosecutors and counsels for the aggrieved aided the youngsters in their testimonies by asking them questions that underscored neither the course of events nor guilt, nor sanity, but that served to illuminate the consequences of the crimes. Witnesses were asked to describe what they were thinking while they waited for help, how their surgical operations had gone, the consequences of gunshot wounds, and the long-term psychological effects of their ordeal. When a witness was younger than sixteen and/or had just joined the AUF and/or had no key position in the youth organization, these facts were emphasized, and it was pretty obvious for whom the message was meant: the defendant.

The youngsters had to balance their words delicately. On the one hand, they couldn't show their most vulnerable side because it would make them weak and the defendant strong. On the other hand, they had to express how much their lives have changed since July 22. They couldn't be too angry or aggressive, and they couldn't use rhetoric that made them appear to be hateful or vengeful. Subtle signals, however, were an acceptable way to vent their feelings and frustrations. Others chose a more direct form of communication. At least one girl who testified did so. The eighteen-year-old had a refreshing vocabulary. The defendant was called "that jerk" and "that thing," who also, obviously, was "lacking in social skills." But she also had another message for him that was somewhat drowned out among the invectives. When asked by counsel about how she was doing at present, she answered that she was doing fine. "It's worse for him, who has to live with what he's done," she said, pointing at him. In addition, she said that after July 22 she had become much more politically active, and she rattled off her new party duties. Hence her final word was directed at him and it was, "Thanks." He looked down and smiled his nervous smile.

It was uncomfortable when he smiled at the wrong time, as he often did, but it was even more uncomfortable when he smiled at the right time.

The smile of the mass murderer of July 22 has been an issue since the trial began. On one of the first days he tried to refute the allegation that he had smiled, laughed, and expressed joy when he had killed sixty-nine people on Utøya, injured many, and tried to kill the rest by scaring them into Lake Tyri so they'd get cramps and drown. He was indignant and said that the rumor stemmed from a single person. "Are you always in control when you smile?" prosecutor Holden asked. "Yes. No. Yes." He had already admitted that the smile was a sign of nervousness, a defense mechanism. But he said that it couldn't have happened on Utøya, as what he did there "was nothing to smile about."

At least three witnesses at the trial affirmed that he had smiled as he killed people on Utøya; two of them heard shouts of joy, while several said that he looked satisfied during the massacre. The issue of his smile, laughter, and shouts of exhilaration evolved into the hub around which the trial revolved. Prosecutors and counsels for the aggrieved asked questions that ran the gamut, including what the witnesses heard the killer utter, while the defense consistently asked questions only about his appearance, his behavior, and his expressions. After the last AUF members from Utøya had testified, he took the stand and reiterated that he had never smiled or laughed on Utøya. That issue was crucial to him.

His emotional state was key in determining whether he was sane or not. Each time there was a reply of "No" or "Nothing" to the question of whether a witness had heard him say something weird or whether there had been something peculiar about his behavior on the island, the defense's claim that the killer had been fully aware of what he was doing on July 22 was bolstered.

He smiled often in court. He smiled as prosecutors attempted to "mock" (his word) him about his network, his visions of being a knight, and his homemade uniforms, and he smiled as witnesses gave evidence. The first time was when the AUF general secretary testified that she heard shouts of joy from Lovers' Lane. He grinned and shook his head. And he smiled when the witnesses pricked him with barbs such as "That jerk" or "He looked like a neo-Nazi."

When he smiled at inappropriate times and during inexplicable moments, our suspicion that he was on a different planet from the rest of us was reinforced. Far worse was when he smiled along with us. Fourteen-year-old Ylva was shot five times on Utøya, and she spent a lot of time in rehabilitation after July 22. Counsel for the aggrieved wondered how things were going at school. "They've gone well," she said. "Actually I've never had such good grades before because now I don't have to go to gym, so my point average has gone up," she said with an infectious laugh. The judge smiled, the families smiled, the journalists smiled, the prosecutors and counsels for the aggrieved smiled, and *he* smiled. Suddenly he was part of our community; he shared our closeness and relief. We were in this together in Courtroom 250. He went from being a "he" or "the perpetrator" or "that thing" to a human being with a face and a name: Anders Behring Breivik. If he could laugh at the same things we could, could he not also cry at the same things?

For the court the smiles, laughter, humor, and tears were relevant in determining not only whether he was sane and whether he was capable of showing healthy human reactions, but also whether we could place him outside or within our community. The most expedient thing to do was to dismiss him as a random outcast on the periphery of Norwegian society, a man who couldn't act otherwise because he was either sick or a robot. It was more uncomfortable to see him as sane, as someone from within, a man who could not only snicker at us, but also smile along with us.

In at least one instance it was apparent that even he was aware of a drift toward the community that he didn't condone. He strangled his smile and strove to recapture his rigid mask. He was on the verge of laughing, a non-nervous laugh, and he quashed it. It was a consolation of sorts. We didn't want to laugh along with him, and he didn't want to laugh along with us.

The trial ended on June 22, 2012. The verdict was due in August. In the meantime the first anniversary of the attack was commemorated in Oslo and by Lake Tyri. During the commemoration after speeches by (among others) Prime Minister Jens Stoltenberg, union leader Roar Flåthen, and AUF leader Eskil Pedersen, the aggrieved families reacted to the fact that there had been too much emphasis on the Labor movement. It was just a foretaste of the debate to come on the future of Utøya. The AUF wanted to "take the island back," while various groups of aggrieved families wanted it turned into a memorial. About fifty thousand people showed up at City Hall in Oslo on July 22, 2012. The weather was as gray and harsh as the year before. Many brought red roses. "We said we would die together. Some die young," sang the Iranian-born Swedish artist Laleh, and the song brought forth tears even from royal eyes. Singer Lillebjørn Nilsen was last out with "Goodnight, Oslo" before the Norwegian Radio Orchestra and church bells played "To Youth."

The verdict was handed down on August 24. He was pronounced legally sane by the judge. Anders Behring Breivik was sentenced to twenty-one years of preventive detention.

Over the autumn there were several debates in the public arena. The main issues were the future of the government quarter and Utøya; the killer's childhood; his prison conditions; the failure of the system; closing off Grubbegata; a vote of no confidence against the government; and the fact that right-wing extremism in Europe these days had a Norwegian face. But life returned to normal in its own muddled, bumpy way. The wave of sympathy toward immigrants that was evident after the terrorist attacks dissipated. The Labor Party gleaned no more sympathy votes. Youth, to which we sang an ode at the one-year anniversary, was again pushed into the background. Maybe it was a blessing. Silence and the daily grind. Banalities. Routines. Many would have wanted it that way. We're done with it. Let's move on. But the story isn't over. The consequences are still not clear. Life has just begun. We still don't know what it means to be bombed in a terrorist attack and targeted by a mass murderer in secure, innocent Norway. On December 14, 2012, an AUF member posted a message on Facebook that he has long feared becoming victim number 78—the first of the survivors to commit suicide. The following Monday he admitted himself to a psychiatric ward. He was exhausted but wished to live.

How has life been since the trial? I asked a handful of July 22 survivors this question just before Christmas 2012, four months after the verdict was handed down. All were interviewed for this book, but here they remain anonymous so that they could speak freely.

A boy, barely sixteen in the summer of 2011, says that he has been very depressed during the past year and especially during the trial. The Oslo boy didn't know how he should feel, and he read everything he came across on Facebook and blog posts to get an idea. Many said that things were much better now. He didn't feel the same way. He felt just as bad, maybe worse. Nowadays he is in stable condition. Stable but poor, that is. "The most positive thing I've gotten out of the last year may be that of feeling relatively bad over a period of time. I think that must be a good experience to have. One also thinks in different ways when one is depressed like that, so I've gotten a lot of good out of it too."

The year started well for a twenty-one-year-old girl who was originally from North Trøndelag County. Was it right to feel good after only half a year? She felt guilty and forced herself to think about July 22 so as to be sad. She was in good shape until the trial neared. Then she broke down. She cried and cried without really knowing why. She wasn't dreading the trial. Her depression came to an end when the trial started on April 16. She felt a sense of victory from seeing him so powerless. The plan was to follow the trial every day, but exams got in the way. The last day of the trial was dreadful according to her. Possibly she had expected that it would mark a transition from the old to the new. She traveled by plane that day alone and burst into tears.

The one-year anniversary commemoration was fine. "For once the focus was on the victims again and not on Breivik," she said. But the same ambivalence emerged. She and several of her friends were trying to be sadder than they actually were. It wasn't possible to say that she was doing fine, although she was actually doing fine. And there's no real reason why you should miss your friends more on a specific date, is there? It is unreal every single day that they're gone. "And it's absolutely unreal that I'm fine, that life continues as before, and that the front pages of the tabloids can return to the usual trivial news of summer, even though this happened not so long ago. That, I think about quite often."

Now days may go by without her thinking about July 22. She had never imagined it would happen. It may happen that she feels guilty about feeling good, especially when the subject is brought up by other AUF members, who, according to her, have difficulty understanding why people react differently. She has changed. She has a more laissez-faire attitude toward life. She cares less about the little, unimportant things. "However, I care more about the little, important things. And now I start to cry when I see romantic and sad movies. I don't like that very much," she says. Her boyfriend's mother says it's an indication of high values. "So there's a positive side to everything."

A girl from southern Norway, who was nineteen the summer before, says that now several days may go by without her thinking about July 22. She no longer hyperventilates when she hears loud noises. She is no longer worried that things that one can't imagine happening will happen. She can now walk into a room without checking where the emergency exits are. "I worry about ordinary stuff. Exams, that I'm too fat, that I need to exercise more, what to have for dinner, whether to buy beer or potatoes at the store, and that guy who. . . ." She has a guilty conscience about letting life pass her by. And sometimes she misses herself as the survivor associated with Utøya. The girl who was known to be so wise, thoughtful, and wonderful. The girl who had gone through so much, but who still stood upright and resolute.

A twenty-five-year-old boy from Oslo was on Einar Gerhardsen Square by chance at 3:25 p.m. on Friday afternoon, July 22. He was critically injured and has since spent much time in surgery and rehabilitation. Yet it was the trial that was the most difficult ordeal for him in 2012. He was supposed to testify and had never been more nervous. He had to omit certain details in order not to break down. "I felt, for some strange reason, that it was important to show the other slightly younger witnesses that the testimony would go well." He is in better shape physically, even though he can't jog anymore. "That's a real bummer." The bright side has been the outpouring of support. Strangers have hugged him. He has since gotten a new job and is getting married. He is still scared when he hears loud noises, and he gets sad easily and starts to cry about "very small matters." It cuts both ways. "On the other hand, I'm quicker to value and appreciate the stuff I hadn't thought so much about before," he says and adds, "Fortunately, I'm more happy than sad."

An AUF member from the Mjøsa lake district, who was twenty in summer 2011, started the year with renewed initiative. He was finally ready to resume his studies. But when the trial began, he broke down. He couldn't sleep. His doctor gave him anti-anxiety medication and he went into therapy. The fact that he was not designated as a victim, just a witness, irked him. This also meant that he was not allowed to enter the courtroom. He wanted to see Breivik and try to understand who he was. However, he managed to enter the courtroom for a couple of days as a chaperon for a victim. He felt no hatred. "I came to the conclusion that I've a view of humanity that makes it impossible for me to hate someone. In my world everyone is basically good, and the fact that people end up on the outside and commit gruesome acts is a result of poor choices and their environment," he says. Thinking about why no one had been able to help Breivik only gave him more reason to be angry. "That feeling I still have today, and it has changed me forever."

It has been agonizing to follow the debate on the scapegoats. As he sees it, politicians and government officials have been condemned in the media. "I've wanted to scream in despair and anger." There's only one person to blame, and that's the perpetrator. The debate on the failure of the emergency preparedness services has demolished the dignity associated with July

22. "It has been very painful." The same applies to the debate on the future of Utøya, which has driven a wedge between the AUF and the bereaved.

Now he has moved to another town and feels he is starting to reclaim his life, one step at a time.

An Oslo girl characterizes the year as "eternal." She was nineteen in summer 2011. The year sort of never came to an end. Life was put on hold once again in anticipation of new significant dates—incarceration meetings, the trial, the first-anniversary commemoration, the verdict, the commission report, parliamentary hearings. She wished she had known about the ramifications of those dates so that she hadn't had have to postpone everything. At one point she and others had worried that the attention would end, that people would stop caring, and that they would be left alone with their traumas. "But it's almost as if the opposite has happened, where you yourself want to move on and others want to bring it up over and over again."

One of the most difficult problems to deal with has been to separate the private from the public. July 22 is her story, her trauma, her dead friends, her perceptions, her nightmare. July 22 is also in the public domain. Others know the details better than she; they can reconstruct the sequence of events perfectly, and they know all about the manifesto. "I've kind of lost ownership of my own story; my thoughts and emotions have been inquired into, investigated, excavated down to the last morsel because they all want to immerse themselves in our personal experiences. It's pretty frustrating when one's identity, emotions, and story are linked to this event and the case is lifted up to such a high professional level that we don't even know what's happening. If you know what I mean?"

She has given her time to so many: psychologists, doctors, municipal support teams, police, the National Criminal Investigation Service, lawyers, journalists. It has been nice to talk to people who understand and who ask the right questions. But it has also been difficult. She has had long conversations with pleasant journalists but then discovered the next day that they hadn't understood certain things or had chosen to angle the story cynically. One journalist opened the interview with a fixed stare and said in a trembling voice, "Oops. This is the first time I've faced a survivor." Totally unsolicited an American journalist who has followed the 9/11 survivors for ten years drew a chart in the air of what her life would be like for the next ten years. It looked like a stock price chart showing mostly troughs. "What can you say? Thanks?"

People behave differently. Peripheral friends try to get closer. At Christmas parties people look at her with doe eyes and want to know how she's really doing. And then there are those who need to share their own bad experiences such as neck pain, unemployment problems, and dead relatives. "Maybe people find it liberating that I share my suffering, but I'm not doing it to create a poor-me image," she says. On Facebook and her mobile phone she is being harassed by a "suicidal stalker." She often feels lonely, even though she is showered with love. She is alone. She has to fix matters herself.

Several AUF members have said to her that they wish they had also been on Utøya on July 22. "This sounds utterly absurd to one who was actually there, but it's clear that the spotlight, love, solidarity, and attention with which we've been showered probably create jealousy." In the youth party the survivors are expected to be thoughtful, clever, and accomplished. This causes her to have performance anxiety.

Nevertheless, the year has had some bright spots. One of them is solidarity in the nation, in the organization, and among friends. Her university education has started again. The brain is "back in business." She feels she had to study for a particular friend who died on Utøya. She thinks that if she doesn't get good grades at Christmas, the mass murderer will have won. And that he will still have control over her. But if she gets good grades, she will be free. She cried and cried when she got an A and A+ on the midterm exams. "These weren't just grades; they were victory."

The year has been marked by contradicting emotions. "On one hand, you want to move on; you want to be free to focus on all the parts of you that aren't Utøya; you want to put it completely behind you. On the other hand, you don't really want to let go; you want to be in it, re-experience it, feel it. It has been difficult to have these two sides all the time, especially when you have to make choices about things like projects and interviews. In a way you become very serious, solemn, pensive. But in another way you long to be amusing, flippant, spontaneous," she says.

Is there anything here that we can understand? That grades are not just grades but a tribute to a young man who was killed by a mass murderer at a summer camp? That bad grades are tantamount to having lost again?

The observations above are just a slice of the post–July 22 daily lives that go on in the midst of the current debates that, they believe, lie at the core of their experience. The little things, if you will. The impressions we get are multifaceted and might have been different if the questions had been asked on another day. But much is certainly still fragile, painful, and taboo. The way we discuss and debate July 22 affects the survivors concretely, physically, and mentally. Several express ambivalence about being in the spotlight. Some dwell on the past, while others wish to move on. But all of them want to convey how complex it all is. There is still much they, and we, don't know about the long-term effects of such a dramatic, surreal, and life-changing experience.

The Norwegian short story writer Hans Herbjørnsrud writes in a way that evokes a sense of "prepare for the worst"; it is complex, ambiguous literature that undermines the urge to think in totalitarian, simplified, and comprehensive terms. It is literature to read before an event, not afterward, and it doesn't provide factual information about Nazism, for example, but evokes empathy and compassion. If Herbjørnsrud's literary technique is applied to journalism or documentary literature and the public debate in general, we may ask ourselves whether we actually know considerably more than we realize. The answer to emergency preparedness services that failed is not just a matter of closing off streets. We should ask ourselves what lies behind statements such as "He was somewhat right then" or "I'm so tired of July 22" or "I wish I had been there." And we should ask ourselves whether we, as a community, have done enough to prevent someone from becoming victim "number 78." Regardless, this should be done ahead of time.

Acknowledgments and Comments on Sources

A story about July 22, 2011, has neither a beginning nor an end. The backstory could begin with the birth of the Labor Party, the French Revolution, or even earlier, and the date will mark both individual and collective Norwegian self-understanding for the foreseeable future, long after we have passed the year 2083. The victims of the terror attacks in the government quarter and in the Utøya youth camp are, to start with, exceptional people. The Utøya youngsters are blessed with an unusual, optimistic view of mankind and society. Yet countless news stories emerged after July 22 about survivors who were struggling to cope with insomnia, difficulties with concentration, trauma, and depression, and more such stories are certain to emerge in the future. While working on the book, the author interviewed a witness at a McDonald's restaurant in Oslo. The witness wasn't able to concentrate on the meal or the conversation until he had checked the trunk of a big, white, empty van that was parked outside with its blinkers on.

People who had not been directly affected but had witnessed the events or participated in the rescue efforts also struggle with the psychological consequences. For several mornings after July 22, the inhabitants of Utstranda perused the shore, checking to see whether there were still any clothes, shoes, or corpses before they could finally accept the youngsters' fates and let them go. AUF leader Eskil Pedersen has worn a security alarm since the massacre because there have been death threats. Some survivors from Utøya got distressing calls on Christmas Eve. Security measures around government ministers have been heightened, even in their private lives. At the moment, it is impossible to predict whether Norway's response to the terror attacks will result in more openness or whether the political climate will become less hostile to immigrants. It is difficult now to see any obvious positive consequences of July 22 other than the fact that awareness of right-wing violence has been heightened. However, it is easy to point to what was lost. First and foremost, human lives. Many young lives. These were people who had fought for radical values, whether these values referred to multiculturalism, gender stereotyping, or peace in the Middle East. More democracy in action, not just in words, is a compelling response to the July 22 attacks. But we mustn't forget that many of the people who lost their lives that day were idealists with an increased commitment to the poor and oppressed in the world and the marginalized and excluded in Norway. Naive and unrealistic? Precisely.

Thanks to all who have shared their stories via email, Skype, or in person, especially the following: Jorid Nordmelan; Hildegunn Fallang; Ingrid Endrerud; Morten Djupdal; Johanne Butenschøn; Hanne Hestø Ness; Arshad Ali; Emma Martinovic; Matti Brox; Khamshajiny Gunaratnam; Jannike Arnesen; Johannes Giske; Harpreet Singh; Eivind Thoresen; Delshad Rasul; Oda Faremo Lindholm; Andreas Olsen; Stine Renate Håheim; Eskil Pedersen; Tore Sinding Bekkedal; Simen Brænden Mortensen; Kjetil Klakegg Bergheim; Hanne Gro Lille-Mæhlum; and Brede, Anita, and Torill Johbraaten. Thanks to the publishing staff—first and foremost Anders Heger, Ida Berntsen, and Birger Emanuelsen, who initiated the project and greatly inspired the author. Thanks to my friend and former AUF member Kjetil Staalesen for his good memory and his company on Utøya. Thanks to Marit, Selma, Sander, and Silja, who have put up with a father and husband with mood swings and an irregular presence.

There are many versions of the truth about July 22. This book offers one version. *Massacre in Norway* is largely based on interviews with the people involved. In addition, some general information has been extracted from the survivors' stories in the press or from their blogs. No one who witnessed the events of that day had an experience identical to anybody else's. Each individual's truth abuts that of others, who may have divergent perceptions of the details and course of events. To the extent possible, information has been fact checked, but much of the book is deliberately devoted to what people were thinking in different situations to bring forth the human perspective, and thoughts are difficult to verify. The author has relied heavily on the continuous news coverage since July 22 to create a broader perspective for the depiction of the day (for example, information about where various ministers were when the bomb exploded in Oslo) but has compared multiple sources and made a critical selection. The information on Anders Behring Breivik is taken from daily newspapers (especially *Dagbladet Magasinet*, December 12, 2011; *Dagbladet*, November 30, 2011; *Aftenposten*, November 25, 2011; and VG, October 22, 2011), including his own text from *2083*, and the forensic psychiatric evaluation written by Torgeir Husby and Synne Sørheim.

Source literature is used directly and indirectly, and the main source books have been the following: Kjetil Stormark, *When Terror Struck Norway*; Øyvind Strømmen, *The Dark Net*; Lisa Bjurwald, *Europe's Shame*; Bjørn Kumm, *Terrorism's History*; Andreas Malm, *Hatred against Muslims*; Jo Stein Moen and Rolf Sæther, *A Thousand Days*; 22/07/11 (*a memorial book*); *Last Letter (an anthology)*; Ayaan Hirsi Ali, *Nomad*; Geir Kjetsaa, *Fyodor Dostoevsky: A Writer's Life*; Siri Marie Seim Sønstelie and Erik H. Sønstelie, *I'm Alive, Dad*; Hallgrim Berg, *Letter to Lady Liberty: Europe in Danger*; and Terje Halvorsen, *The Party's Salt*. Finally, a word about the author: he is a former AUF member and knows Utøya from the early 1990s; he made a return visit in December 2011. He works for the *Dagsavisen* daily at Grubbegata.

Massacre in Norway is a report written in a journalistic style interwoven with reflections and opinions about current policy articulated by both the interview subjects and the author. The author is solely responsible for any errors or misunderstandings.

STIAN BROMARK